JOURNAL FOR THE STUDY OF THE OLD TESTAMENT
SUPPLEMENT SERIES
4

Editors
David J A Clines
Philip R Davies
David M Gunn

Department of Biblical Studies
The University of Sheffield
Sheffield S10 2TN
England

Thanksgiving for a Liberated Prophet

An Interpretation of Isaiah Chapter 53

R.N.Whybray

Journal for the Study of the Old Testament
Supplement Series 4

Sheffield
1978

ISBN 0 905774 09 4 (hardback)
ISBN 0 905774 04 3 (paperback)

ISSN 0309 0789

Copyright © 1978, Journal for the Study of the Old Testament

Published by
JSOT
Department of Biblical Studies
The University of Sheffield
Sheffield, S10 2TN
England

Reprinted with corrections, 1985

In memory of my wife
who gave me
much help and encouragement

CONTENTS

PREFACE

Some parts of this book were presented in outline as a paper at the Summer Meeting of the Society for Old Testament Study at Manchester in July 1973, and other parts to my colleagues in the Department of Theology at the University of Hull. I desire to express my thanks to those who offered criticisms and suggestions in the discussions which followed the reading of those papers, and in addition to Professor W.G. Lambert of Birmingham University for his help and advice on matters Babylonian, and to Drs. G. Vermes and P. Wernberg-Møller, both of Oxford University, for supplying me with information on other points. These scholars are, however, in no way responsible for the opinions expressed in the book. I am also indebted to the editors of the *Journal for the Study of the Old Testament* for accepting the work for publication in their Supplement Series.

R.N. Whybray

ABBREVIATIONS

AB	*The Anchor Bible*, New York
ANET	*Ancient Near Eastern Texts Relating to the Old Testament*, ed. J.B. Pritchard, Princeton, 1955^2
Aq.	Aquila
ASTI	*Annual of the Swedish Theological Institute in Jerusalem*, Leiden
ATANT	*Abhandlungen zur Theologie des Alten und Neuen Testaments*, Zurich
ATD	*Das Alte Testament Deutsch*, Göttingen
AV	*The Authorised Version of the Bible*
BHS	*Biblia Hebraica Stuttgartensia*, ed. K. Elliger and W. Rudolph, Stuttgart
BJ	*La Bible de Jérusalem*
BJRL	*Bulletin of the John Rylands Library*, Manchester
BKAT	*Biblischer Kommentar, Altes Testament*, Neukirchen
BOT	*De Boeken van het Oude Testament*, Roermond
BS	*Biblische Studien*, Neukirchen
BSOAS	*Bulletin of the School of Oriental and African Studies*, University of London
BWANT	*Beiträge zur Wissenschaft vom Alten und Neuen Testament*, (Leipzig), Stuttgart
BZAW	*Beihefte zur Zeitschrift für die Alttestamentliche Wissenschaft*, (Giessen), Berlin
CAT	*Commentaire de l'Ancien Testament*, Neuchâtel
CB	*The Cambridge Bible for Schools and Colleges*, Cambridge
CBC	*The Cambridge Bible Commentary on the New English Bible*, Cambridge
EB	*Etudes Bibliques*, Paris
ET	English translation
ETL	*Ephemerides Theologicae Lovanienses*, Louvain
EVV	English translations of the Bible
FRLANT	*Forschungen zur Religion und Literatur des Alten und Neuen Testaments*, Göttingen

G-K	*Gesenius' Hebrew Grammar as Edited and Enlarged by ... E. Kautzsch, Revised ... by A.E. Cowley*, Oxford, 1910^2
HAT	*Handbuch zum Alten Testament,* ed. O. Eissfeldt, Göttingen
HK	*Göttinger Handkommentar zum Alten Testament*, ed. W. Nowack, Göttingen
IB	*The Interpreter's Bible,* New York and Nashville
ICC	*The International Critical Commentary*, Edinburgh and New York
JB	*The Jerusalem Bible*
JBL	*The Journal of Biblical Literature,* (New York, New Haven), Cambridge, Mass.
JSOT	*The Journal for the Study of the Old Testament*, University of Sheffield
JSS	*The Journal of Semitic Studies,* Manchester
JTS	*The Journal of Theological Studies,* Oxford
KAT	*Kommentar zum Alten Testament,* ed. (E. Sellin), W. Rudolph, K. Elliger and F. Hesse, (Leipzig), Gütersloh
K-B	*Lexicon in Veteris Testamenti Libros*, ed. L. Koehler and W. Baumgartner, Leiden, 1953
KD	*Biblischer Commentar über das Alte Testament,* ed. K.F. Keil and F. Delitzsch, Leipzig
KHC	*Kurzer Hand-Commentar zum Alten Testament*, ed. K. Marti, Tübingen and Leipzig
LXX	The Greek translation of the Old Testament known as the Septuagint
MT	The Massoretic Text of the Old Testament
NCB	*The New Century Bible Based on the Revised Standard Version,* London
NEB	*The New English Bible*
NF	Neue Folge
OTL	*The Old Testament Library,* London and Philadelphia
OTS	*Oudtestamentische Studiën,* Leiden
Pesh.	The Old Testament in Syriac known as the Peshiṭṭa
REL	*Revue Ecclésiastique Liège,* Liège
RSV	*The Revised Standard Version of the Bible*

RV	*The Revised Version of the Bible*
SB	*Sources Bibliques,* Paris
SBOT	*The Sacred Books of the Old Testament,* ed. P. Haupt, Leipzig; Baltimore
SBT	*Studies in Biblical Theology,* London
SNVAO	*Skriften utgitt av det Norske Videnkaps-Akademi i Oslo*
SOTS	The Society for Old Testament Study
Targ.	Targum
TB	*Theologische Bücherei AT*, Munich
TBC	*Torch Biblical Commentaries,* London
THAT	*Theologisches Handwörterbuch zum Alten Testament,* ed. E. Jenni and C. Westermann, 2 vols., Munich and Zurich, 1971 and 1976
VT	*Vetus Testamentum,* Leiden
VT Suppl	*Supplements to Vetus Testamentum,* Leiden
Vulg.	The Latin Version of the Old Testament known as the Vulgate
WMANT	*Wissenschaftliche Monographien zum Alten und Neuen Testament,* Neukirchen
ZA	*Zeitschrift für Assyriologie,* (Leipzig), Berlin
ZAW	*Zeitschrift für die Alttestamentliche Wissenschaft,* (Giessen), Berlin
ZB	*Zürcher Bibelkommentare,* Zurich and Stuttgart
ZTK	*Zeitschrift für Theologie und Kirche* (Freiburg i. Br.; Leipzig), Tübingen
1QIs[a]	The First Isaiah Scroll from Qumran Cave I
1QIs[b]	The Second Isaiah Scroll from Qumran Cave I

BIBLIOGRAPHY

N.B. Books in the following bibliography will be referred to in the notes only by the surname of the author, except when more than one title is listed for a single author. In these cases shortened titles will be used. In addition, books marked with an asterisk will be referred to by surname only, even if more than one title is listed for that author.

Albright, W.F., "The High Place in Ancient Palestine", in *Volume du Congrès: Strasbourg 1956* (*VT Suppl* 4), 1957, pp. 242-258

Baltzer, K., *Die Biographie der Propheten*, Neukirchen, 1975

— — "Zur formgeschichtlichen Bestimmung der Texte vom Gottes-Knecht im Deutero-Jesaja-Buch", in H.W. Wolff, ed., *Probleme Biblischer Theologie. Gerhard von Rad zum 70. Geburtstag*, Munich, 1971, pp. 27-43

Barth, C., *Einführung in die Psalmen*, Neukirchen, 1961

— — *Die Errettung vom Tode in den individuellen Klage- und Dankliedern*, Basel, 1947

Begrich, J., "Das priesterliche Heilsorakel", *ZAW* 52 (1934), pp. 81-92

— — * *Studien zu Deuterojesaja* (*BWANT 77*), 1938 (reprinted as *TB* 20, 1963)

Bentzen, A., *Daniel* (*HAT* 19), 1952[2]

— — *King and Messiah*, London, 1955 (translated from *Messias – Moses redivivus – Menschensohn: Skizzen zum Thema Weissagung und Erfüllung* (*ATANT* 17), 1948)

Beyerlin, W., *Die Rettung der Bedrängten in den Feindpsalmen der Einzelnen auf institutionelle Zusammenhänge untersucht* (*FRLANT* 99), 1970

Birkeland, H., *The Evildoers in the Book of Psalms* (Avhandlinger utgitt av Det Norske Videnskaps-Akademi i Oslo II. Hist.-Filos. Klasse. 1955. No. 2), Uppsala, 1955

Bonnard, P.-E., *Le second Isaïe* (*EB*), 1972

Brunner, R., *Das Buch Ezechiel, I. 1-24* (*ZB*), 1969[2]

Büchler, A., *Studies in Sin and Atonement in the Rabbinic Literature of the First Century*, London, 1928

De Buck, A., "La fleur au front du grand-prêtre", *OTS* 9 (1951), pp. 18-29

Carley, K.W., *The Book of the Prophet Ezekiel* (*CBC*), 1974

Childs, B.S., *Memory and Tradition in Israel* (*SBT* 37), 1962

Clements, R.E., *Exodus (CBC)*, 1972

Clines, D.J.A., *I, He, We, and They. A Literary Approach to Isaiah 53 (JSOT* Supplement Series 1), 1976

Cooke, G.A., *The Book of Ezekiel (ICC)*, 1936

Cornill, C.H., *Das Buch des Propheten Ezechiel*, Leipzig, 1886

Cowley, A.E., *Aramaic Papyri of the Fifth Century B.C. Edited with Translation and Notes*, Oxford, 1923

Crüsemann, F., *Studien zur Formgeschichte von Hymnus und Danklied in Israel (WMANT* 32), 1969

Dahood, M.J., "Hebrew-Ugaritic Lexicography IX", *Biblica* 52 (1971), pp. 337-356

− − "Phoenician Elements in Isaiah 52,13 − 53,12", in H. Goedicke, ed., *Near Eastern Studies in Honor of William Foxwell Albright*, Baltimore, 1971, pp. 63-73

− − *Psalms I. 1-50 (AB* 16), 1966

− − *Psalms II. 51-100 (AB* 17), 1968

− − *Psalms III. 101-150 (AB* 17A), 1970

Delcor, M., *Le livre de Daniel (SB)*, 1971

Delekat, L., *Asylie und Schutzorakel am Zionheiligtum. Eine Untersuchung zu den privaten Feindpsalmen*, Leiden, 1967

Delitzsch, F., *Biblical Commentary on the Prophecies of Isaiah (Foreign Theological Library)*, Edinburgh, 1890 (translated from *Der Prophet Jesaia (KD)*, 1889[4])

Dhorme, E., *Le livre de Job (EB)*, 1926 (ET *A Commentary on the Book of Job*, London, 1967)

Dion, P.−E., "Les chants du Serviteur de Yahweh et quelques passages apparentés d'Is 40-55. Un essai sur leurs limites précises et sur leurs origines respectives", *Biblica* 51 (1970), pp. 17-38

Driver, G.R., "Isaiah 52:13 − 53:12: The Servant of the Lord", in M. Black and G. Fohrer, ed., *In Memoriam Paul Kahle (BZAW* 103), 1968, pp. 90-105

− − *Problems of the Hebrew Verbal System (Old Testament Studies* 2), Edinburgh, 1936

Driver, S.R., *The Book of Exodus (CB)*, 1911

Driver, S.R. and Gray, G.B., *The Book of Job (ICC)*, 1921

Driver, S.R. and Neubauer, A., *The Fifty-Third Chapter of Isaiah According to the Jewish Interpreters*, 2 vols., New York, 1969[2]

Duhm, B., *Das Buch Hiob (KHC* 16), 1897

– – * *Das Buch Jesaia (HK* 3/1), 1922[4]

– – *Die Psalmen (KHC* 2/2), 1899

Eaton, J.H., *Kingship and the Psalms (SBT* Second Series 32), 1976

Ehrlich, A.B., *Randglossen zur hebräischen Bibel. Ezechiel*, Leipzig, 1912

Eichrodt, W., *Der Prophet Hesekiel (ATD* 22), 1966

– – *Theology of the Old Testament*, 2 vols., London, 1961, 1967 (translated from *Theologie des Alten Testaments*, 2 vols., Stuttgart and Göttingen, 1957[5], 1961[4])

Eissfeldt, O., *The Old Testament. An Introduction*, Oxford, 1965 (translated from *Einleitung in das Alte Testament*, Tübingen, 1964[3] (=1976[4]))

Elliger, K., *Deuterojesaja in seinem Verhältnis zu Tritojesaja (BWANT* 63), 1933

– – "Jes 53$_{10}$: alte crux - neuer Vorschlag", *Mitteilungen des Instituts für Orientforschung*, Berlin, 15 (1969), pp. 228-233

– – *Jesaja II (BKAT* 11/1), 1970 –

– – *Leviticus (HAT* 4), 1966

Engnell, I., "The ʿEbed Yahweh Songs and the Suffering Messiah in Deutero-Isaiah", *BJRL* 31 (1948), pp. 54-93

Fahlgren, K.H., *sᵉdaqâ, nahestehende und entgegengesetzte Begriffe im Alten Testament*, Uppsala, 1932

Fohrer, G., *Das Buch Hiob (KAT* 16), 1963

– – * *Das Buch Jesaja. 3. Band: Kapitel 40-66 (ZB)*, 1964

– – *Ezechiel (HAT* 13), 1955

– – "Die Gattung der Berichte über symbolische Handlungen der Propheten", *ZAW* 64 (1952), pp. 101-120 (reprinted in G. Fohrer, *Studien zur alttestamentlichen Prophetie (1949-1965) (BZAW* 99), 1967, pp. 92-112)

– – *The History of Israelite Religion*, London, 1973 (translated from *Geschichte der israelitischen Religion*, Berlin, 1969)

– – "Prophetie und Magie", *ZAW* 78 (1966), pp. 25-47 (reprinted in G. Fohrer, *Studien zur alttestamentlichen Prophetie (1949-1965) (BZAW* 99), 1967, pp. 242-264)

Frost, S.B., "Asseveration by Thanksgiving", *VT* 8 (1958), pp. 380-390

Ginsberg, H.L., "The Oldest Interpretation of the Suffering Servant", *VT* 3 (1953), pp. 400-404

Gray, G.B., *Numbers* (*ICC*), 1903

Gressmann, H., *Der Messias* (*FRLANT* 43), 1929

Guillaume, A., "A Contribution to Hebrew Lexicography", *BSOAS* 16 (1954), pp. 1-12

Gunkel, H., *Ausgewählte Psalmen*, Göttingen, 1917[4]

– – *Einleitung in den Psalmen. Die Gattungen der religiösen Lyrik Israels. Zu Ende geführt von Joachim Begrich* (*HK*, Ergänzungsband zur II. Abteilung), 1933

– – "Jesaia 33, eine prophetische Liturgie", *ZAW* 42 (1924), pp. 177-208

– – *Die Psalmen* (*HK*), 1929[4]

Heller, J., "Hiding of the Face. A Study of Is. 53:3", *Communio Viatorum*, Prague, 1 (1958), pp. 263-266

Hertzberg, H.W., "Sind die Propheten Fürbitte?", in E. Würthwein and O. Kaiser, ed., *Tradition und Situation. Studien zur alttestamentlichen Prophetie. Artur Weiser zum 70. Geburtstag . . . dargebracht*, Göttingen, 1963, pp. 63-74

Hillers, D.R., *Lamentations* (*AB* 7A), 1972

Hogg, J.E., "A Note on Two Points in Aaron's Headdress", *JTS* 26 (1925), pp. 72-75

Hölscher, G., *Das Buch Hiob* (*HAT* 17), 1952[2]

Holzinger, H., *Numeri* (*KHC*), 1903

Hooker, M.D., *Jesus and the Servant. The Influence of the Servant Concept of Deutero-Isaiah in the New Testament*, London, 1959

Hyatt, J.P., *Exodus* (*NCB*), 1971

Van Imschoot, P., *Théologie de l'Ancien Testament II*, Paris, 1956

Jacob, E., *Theology of the Old Testament*, London, 1958 (translated from *Théologie de l'Ancien Testament*, Neuchâtel, 1955)

Jahnow, H., *Das hebräische Leichenlied im Rahmen der Völkerdichtung* (*BZAW* 36), 1923

Kaiser, O., *Isaiah 13-39* (*OTL*), 1974 (translated from *Jesaja. Kap. 13-39* (*ATD* 18), 1973)

– –[*] *Der königliche Knecht. Eine traditionsgeschichtlich-exegetische Studie über die Ebed-Jahwe-Lieder bei Deuterojesaja* (*FRLANT* 70), 1962[2]

Koch, K., *ṢDQ im Alten Testament. Eine traditionsgeschichtliche Untersuchung*, Heidelberg, 1965

– – "Der Spruch 'Sein Blut bleibe auf seinem Haupt' und die israelitische

Auffassung vom vergossenen Blut", *VT* 12 (1962), pp. 396-416 (reprinted in K. Koch, ed., *Um das Prinzip der Vergeltung in Religion und Recht des Alten Testaments* (*Wege der Forschung* 125), Darmstadt, 1972, pp. 432-456)

Koehler, L., *Old Testament Theology*, London, 1957 (translated from *Theologie des Alten Testaments*, Tübingen, 1953[3])

Kraus, H.-J., *Klagelieder (Threni)* (*BKAT* 20), 1960[2]

– – *Psalmen*, 2 vols. (*BKAT* 15/1, 2), 1961[2]

Kutsch, E., *Sein Leiden und Tod – unser Heil. Eine Exegese von Jesaja 52,13 – 53,12* (*BS* 52), 1967

Lambert, W.G., *Babylonian Wisdom Literature*, Oxford, 1960

– – "Myth and Ritual as Conceived by the Babylonians", *JSS* 13 (1968), pp. 104-112

– – "Nabonidus in Arabia", in *Proceedings of the Fifth Seminar for Arabian Studies . . .*, London, 1972, pp. 53-64

Van Leeuwen, C., "Die Partikel אם", in C.J. Labuschagne and others, *Syntax and Meaning. Studies in Hebrew Syntax and Biblical Exegesis* (*OTS* 18), 1973, pp. 15-48

Lindblom, J., *The Servant Songs in Deutero-Isaiah. A New Attempt to Solve an Old Problem* (*Lunds Universitets Årsskrift*, N.F. Avd. 1. Bd. 47. Nr. 5), Lund, 1951

* Lipiński, E., "Psaumes - 1. Formes et genres littéraires", in *Supplément au Dictionnaire de la Bible*, ed. H. Cazelles and A. Feuillet, vol. 9, fasc. 48, cols. 1-125

– – "Les psaumes d'action de grâces individuelle", *REL* 53 (1967), pp. 348-366

Loewe, R.J., "Prolegomenon", in S.R. Driver and A. Neubauer, *The Fifty-Third Chapter of Isaiah According to the Jewish Interpreters*, New York, 1969[2], vol. 2, pp. 1-38

McKane, W., *Proverbs* (*OTL*), London, 1970

McKenzie, J.L., *A Theology of the Old Testament*, London, 1974

Mand, F., "Die Eigenständlichkeit der Danklieder des Psalters als Bekenntnislieder", *ZAW* 70 (1958), pp. 185-199

Marti, K., *Das Buch Jesaja* (*KHC*), 1900

Martin-Achard, R., *De la mort à la résurrection d'après l'Ancien Testament* (*Bibliothèque Théologique*), Neuchâtel, 1956

Mettinger, T.N.D., "The Hebrew Verbal System", *ASTI* 9 (1973), pp. 64-84

Miller, J.W., "Prophetic Conflict in Second Isaiah. The Servant Songs in the Light of their Context", in J. Stoebe, ed., *Wort – Gebet – Glaube. Walter Eichrodt zum 80. Geburtstag (ATANT* 59), 1970, pp. 77-85

Morgenstern, J., "The Suffering Servant – A New Solution, I", *VT* 11 (1961), pp. 292-320

Mowinckel, S., *He That Cometh,* Oxford, 1956 (translated from *Han som kommer,* Copenhagen, 1951)

– – *Psalmenstudien II. Das Thronbesteigungsfest Jahwäs und der Ursprung der Eschatologie (SNVAO,* Hist.-Filos. Klasse 1921, 6), Kristiana, 1922

– – *Psalmenstudien V. Segen und Fluch in Israels Kult und Psalmdichtung (SNVAO,* Hist.-Filos. Klasse 1923, 3), Kristiana, 1923

– – *The Psalms in Israel's Worship,* Oxford, 2 vols., 1962 (translated from *Offersang og Sangoffer,* Oslo, 1951)

Muilenburg, J., *The Book of Isaiah, Chapters 40-66 (IB* 5), 1956

Müller, H.-P., "Ein Vorschlag zu Jes $53_{10f.}$", *ZAW* 81 (1969), pp. 377-380

* North, C.R., *The Second Isaiah,* Oxford, 1964

– – *The Suffering Servant in Deutero-Isaiah. An Historical and Critical Study,* Oxford, 1948

* Noth, M., *Exodus (OTL),* 1962 (translated from *Das zweite Buch Mose. Exodus (ATD* 5), 1959)

– – *Leviticus (OTL),* 1965 (translated from *Das dritte Buch Mose. Leviticus (ATD* 6), 1962)

– – *Numbers (OTL),* 1968 (translated from *Das vierte Buch Mose. Numeri (ATD* 7), 1966)

– – "Office and Vocation in the Old Testament", in M. Noth, *The Laws in the Pentateuch and Other Studies,* Edinburgh and London, 1966, pp. 229-249 (translated from *Amt und Berufung im Alten Testament* (Rektoratsrede an der Rheinischen Friedrich-Wilhelms Universität zu Bonn, 1958 *[Bonner Akademische-Reden 19]*), Bonn, 1958)

Orlinsky, H.M., "The So-Called 'Servant of the Lord' and 'Suffering Servant' in Second Isaiah", in H.M. Orlinsky and N.H. Snaith, *Studies on the Second Part of the Book of Isaiah (VT Suppl* 14), 1967, pp. 1-133

Plöger, O., *Das Buch Daniel (KAT* 18), 1965

– – *Die Klagelieder (HAT* 18), 1969[2]

Pope, M.H., *Job (AB* 15), 1973[2]

Porteous, N.W., *Daniel (OTL),* 1965 (German version, *Das Danielbuch (ATD* 23), 1962)

Preuss, H.D., *Deuterojesaja. Eine Einführung in seine Botschaft,* Neukirchen, 1976

Rad, G. von, "כפל ים in Jes 40_2 = 'Äquivalent'?", *ZAW* 79 (1967), pp. 80-82

– – *Old Testament Theology I,* Edinburgh and London, 1962 (translated from *Theologie des Alten Testaments I,* Munich, 1957)

Reventlow, H. Graf, *Liturgie und prophetisches Ich bei Jeremia,* Gütersloh, 1963

– – "Prophetamt und Mittleramt", *ZTK* 58 (1961), pp. 269-284

– – " 'Sein Blut komme über sein Haupt' ", *VT* 10 (1960), pp. 311-327 (reprinted in K. Koch, ed., *Um das Prinzip der Vergeltung in Religion und Recht des Alten Testaments (Wege der Forschung* 125), Darmstadt, 1972, pp. 412-431)

– – *Wächter über Israel. Ezechiel und seine Tradition (BZAW* 82), 1962

Riesenfeld, H., *The Resurrection in Ezekiel xxxvii, and in the Dura-Europos Paintings,* Uppsala, 1948

Ringgren, H., *Israelite Religion,* Philadelphia, 1966 (translated from *Israelitische Religion (Die Religionen der Menschheit* 26), Stuttgart, 1963)

– – *The Messiah in the Old Testament (SBT* 18), 1956

Rowley, H.H., *The Faith of Israel,* London, 1956

– – *Job (NCB),* 1970

Rudolph, W., *Hosea (KAT* 13/1), 1966

– – *Die Klagelieder (KAT* 17/3), 1962

Sanders, J.A., *The Psalms Scroll of Qumran Cave 11 (11QPs^a) (Discoveries in the Judaean Desert of Jordan 4),* Oxford, 1965

Saydon, P.P., "The Use of Tenses in Deutero-Isaiah", *Biblica* 40 (1959), pp. 290-301

Schaeffer, C.F.A. (ed.), *Ugaritica V,* Paris, 1968

Scharbert, J., *Heilsmittler im Alten Testament und im Alten Orient (Quaestiones Disputatae* 23/24), Freiburg i. B., 1964

Schmid, H.H., *Gerechtigkeit als Weltordnung (Beiträge zur Historischen Theologie* 40), Tübingen, 1968

Schmidt, H., Erklärung des 118. Psalms", *ZAW* 40 (1922), pp. 1-14

– – *Das Gebet der Angeklagten im Alten Testament (BZAW* 49), 1928

– – *Die Psalmen (HAT* 15), 1934

Schoors, A., *I am God Your Saviour. A Form-Critical Study of the Main*

Genres in Is. XL-LV(VT Suppl 24), 1973

– – *Jesaja II (BOT* 9B), 1973

Scott, R.B.Y., *The Book of Isaiah, Chapters 1-39 (IB* 5), 1956

Sellin, E., *Das Rätsel des deuterojesajanischen Buches,* Leipzig, 1908

– – *Studien zur Entstehungsgeschichte der jüdischen Gemeinde nach dem babylonischen Exil, I. Der Knecht Gottes bei Deuterojesaja,* Leipzig, 1901

Skinner, J., *The Book of the Prophet Isaiah, Chapters XL-LXVI (CB),* 1917[2]

Snaith, N.H., *Leviticus and Numbers (NCB),* 1967

Soden, W. von, "Gibt es ein Zeugnis dafür, dass die Babylonier an die Wiederaufstellung Marduks geglaubt haben?", *ZA* 51, NF 17 (1955), pp. 130-166

Soggin, J.A., "Tod und Auferstehung des leidendes Gottes-Knechtes: Jesaja 53_{8-10}", *ZAW* 85 (1975), pp. 346-355

Sonne, I., "Isaiah 53, 10-12", *JBL* 78 (1959), pp. 335-342

Staerk, W., *Die Ebed-Jahwe Lieder in Jesaja 40ff,* Leipzig, 1913

Stalker, D.M.G., *Ezekiel (TBC),* 1968

Stamm, J.J., *Erlösen und Vergeben im Alten Testament,* Berne, 1940

– – "Eine Erwägung zu Hosea 6_{1-2}", *ZAW* 57 (1939), pp. 266-268

Stoebe, H.J., *Das erste Buch Samuelis (KAT* 8), 1973

Terrien, S., *Job (CAT* 13), 1963

* Thomas, D.W., "A Consideration of Isaiah LIII in the Light of Recent Textual and Philological Study", *ETL* 44 (1968), pp. 79-86

– – "A Consideration of Some Unusual Ways of Expressing the Superlative in Hebrew", *VT* 3 (1953), pp. 209-224

– – "Some Further Remarks on Unusual Ways of Expressing the Superlative in Hebrew", *VT* 18 (1968), pp. 120-124

Torrey, C.C., *The Second Isaiah,* Edinburgh, 1928

Toy, C.H., *The Book of Ezekiel (SBOT),* 1899

Vaux, R. de, "Les combats singuliers dans l'Ancien Testament", in *Studia Biblica et Orientalia I: Vetus Testamentum,* Rome, 1959, pp. 361-374 = *Biblica* 40 (1959), pp. 495-508 (reprinted in R. de Vaux, *Bible et Orient,* Paris, 1967, pp. 217-230)

– – *Les Institutions de l'Ancien Testament,* 2 vols., Paris, 1958, 1960 (ET *Ancient Israel. Its Life and Institutions,* 1 vol., London, 1961)

– – *Les Sacrifices de l'Ancien Testament (Cahiers de la Revue Biblique* 1), Paris, 1964

Vawter, B., "Intimations of Immortality and the Old Testament", *JBL* 91 (1972), pp. 158-171

Volz, P., *Jesaja II (KAT* 11), 1932

Vriezen, T.C., *An Outline of Old Testament Theology,* Oxford, 1958 (translated from *Hoofdlijnen der Theologie van het Oude Testament,* Wageningen, 1954[2])

* Waldow, H.-E. von, *Anlass und Hintergrund der Verkündigung des Deuterojesaja* (Dissertation), Bonn, 1953

– – "... *denn ich erlöse dich". Eine Auslegung von Jesaja 43 (BS* 29), 1960

– – "The Message of Deutero-Isaiah", *Interpretation* 22 (1968), pp. 259-287

Weiser, A., *Das Buch Hiob (ATD* 13), 1956[2]

– – *Hosea (ATD* 24), 1967[5]

– – *Klagelieder (ATD* 16), 1967[2]

– – *The Psalms (OTL),* 1962 (translated from *Die Psalmen (ATD* 14, 15), 2 vols., 1959)

Wellhausen, J., *Die Composition des Hexateuchs und der historischen Bücher des Alten Testaments,* Berlin, 1885

Westermann, C., *Genesis I: Genesis 1-11 (BKAT* 1/1), 1974

– –* *Isaiah 40-66 (OTL),* 1969 (translated from *Das Buch Jesaja Kap. 40-66 (ATD* 19), 1966)

– – *The Praise of God in the Psalms,* London, 1966 (translated from *Das Loben Gottes in den Psalmen,* Göttingen, 1961[2])

– – "Sprache und Struktur der Prophetie Deuterojesajas", in C. Westermann, *Forschung am Alten Testament (TB* 24), 1964, pp. 92-170

– – "Struktur und Geschichte der Klage im Alten Testament", *ZAW* 66 (1954), pp. 44-80

Wevers, J.W., *Ezekiel (NCB),* 1969

– – "A Study in the Form Criticism of Individual Complaint Psalms", *VT* 6 (1956), pp. 80-96

Whybray, R.N., *The Heavenly Counsellor in Isaiah xl 13-14. A Study of the Sources of the Theology of Deutero-Isaiah (SOTS Monograph Series 1),* Cambridge, 1971

– –* *Isaiah 40-66 (NCB),* 1975

Wolff, H.W., *Hosea (Hermeneia),* Philadelphia, 1974 (translated from *Hosea (BKAT* 14/1), 1965[2])

Zimmerli, W., "Die Eigenart der prophetischen Reden des Ezechiel", *ZAW*
66 (1954), pp. 1-26

– – *Ezechiel I: Ezechiel 1-24 (BKAT* 13/1), 1969

– – "Zur Vorgeschichte von Jes. LIII", in *Congress Volume: Rome 1968
(VT Suppl* 17), 1969, pp. 236-244

INTRODUCTION

Isaiah chapter 53[1] portrays a person – Yahweh's "Servant" – who undergoes a wholly unmerited punishment. It also speaks of his subsequent vindication and divine reward. Amid all the various opinions about the identity of this "Servant" and about the chronology envisaged by the author – whether these events are seen as wholly or partly past or future – so much is universally admitted. Almost as widely accepted, at least among Christian exegetes, are two further propositions: 1. that the chapter speaks of the death and subsequent restoration to life of the Servant; and 2. that it states that the penalty which he suffered had a vicarious character: that is, that others who deserved to be punished were not required to do so because God accepted his suffering in lieu of theirs.

These last two propositions create very serious exegetical and theological problems even if the Servant is not a real historical individual but symbolizes the Israelite people in the sixth century B.C.: a people humiliated and oppressed, but subsequently to be restored to God's favour. If the Servant is understood to be a real individual the problems are even greater. Some recent scholars have, however, denied these propositions: it has been argued that the chapter does not state that the Servant's sufferings were fatal;[2] and also that it does not speak of them as vicarious.[3]

The purpose of the present study is to offer arguments in further support of these recent theories, and also to offer a positive theory about the chapter's character and meaning. With regard to the Servant's identity, many differing views have been and are still held by those who believe him to have been a historical individual.[4] Here the view will be taken that he was the prophet, "Deutero-Isaiah", himself: the exilic prophet of the sixth century B.C. whose ministry was exercised in Babylon and whose teachings are recorded in chapters 40-55 of the book of Isaiah. This view, which is held at the present time by a substantial minority of scholars,[5] will not be discussed in detail in the following pages but will, it is hoped, commend itself as the study proceeds as the only view which makes a full understanding of the chapter possible.[6]

Part I. Was the Servant's Suffering Vicarious?

PART I. WAS THE SERVANT'S SUFFERING VICARIOUS?

A. Supposed References to Vicarious Suffering

A number of words and phrases in the chapter have been interpreted as asserting or implying the vicariousness of the Servant's suffering. These must now be examined. It is also necessary to investigate afresh the meaning of the phrase נשא עון , which, although it does not occur in the chapter, has played an important role in the discussion. This will be done in a separate Excursus.[1]

1. Statements that the Servant "bore the sin (guilt, punishment)" of others

a. ועונתם הוא יסבל (verse 11b)[2]

The phrase סבל עון occurs in only one other Old Testament passage, viz. Lam. 5:7:[3] אבתינו חטאו ואינם ואנחנו עונתיהם סבלנו ("Our fathers sinned, and are no more; but we bear their iniquities").

It has long been recognized that of the various inter-related senses of עון — sin, guilt, punishment — it is frequently difficult to determine which is intended in a particular passage. In particular, the question whether in a specific case the word refers primarily to the deed or its consequences can present a major problem of interpretation. K. Koch has argued convincingly [4] that this twofold meaning illustrates the *Tun-Ergehen* principle which he finds in Old Testament thought: the act and its consequences are seen as one and the same thing because the act bears within itself, irrespective of any punishment which may be imposed from without, its own inevitable consequences. There is therefore a sense in which it is impossible to say in any particular case that the meaning of עון is *either* "sin" *or* "punishment". This is a point which it will be necessary to bear in mind in all the discussions of עון which follow. Nevertheless in practice in particular cases one or other of the meanings is generally primary; [5] and in Lam. 5:7 the context, in which the speaker specifies in detail the suffering which the community is at present undergoing, leaves no doubt that it is the consequences of sin rather than the sin itself which are the more prominent in his mind.

The modern commentators [6] are agreed that the author of this lamentation is not seeking to throw the blame for the present sufferings of the community on the "fathers" in order to exculpate his own generation. He is not concerned to contrast the guilt (חטאו) of the fathers with the undeserved sufferings of himself and his contemporaries (סבלנו). The exclamation "Woe to us, for we have sinned!" of verse 16 makes this clear. Sin, guilt and punishment belong together, and bind the generations together in a common fate. The punishment received by the present generation is a continuation of that of the

29

previous generation, and so is its sin. The principle is the same as that expressed in Exod. 20:5, where the עון of the fathers is visited on the children to the third and fourth generation. There is therefore no question here of vicarious suffering: there is cause and effect, but not substitution.

In Isa. 53:11 as in Lam. 5:7 a statement is made that someone (viz. the Servant) bears the punishment "of " others. The suffix "their" (עונם) refers to the "many" (רבים). Although the immediate context, which is beset with textual difficulties, does not make clear the identity of these "many", the general situation reflected in the book of Deutero-Isaiah indicates that they are the Jewish exiles in Babylonia.[7] If this is so, the Servant cannot be said to be suffering, or to have suffered, *in place* of the exiles in such a way that they escape the consequences of their sins, since, as in the case of the speakers in Lam. 5:7, it cannot be said that these have escaped punishment: they are all actually suffering the consequences of defeat and banishment. The Servant, if, as is here maintained, he is one of them, shares their suffering. Chapter 53 indeed makes it clear that he has suffered more intensely than they, and the "we" who speak there confess that, at any rate compared with themselves, he is innocent;[8] nevertheless this is shared and not vicarious suffering. This consideration applies equally to the other passages which are to be considered in this section, and should itself be sufficient to dismiss the theory of vicarious suffering here as impossible. It is however desirable to confirm this conclusion by a detailed demonstration that none of the words and phrases in chapter 53 which have been interpreted in a vicarious sense has that meaning elsewhere in the Old Testament.[9]

b. והוא חטא-רבים נשא (verse 12c)[10]

The phrase נשא חטא occurs – apart from Isa. 53:12 – in eight passages in the Old Testament: Lev. 19:17; 20:20; 22:9; 24:15; Num. 9:13; 18:22, 32; Ezek. 23:49, always in the context of priestly legislation. The offences in question are those of various kinds: hatred of one's neighbour, incest, breaches of the laws concerning uncleanness, blasphemy, failure to observe the Passover, approaching too closely to the Tent of Meeting and idolatry. In one case (Num. 18:32) the phrase occurs in a negative form: the Levites are permitted to eat their portion of the offerings wherever they wish, without incurring a penalty (ולא-תשאו עליו חטא). In some cases death is specified as the penalty; in others no penalty is specified, although death may be implied. In the case of incest (Lev. 20:20) the phrase "they shall die childless" is ambiguous: it may or may not imply immediate death. Probably it does not, since in the following verse the punishment for a similar offence is simply "they shall be childless".[11] In some cases the phrase used is simply "bear sin" (חטא); in others it is "bear his/their sin" (חטאם / חטאו).

30

In every one of these cases the verb נשא clearly has the meaning "bear, carry, incur". In each case also, as with סבל עון in Lam. 5:7, a penalty or punishment, directly sent by God or mediated through human agency, is either specified or implied. This is always a punishment which the sinner has deserved and brought upon himself: the idea of vicarious bearing of a punishment on behalf of others is never present.

The phrase והוא חטא-רבים נשא in Isa. 53:12 is thus the only example of נשא חטא in which a person is said to bear or incur the חטא of others. The immediate context, though free from textual difficulties, does not help to elucidate its meaning. The parallel phrase ולפשעים יפגיע is itself of uncertain meaning though, as will be shown below, [12] unlikely to bear a vicarious sense.

It may however be said that the similarity of והוא חטא-רבים נשא here to וע‍ונתם הוא יסבל in verse 11 can hardly be accidental, and it is extremely improbable that any difference of meaning between the two should have been intended by the author, especially since נשא in the sense used here is exactly equivalent to סבל, and חטא and עון are used interchangeably in the priestly writings.

There is however another phrase which, although it does not occur in Isa. 53, and is never in any passage applied to the Servant of Yahweh in Deutero-Isaiah, cannot be omitted from the discussion. This is נשא עון (with a variant נשא בעוֹן in Ezek. 18:19, 20). It occurs in a number of passages which have frequently been pressed into service in support of the theory of vicarious suffering in Isa. 53; and this is in itself a not unreasonable method of procedure, since it appears to be virtually identical in meaning with נשא חטא : the two phrases occur in very similar contexts in adjacent verses in the same legal pericope in Lev. 20:19, 20 and are probably also interchangeable when they occur in close proximity in Num. 18:22, 23. [13] The pages which follow will therefore be devoted to a detailed investigation into the uses of נשא עון.

B. Excursus: נשא (ב) עון in the Old Testament

1. Introduction

This phrase has been discussed in detail by W. Zimmerli. [14] Some of his conclusions, however, are open to criticism, and a fresh analysis of all the passages in which the phrase occurs needs to be undertaken.

The verb נשא in the Qal with עון (sing. or plur., with or without a pronominal suffix) as its direct object occurs 29 times in the Old Testament: Exod. 28:38, 43; 34:7; Lev. 5:1, 17; 7:18; 10:17; 16:22; 17:16; 19:8; 20:17, 19; Num. 5:31; 14:18, 34; 18:1 (twice), 23; 30:16 (EVV 15); Ps. 32:5;

85:3 (EVV 2) ; Ezek. 4:4, 5, 6; 14:10; 44:10, 12; Hos. 14:3 (EVV 2) ; [15] Mic. 7:18. In two other texts the same relationship between נשא and עון is implied: Gen. 4:13 (גדול עוני מנשׂא) and Isa. 33:24 (נשׂא עון). There is one case in which the verb is in the Hiphil: Lev. 22:16. Three further texts have the form נשא בעון : Ezek. 18:19, 20 (twice). [16] There are thus 35 examples to be considered.

In seven of these cases [17] (Exod. 34:7; Num. 14:18; Ps. 32:5; 85:3; Isa. 33:24; Hos. 14:3; Mic. 7:18) God is the subject of the verb: he "takes away" human sin, that is, he forgives the sinner. As Zimmerli has pointed out, it is significant that all these passages lie outside the "priestly" writings of P and Ezekiel, while all the remaining passages occur within those writings. In these latter —with one exception: that of the scapegoat in Lev. 16:22 — it is always a human being (or beings) who is the agent. God is never the subject.

These remaining 27 cases, of which 18 occur in P and 9 in Ezekiel, Zimmerli [18] divides into three categories. [19]

a. In 14 cases (Exod. 28:43; Lev. 5:1, 17; 7:18; 17:16; 19:8; 20:17, 19; 22:16; Num. 5:31; 30:16; Ezek. 14:10; 44:10, 12) to which Zimmerli also attached the eight cases of נשא חטא in P and Ezek. discussed above,[20] the phrase נשא עון is seen by him as a priestly "verdict" or diagnosis in which the priest states that certain sinful actions, which are offences against the realm of the holy, inevitably bring upon the guilty person the punishment of the holy God. The fact that in some of these cases there is also a punishment to be imposed by the community, principally to protect itself from "contamination", does not alter the principle that these are sins against God which can be punished only by God himself. Zimmerli points to the fact that in almost all these passages the formula is "he shall bear his עון " or an equivalent phrase, and that it stands at the end of a pericope as a formula prescribing the penalty for the sin described in the preceding sentence. These are the concerns of the priests; Ezekiel has adopted the familiar priestly formula in his use of the expression. [21]

b. In 7 cases (Exod. 28:38; Lev. 10:17; 16:22; Num. 14:34; Ezek. 4:4, 5, 6), and also in the case of נשא חטא in Isa. 53:11, the expression, according to Zimmerli, denotes the vicarious bearing of the guilt of others. [22] This, he says, is the function of the scapegoat (Lev. 16:22; cf. 10:17) and also perhaps [23] of Aaron in Exod. 28:38. It is certainly true, he affirms, of Ezekiel in Ezek. 4:4-6 and of the Servant in Isa. 53:11. Zimmerli sees [24] some relationship between these passages and the non-priestly passages in which the phrase נשא עון is used of God's forgiveness of sins.

c. In 6 cases (Num. 18:1 (twice); 18:23 (probably); Ezek. 18:19; 18:20

(twice)) the phrase is used, according to Zimmerli, in a weakened sense: " to bear עון " has become simply an expression denoting " to assume responsibility".

Zimmerli's first category does not require discussion here. These are all cases, like those in which נשא חטא is used, in which the sinner is held personally responsible for his own sin. Whether they are to be interpreted as referring primarily to a punishment inflicted directly by God or [25] in a purely juridical sense, there is clearly no idea of vicarious punishment here. Zimmerli's other two categories, however, require further investigation. It may be asked on the one hand whether the passages in his second category must of necessity be interpreted in terms of vicarious guilt or punishment, and on the other whether the distinction between his second and third categories is justified: whether his theory of a "weakened sense" of the phrase נשא עון can be substantiated. A fresh investigation is therefore required of the passages in these two categories, i.e. Exod. 28:38; Lev. 10:17; 16:22; Num. 14:34; 18:1, 23; Ezek. 4:4-6; 18:19, 20.

2. Aaron, his sons, and the Levites

In all these passages (Exod. 28:38; Lev. 10:17; Num. 18:1, 23) either Aaron or his sons or the Levites are to bear the עון "of" or "in connection with" (construct state) something or someone other than themselves. All occur in the Priestly literature.

a. ונשא אהרון את-עון הקדשים (Exod. 28:38) [26]

In order to understand the meaning of this statement it is important to observe the contents and structure of the section within which it occurs — verses 36-38 — and of the chapter as a whole.

Chapter 28 constitutes a distinct section within the priestly legislation. Yahweh commands Moses to provide for the making of priestly vestments and ornaments, particularly for Aaron, and gives detailed instructions concerning the materials from which they are to be made, their character and shape, and the way in which they are to be made. Something is also said about their function.

The four main sections of the chapter are each concerned with one of these objects: the ephod (verses 5-14), the so-called " breastpiece of judgement " (חשן משפט) within which the Urim and Thummim are to be placed (verses 15-30), the "robe of the ephod" (verses 31-35) and the golden "flower" or rosette (?) (ציץ זהב) to be fixed on Aaron's forehead, on the front of his turban (verses 36-38). These four sections are preceded by an introductory section (verses 1-4) and followed by briefer instructions concerning the remaining vestments for Aaron (verse 39), the coats, caps and girdles of Aaron's sons (verse 40), the investiture, anointing and consecration of Aaron and his sons (verse 41); and by a separate section about the making of breeches for them (verses 42-43).

Although it is clear that the chapter is not from a single hand, [27] the four central sections in their present form are constructed according to a common pattern which is easily discernible in spite of certain variations. At or near the beginning of each section comes the naming of the object with the command for its manufacture: "And you/they shall make . . .". Near or at the end of each section (verses 12, 29f., 35, 38) comes a statement concerning the function or purpose of the object in question. In the section on the "breast-piece of judgement" in its present form there are two such statements: one on the purpose of the twelve stones sewn on to the breastpiece (verse 29) and another on the purpose of the Urim and Thummim to be placed within it (verse 30b).

It is important to observe that these five explanatory statements, although they do not form an entirely rigid pattern, are mainly composed of words and phrases common to all, or at least to more than one:

"before Yahweh" occurs in all five sections and six times in all.

References to Aaron's bearing certain objects on his person also occur in all five sections: "upon his two shoulders" (verse 12); "upon his heart" (verses 29, 30); "upon Aaron" (verse 35); "upon his forehead" (twice) (verse 38).

"remembrance" (זכרן) occurs twice (verses 12, 29).

"when he goes in" occurs three times (verses 29, 30, 35).

"perpetually" (תמיד) occurs three times (verses 29, 30, 38).

"And Aaron shall bear" (ונשא אהרן) occurs four times:
"And Aaron shall bear their names before Yahweh" (verse 12);
"And Aaron shall bear the names of the sons of Israel" (verse 29);
"Thus shall Aaron bear the judgement of the people of Israel"
    (verse 30);
"And Aaron shall bear the עון of the holy offerings (הקדשים)"
    (verse 38).

These passages not only follow a formal pattern of words and phrases; they also have a similarity of content and purpose. In each case, after the description of the vestment in question and the way in which it is to be made attention is drawn to a material object which forms part of it, or is attached to it: two engraved stones set in the ephod; twelve engraved stones set in the breastpiece; the Urim and Thummim placed within the pocket of the breast-piece; the bell attached to the skirt of the robe; the "flower" fixed to the turban. The explanatory statement of purpose or function is related not to the vestment itself but to this attached object. [28]

These objects naturally accompany Aaron, their wearer, into the sanctuary when he enters it to perform his cultic duties "before Yahweh", a phrase which is sometimes elaborated, [29] sometimes not.

For the elucidation of the meaning of נשא עון in verse 38 it is important to consider the statements about the purpose and function of these objects which Aaron takes with him into the sanctuary. For it can hardly be a coincidence that the phrase ונשא אהרן את-עון הקדשים in verse 38 is so closely paralleled by ונשא אהרן את-שמותם in verse 12, ונשא אהרן את-שמות בני-ישראל in verse 29 and ונשא אהרן את-משפט in verse 30. In each of these cases Aaron brings before Yahweh something (names, judgement, עון) which is symbolized by, and as it were inherent in, material objects (engraved stones, Urim and Thummim, the "flower" on the turban). It is of course possible that the passage about the " flower " (verses 36-38) has been modelled upon the other passages by a later hand but with a different intention, and that the verb נשא is used here in two different senses ("incur" in verse 38, "carry" in the other cases); but in the absence of any evidence in favour of such an hypothesis it is more natural to suppose that it has the meaning of "carry" in the most literal sense in verse 38 as well as elsewhere in the chapter. Verse 35, although נשא does not occur there, will also be included in this investigation since the verse otherwise has some similarities to the others.

In *verse 12* the two onyx stones, on which have been engraved the twelve names of the sons of Israel, the ancestors of the twelve tribes (verses 9-11), are to be "set upon the shoulder-pieces of the ephod, as stones of remembrance for the sons of Israel" (אבני זכרן לבני ישראל). When Aaron goes into the sanctuary "before Yahweh" he will "bear their names before Yahweh . . . as a memorial (לזכרן . . . לפני יהוה את-שמותם אהרן ונשא)". The meaning of זכרן in these two instances is, as it is in more than half of the total number of its occurrences in the Old Testament, "reminder".[30] In this sense it is always used in a religious context: Israel is "reminded" of God, his deeds, requirements, laws, ordinances etc. (Exod. 12:14; 13:9; 17:14; Num. 17:5 [EVV 16:40] ; Josh. 4:7; Zech. 6:14). But equally Israel "reminds" God (Exod. 30:16; Num. 10:10; 31:54), presumably of its existence and of God's promise of good will towards his people.[31]

Who is to be "reminded" here? God, or the people? The phrase "stones of remembrance for the sons of Israel" is in itself ambiguous; but the second phrase "bear their names before Yahweh . . . as a memorial" makes it clear, as the commentators point out, that it is God who is to be reminded.

It is not said of what God is to be reminded here; but we may presume that it is of his promises of good will towards his people. A similar idea is found in the psalms of lamentation, where the speaker complains that Yahweh has "forgotten" his people or an individual. This "forgetting" is a "forgetting to be gracious", as is specifically stated in Ps. 77:10 (EVV 77:9): "has God forgotten to be gracious?" (השכח חנות אל). The classical example of God's "reminding himself" is in Gen. 9:12-17 (P), where he establishes his covenant with Noah and sets the rainbow in the sky so that "when . . . the bow is seen in the clouds, I will remember (וזכרתי) my covenant which is between me and you and every living creature . . .; and the waters shall never again become a flood to destroy all flesh" (verses 14f.); and, "When the bow is in the clouds, I will look at it and remember (וראיתיה לזכר) the ever-lasting covenant between God and every living creature" (verse 16). As the rainbow is the "sign" (אות) of this covenant, so also the names of the sons of Israel engraved on the onyx stones function as "signs" which God sees and which cause him to "remember".

A passage which sheds the greatest light, because of its cultic context, on what is effected by God's being "reminded" by objects brought into the sanctuary is, however, Exod. 30:16. Here Moses is to take the half-shekel which has been collected from each member of the people of Israel as "atonement money" (כסף הכפרים) and "it will be for the sons of Israel a זכרון before Yahweh to make atonement for yourselves" (לכפר על-נפשתיכם).

Verse 29 resembles verse 12 in some ways but differs from it in others. Here again Aaron is to "carry the names of the sons of Israel" into the holy place "for a continual remembrance before Yahweh" (לזכרן לפני-יהוה תמיד). Here again, as in verse 12, it is Yahweh who is to be "reminded". But in this case there are twelve stones, each of a different kind, "with their names according to the names of the sons of Israel; they shall be like signets, each engraved with its name, for the twelve tribes" (verse 21). It is unlikely that any significant difference of meaning is intended: this is probably a variant of the earlier passage by a different hand. If there is a significant difference it lies in the name of the vestment in which these stones are set: the "breastpiece of judgement" (חשן משפט). But neither verse 29 nor the preceding verses (15-28) which describe this vestment make any reference to the meaning of this name. The only clue to its meaning is to be found in the following verse (30), the third of the verses under discussion, which is probably again by a different hand.

In *verse 30* the word זכרן does not occur. The context is once more Aaron's "going in before Yahweh"; but two new features are added: the Urim and Thummim are "placed in" (ונתת אל-) the "breastpiece of judgement".

The significance of these objects is defined in the last clause which prescribes that Aaron "shall bear the judgement of the people of Israel(משפט בני-ישראל) upon his heart before Yahweh continually".

Little clear information is available concerning the nature of the objects known as Urim and Thummim. The accounts of their use as a sacred lot suggest that they were two material objects. If they were two stones, as is perhaps most probable, this verse constitutes yet a third reference in this chapter to the carrying by Aaron into the sanctuary of certain kinds of stones attached to his vestments. Once more the possibility of variants suggests itself. Since there were (probably) two stones here, they correspond rather to the two stones attached to the ephod (verses 9-14) than to the twelve stones in the breastpiece referred to in the passage in which this verse now stands. But it is not stated that the names of the sons of Israel were engraved upon them.

That the Urim and Thummim[32] were the instruments of the sacred lot whose operation was reserved for the priests (or Levites), and that they were the instruments by which the priests used to "enquire" (שאל) of God what was his will for Israel or for an individual is not disputed.[33] How the lots were manipulated and interpreted is not known; but it was believed that God in some way "answered" (ענה) the enquirer (I Sam. 28:6). This divine "answer" was known as a "decision" (משפט), as can be seen from Num. 27: 21, where Eleazar the priest is to enquire on behalf of Joshua (ושאל לו) "through the decision of the Urim(במשפט האורים) before Yahweh"; similarly in Prov. 16:33 "The lot (גורל) is cast into the lap, but every decision (כל-משפטו) is from Yahweh". It may be assumed that this is the meaning of משפט in the phrase "breastpiece of judgement"(חשן משפט) : it is the vestment connected with the giving of the divine decision by lot.[34]

As we have seen, the casting of the lot by Urim was carried out by the priest "before Yahweh" (Num. 27:21), that is, in the sanctuary. In carrying the משפט בני-ישראל "upon his heart continually before Yahweh", therefore, Aaron is appearing before Yahweh on all occasions equipped, as it were, with the tools of his trade: tools which were ready for use and were actually used on some occasions. There can be little doubt that it is this situation which P intends to depict here: even if, as is possible, the Urim and Thummim in P are merely an element in a purely theoretical and imaginary Tabernacle cult, what little older evidence we have suggests that his use of משפט here is based on some knowledge of older practice.

It is, indeed, difficult to see what other meaning is possible. The view expressed recently by R.E. Clements[35] is improbable: "The author here regards the Urim and Thummim primarily as symbols of justice. By wearing them above his heart when he performed his priestly duties, Aaron was to give visible expression to the belief that justice originates from God, and to remind God to watch over the administration of justice in Israel". This interpretation ignores the obvious meaning of משפט in the context of the casting of lots and interprets it in a sense which it does not otherwise have in P. It is also difficult to believe that the author, if he had intended the word to be taken in this sense, would not have expressed his intention with greater clarity.

The meaning of the phrase "Aaron shall bear the משפט of the sons of Israel . . . before Yahweh" in Exod. 28:30 is therefore that he is regularly to enter the sanctuary equipped with the Urim and Thummim, which can be referred to as "the משפט " because it is through them that Yahweh gives the decisions which are binding upon his people. It must be assumed that both P and his audience were aware of the ancient tradition about the Urim and Thummim. This is not improbable in view of the fact that the author of Ezra 2:63 (= Neh. 7:65) was evidently familiar with them.

In *verse 35* the phrase ונשא אהרן does not occur, nor does זכרן . It is simply stated that " 'It' shall be upon Aaron when he ministers" (והיה על-אהרן לשרת). "It" presumably refers to the "robe" (מעיל) mentioned at the end of verse 34, more fully defined as "the robe of the ephod" (מעיל האפוד) in verse 31. It is further stated that "its sound (קולו) shall be heard when he goes into the holy place before Yahweh, and when he comes out, lest he die". The "sound" is caused, at least mainly, by the "bells of gold" (פעמני זהב) which are attached to the skirts of the robe (verses 33-34), which, as Ecclus 45:9 puts it in its description of the same vestment, "sent forth a sound as he walked".

The bells are thus yet another set of objects which Aaron carries with him into the sanctuary. The consensus of the commentaries is that the original purpose of these bells in the ancient tradition of which P is here making use was apotropaic : to drive away demons, perhaps specifically demons of the threshhold, which might otherwise attack the priest as he went in to perform his sacred duties. Most commentators, however, agree that P was either unaware of, or chose to ignore, this original function.

It is not stated whether it is God or the people who are intended to hear the sound of the bells. It has been suggested by some commentators[36] that it is the people : the sound will warn or alternatively reassure the people that Aaron is actually inside the holy place performing the sacred duties of his office. But this interpretation leaves unexplained the phrase "and so he shall not die" (ולא ימות). This phrase is regularly used in the priestly legislation[37] to describe the fate which will befall the sacred ministers (Aaron and his sons, the Levites) if they defile the holiness of the sanctuary by infringing the commandments regarding their behaviour, dress etc. while they are there.[38]

It would therefore seem that the purpose of the bells as understood by P is to remind God – though זכרן is not used – that it is Aaron, properly dressed and equipped, who has entered the sanctuary to perform the prescribed rites, and not some unauthorized person.[39]

In the light of the above investigation certain observations may be made which assist the interpretation of נשא עון in verse 38.

i. In all the four verses (12, 29, 30, 35) where the phrase ונשא אהרן occurs there is an identification of an object or objects carried (נשא) by Aaron into the sanctuary with something which they symbolize: in verses 12 and 29 the stones engraved with the names of the sons of Israel are identified with the names themselves, so that Aaron can be said to "carry their names" before Yahweh. In verse 30, similarly, by carrying the Urim and Thummim into the sanctuary Aaron can be said to "carry the divine decision" (משפט), that is, the instruments of the divine decision, "before Yahweh". It is therefore natural to suppose that in verse 38 also, where Aaron takes with him into the sanctuary the "flower" fixed to his turban, and is said thus to be carrying "the עון of the offerings" of the sons of Israel, נשא here as in the other passages means "carry" in the physical sense rather than "incur": the עון הקדשים is carried into the presence of Yahweh by virtue of its identification with the "flower".

Why the "flower" should symbolize guilt is not clear. The inscription engraved on it, "Holy to Yahweh", would seem to indicate the opposite; and this is true also of the "flower" itself. In Egypt and elsewhere in the ancient Near East the flower was frequently used in religious iconography as a symbol of life.[40] It has been argued by M. Noth[41] that the "flower" in the High Priest's turban was originally part of the regalia of the Judaean kings. If this were so both the object itself and the inscription engraved on it might be seen as a kind of "prophylactic" to avoid the incurring by the people of the consequences of their guilt. The identification of guilt with an object representing the neutralizing of the guilt has perhaps some partial parallels in the golden offerings made by the Philistines to Yahweh in the form of the things by which he had punished them (I Sam. 6) and the use of a bronze image of the death-dealing serpent to give life (Num. 21:6-9). In these two cases the procedure is reversed in that the object in question represents the guilt but is intended to neutralize it by being brought into the divine sphere, whereas in Exod. 28:38 the object represents forgiveness and brings the guilt with it, as it were under its aegis. The same principle, of the neutralizing of guilt by an identification of opposites, is however present in all three cases. But whether this explanation of Aaron's action in Exod. 28:38 is satisfactory or not, the identification of עון with the "flower" is assured by the similarity of the passage to the others which have been discussed above.

39

ii. In verses 12 and 29 the purpose of this action is to remind God to be gracious to his people, and there is also a "reminder" to God in verse 35, though in this case it concerns Aaron alone. Here, however, the word זכרן does not occur. In verse 38 also זכרן does not occur. On the other hand it is said that "it" (presumably the "flower") will be "a רצון for them before Yahweh continually". Whatever may be the precise meaning of רצון here,[42] it undoubtedly signifies some effect upon Yahweh's attitude towards his people. Verse 38 therefore is parallel with the other verses studied: God is "reminded", by the bringing into his presence of a specially designated material object, of an obligation or promise.

iii. There is a specially close parallel between verses 30 and 38 in that in both cases the object brought into the sanctuary by Aaron is identified with something quite abstract: עון, משפט.

iv. In the four other verses (12, 29, 30, 35) the function of Aaron in bringing these objects before Yahweh is neither a vicarious nor even a representative function but that of a messenger. He does not represent in his own person the names or the משפט of Israel, but merely brings before God the objects which do so. Still less is his action vicarious: he does not in any way substitute himself for Israel in his encounter with God. There is therefore good reason to suppose that in verse 38 also his function is not representative or vicarious: he simply brings into the sanctuary an object (the "flower") which is in some way identified with the עון "of", or connected with, the offerings of the people; and the appearance of this object in Yahweh's presence achieves רצון for them. The phrase נשא עון is to be interpreted not as "incurring punishment" but in a way which brings it into line with the other three occurrences of the phrase· ונשא אהרן in chapter 28.

The meaning of the phrase עון הקדשים in verse 28 will be discussed later together with the equally unusual expressions עון המקדש and עון כהנתכם in Num. 18:1.[43] But whatever may be the precise nature of the עון of Israel here, the purpose of its being carried into the sanctuary is stated in the final phrase of the verse: it is to be a רצון for the people "before Yahweh". The phrase לרצון occurs in Lev. 22:20, 21 in connection with the necessity of offering peace offerings which are without blemish; with suffixes (לרצנו, לרצנכם) it occurs a number of times in the priestly legislation,[44] also in connection with sacrifice. It is generally interpreted as referring to Yahweh's favour in accepting sacrifice, since "favour" is a common meaning of the word elsewhere. It is possible, however, that in the passages referred to above it has a different meaning.

Some recent scholarship[45] distinguishes two verbs רצה in biblical Hebrew: רצה I, "to be pleased", and רצה II, "to pay, pay off". רצון in its usual sense of "favour" is related to רצה I.   רצה II is found in the Qal in Lev. 26: 34, 41, 43 and in the Hiphil also in Lev. 26:34. In Isa. 40:2 (כי נרצה עונה) it is significantly associated with עון : Jerusalem is assured that it has paid off and so completed its punishment. If this identification of a second verb רצה may be accepted, we should perhaps also recognize the existence of a second noun רצון cognate with רצה II, meaning "the payment of a debt". This would ease a number of difficulties in other passages where רצון occurs. Thus in some of the passages in Leviticus, where it is said of a person or persons offering free will offerings, thanksgiving offerings or sacrifices in payment of vows, that they offer the sacrifice לרצנם/ם (Lev. 1:3; 19:5; 22:19, 29), these phrases can, if רצון here means "favour, acceptance", only be translated if the suffixes are taken as equivalent to objective genitives: "for (Yahweh's) acceptance of him/you". But this rendering is very forced. If, however, רצון here means "payment of debt", they can be rendered far more naturally by "for the payment of his/their debt (to Yahweh)", that is, a debt incurred by the receiving of Yahweh's favours in the past (in the case of the freewill and thanksgiving sacrifices) or by the making of vows which had to be paid. Again in Mal. 2:13 "accepting a payment of debt from your hand" is a much more natural translation of לקחת רצון מידכם than "accepting it from your hand with favour", where "it" is unexpressed in the Hebrew and רצון has to be taken somewhat improbably as a kind of "adverbial accusative".

If the above proposal to distinguish between רצון I and רצון II is accepted, and רצון in Exod. 28:38 can be taken as meaning "payment of debt", the verse may then be translated in a sense analogous to נרצה עונה in Isa. 40:2, in which "Jerusalem" is said to have "paid off" its debt to Yahweh, with the difference that whereas in Isa. 40:2 this was achieved by the enduring of the punishment of exile prescribed by Yahweh, in Exod. 28: 38 Israel's עון הקדשים , symbolized by the "flower" in Aaron's turban, is "paid off", as in the sacrificial passages in Leviticus, by a ceremonial action: its being brought "before Yahweh" by Aaron. Of this action Aaron is the instrument, since only he is permitted to approach Yahweh; but he is no more than the instrument.

The above suggestion regarding the meaning of רצון tends to support the interpretation of נשא עון in Exod. 28:38 made above in that it proposes some explanation of the concept of a literal "carrying of Israel's עון " before Yahweh. However, the interpretation of נשא עון does not depend on it. The main conclusion remains valid whether רצון means "favour" or "payment of a debt", that in the context of Exod. 28 as a whole it is overwhelmingly probable that נשא in verse 38 means "carry, bring" rather than "bear, incur" as it does in the other instances in the chapter, and that there is therefore no idea here of Aaron's vicariously bearing the guilt or punishment of the people.

b. אתה ובניך ... תשאו את-עון המקדש ואתה ובניך אתך
תשאו את-עון כהנתכם (Num. 18:1)[46]

In its original form Num. 18 may well have been an independent unit[47] concerned with the status, duties, responsibilities and rewards of Aaron and his descendants with regard to the service of the sanctuary. In its present form, however, the chapter is linked in many ways, particularly in verses 1-7, to chapters 16 and 17 which describe the rebellion of Korah the Levite and its consequences[48] and which raise the question of the difference between the status of the priests (Aaron and his descendants), Levites and people respectively and also emphasize dramatically the fatal consequences of the arrogant assumption by either Levites or people of the approach to or hand-ling of holy things reserved for the priests. Thus in 18:5 the law restricting the service of the sanctuary and the altar to Aaron and his descendants "so that wrath (קצף) shall no more fall upon the sons of Israel" clearly refers back to 17:11 (EVV 16:46) when "wrath (קצף) came forth from Yahweh" in the form of a plague which struck down the rebellious people. Although this incident is distinct from the punishment of the Levite Korah, when it was fire which came out from Yahweh (16:35),[49] and the word קצף is not used, the story of the plague (17:6-15 [EVV 16:41-50]) is intended to show that when Aaron, in contrast to the Levites, uses his censer atonement is brought about and the "wrath" of the plague is stopped. The point is made even clearer by the previous verse (17:5 [EVV 16:40]), where the use of the censer is specifically reserved for Aaron and his descendants. Other references in chapter 18 stressing that neither people nor Levites must "draw near" to the sanctuary but only Aaron and his descendants (verses 3, 4, 7) also refer back to chapter 17.[50]

In this context, and particularly in view of the two preceding verses 17:27f. (EVV 17:12f.), where the people lament that they must all perish because "every one who comes near to Yahweh's tabernacle (משכן) will die", it is probable that the phrases ונשאו את-עון המקדש and תשאו את-עון כהנתכם , which, together with Exod. 28:38's ... ונשא את-עון הקדשים , are quite unique, are connected in some way with the "wrath" of God which had manifested itself in the form of fire in the case of Korah, the man who had challenged the special status of Moses and Aaron over the right to approach the tabernacle (16:4-11). The nature of this connection must now be examined.

In all three phrases עון is associated with things which are not only good in themselves but ordained by God: the sanctuary, the office of priesthood and the holy offerings. In order to explain this apparent anomaly Zimmerli[51]

42

suggested that here – and also in 18:23; Ezek. 18:19, 20 – עון has the "weakened" sense of "responsibility": Aaron and his sons are *responsible* for carrying out the duties of the sanctuary and the other duties pertaining to their priestly office. But it is doubtful whether such a weakened sense can be admitted. Zimmerli gives no explanation of the *raison d'être* of this shift in meaning: presumably it lies in the fact that responsibility includes the taking of the blame when things go wrong. But it is a long step from "guilt" or "punishment" to mere "responsibility"; and in the context of Num. 16-18, where sin in its full sense, and the punishment which follows it, are very much in the forefront of the narrative, such a reduced sense is especially improbable.

עון in Num. 18:1 and Exod. 28:38 must then be regarded as having its full sense of an act or state displeasing to God and having divine punishment as its result. If this is so, then since it is spoken of in connection with things which in themselves are the very opposite of sinful, it can only refer to some failure to perform the sacral duties in the proper manner. This is the genitive of nearer definition: the עון is an עון which occurs *in connection with* the altar, the priestly office, or the offerings of the people. Since further there is no suggestion of a deliberate failure to act according to the prescribed manner, the situation envisaged must be analogous to that in the story of Uzzah in 2 Sam. 6:6-11: Uzzah's intention in steadying the Ark when the oxen drawing it stumbled was good, and indeed, by ordinary standards, praiseworthy (verse 6); but Yahweh's anger was kindled (verse 7), and he "broke out" (פרץ יהוה פרץ) (verse 8) against Uzzah, killing him. The parallel with the thought in Num. 17:27f. is striking. Uzzah had clearly committed an involuntary עון , although the word is not used. It is in this sense that Num. 18:1 – and also Exod. 28:38 – must be explained.[52]

But the situation presupposed in Num. 18:1 must be distinguished from that of Exod. 28:38. The phrase נשא עון has a different meaning in each of the two passages. In Exod. 28:38, as has been shown, Aaron carries (נשא) into the sanctuary an object which symbolizes the sin (עון) of the people: it is sin connected with the holy offerings which *the people* sanctify (אשר יקדישו בני ישראל), and Yahweh receives it לרצון . In Num. 18:1 the עון is not the people's sin but that of Aaron and his sons: it is they who perform these duties, and it is their priesthood (כהנתכם) which is involved. In doing so they admittedly save the people from destruction at the hand of Yahweh such as is envisaged in 17:27f. (EVV 17:12f.), because they, unlike the people, are safe, as authorized persons, when they approach the sanctuary; but there is nothing vicarious about their action. If the duties are not properly performed it is they and they alone, as agents, who commit עון . Thus neither here nor in Exod. 28:38 can it be said that Aaron (or his sons) "bears the guilt", or punishment, of others.

43

c. והם ישאו עונם (Num. 18:23)[53]

Num. 18:21-24 is concerned with the tithe which is to be paid by the
tribes of Israel to the Levites, who have received no other inheritance such
as that given to the other tribes, in return for their service in the sanctuary.
Here the danger of approaching the holy things is again raised. The Levites'
service makes it unnecessary for the people to "come near the tent of meeting
and so bear sin and die (לשאה חטא למות)" (verse 22). Instead the
Levites will "do the service of the tent of meeting, and they will bear their
iniquity (והם ישאו עונם)".

Some of the older commentators[54] regarded this phrase as a later addition
to the basic P document. It has long been recognized that its similarity to
ונשאו עונם in Ezek. 44:10 is unlikely to be accidental. Ezek. 44:9-14 is a
polemic against the Levites, who, in contrast to the faithfulness of the
"Levitical priests, the sons of Zadok", forsook Yahweh and followed idols.
In consequence "they shall bear their punishment" (verse 10) by being de-
graded from the priesthood and placed in a subordinate position (verse 13).
The reference of נשא עון in the two passages is thus quite different; but it
was held by some earlier critics that it is inappropriate in its context in Num.
18:23 and is a later addition unintelligently repeated from the Ezekiel
passage. Wellhausen[55] believed that it was an original part of P but thought
that it was derived by the author of P from Ezekiel and included at this point
deliberately in a new sense analogous to that in which the expression נשא
עון is used in Num. 18:1. It is perhaps curious that the same writer should
have used the phrase נשא חטא of the people's approach to the tent of meeting
in verse 22 but נשא עון of the Levites in verse 23, and there may in fact be
a reminiscence of Ezek. 44:10 here; nevertheless in the general context the
phrase והם ישאו עונם , with its stress on the contrast between people
and Levites, makes good sense, and it is therefore relevant to consider what
its author (or interpolator) intended it to mean.

The main question which arises is that of the reference of the suffix -ם ,
"their". Is it the עון of the people which the Levites bear, or their own עון?
If it is the former, then a vicarious interpretation would be in order: the
Levites would be substituting themselves for the people and incurring the
punishment which would otherwise fall upon the people. The grammatical
form provides no answer to this question. But the situation seems to be
similar to that of the priests earlier in the chapter (18:1). Although the
Levites are excluded from the most holy sphere of the sacred vessels and the
altar, which is reserved for the priests (Aaron and his sons), they have their
own sacred function which is denied to the people: they attend the "service
of the tent" (verse 23, cf. verse 3); and just as the priests' performance of
their duties enables the people to be free of Yahweh's "wrath" (verse 5, cf.

44

verse 7), so the Levites relieve the people of the necessity of approaching the tent, which would be fatal to them (verse 22). Clearly the duty under-taken by the Levites, like that of the priests, was one which involved the possibility of inadvertent breaches of the commandments which might have fatal consequences. It is this עָוֹן which the Levites are to bear according to verse 23. Like Aaron and his sons in 18:1 the Levites here shield the people from the consequences of their approaching the holy things, but this is not a vicarious action: if the Levites incur עָוֹן, it will be their own עָוֹן and not one transferred to them from the people.

d. ואתה נתן לכם לשאת את-עון העדה לכפר עליהם
לפני יהוה (Lev. 10:17)[56]

Lev. 10:16-20 is a narrative concerning an apparent inadvertent breach of the commandments of precisely the kind envisaged in Num 18:1 and 18:23: Eleazar and Ithamar the sons of Aaron have in Moses' estimation committed a fault in the execution (Lev. 9:8-21) of the instructions (Lev. 9:1-7) con-cerning the performance of special sacrifices on the eighth day after the con-secration of Aaron and his sons (Lev. 8). The passage is separated from the events to which it refers by 10:1-15, and appears to be an attempt by a later hand[57] to reconcile two apparently contradictory texts. The sacrifice in question is that of "the goat of the sin offering (חטאת)", one of the animals sacrificed on this occasion with a special intention for the people (9:15). Moses made enquiries about the disposal of the victim and discovered that it had been entirely burned (10:16), whereas according to him it should have been eaten by Eleazar and Ithamar (verse 17), as he had commanded (verse 18). The law in question does not in fact occur in the specific instructions in chapter 9, and the reference is presumably to the general law concerning the חטאת in Lev. 6:17-23 (EVV 24-30), where it is specifically stated (verse 19 [EVV 26]) that it is to be eaten by the sacrificing priest. But in another passage (Lev. 4:12, 21) it is laid down that the whole of the victim of the חטאת is to be burned. There, however, the victim is a bull; in chapters 9 and 10, where the sacrifices are for a special occasion, it is a goat.

It is not necessary here to examine in detail either the character and pur-pose of Lev. 10:16-20 or the rather obscure defence offered by Aaron in verse 19, which, it is stated, satisfied Moses. Our concern is with verse 17. Here Moses' question "Why have you not eaten the חטאת in the place of the sanctuary?" is followed by a series of statements, possibly but not certainly by a later hand or hands, about the חטאת : (i) "for it is a most holy thing (קדש קדשים)"; (ii) "it was given to you העדה לשאת את-עון ":

45

(iii) "making atonement (לכפר) for them before Yahweh".

These three statements all refer to the nature and function of the חטאת sacrifice; the last two refer in addition to the role of the priests in connection with it. The third, which occurs regularly in passages concerning the חטאת (including verse 3 of this chapter), is parallel with the second (the infinitive construction is used in both cases) and may be taken as referring to the same function: making atonement is identified with לשאת את-עון העדה . The first is a statement about the holiness of the חטאת , also found elsewhere.

With regard to the meaning of לשאת עון here, it is clear that the phrase does not refer to the act of eating the flesh of the victim by Aaron's sons. As Elliger pointed out,[58] the pericope as a whole makes it clear that Moses did not question the efficacity of the sacrifice, even though he regarded the burning of the victim rather than its consumption by them as a serious breach of the instructions which he had given. The three statements in verse 17b are all general statements about the חטאת sacrifice. There is therefore no justification for supposing that by eating the victim's flesh the priests were in some way absorbing, and so "bearing", the עון of the people which had been transferred to its flesh.

There is however an even stronger reason for rejecting this view. It is never stated in the laws of the Old Testament or in any other text that there is such a transference of עון to a sacrificial victim.[59] On the contrary, the victim is accepted by God as pleasing to him. The flesh of the חטאה is in fact so far from being "contaminated" by עון that it can be described as "most holy" (קדש קדשים), and according to Lev. 6:22 (EVV 29) it is for that very reason that it is to be eaten by the priests alone.[60]

We may therefore conclude that נשא עון here does not mean "bear guilt/punishment". Rather it means "take away the guilt". Aaron's sons are in no way involved in vicarious guilt; they have been given the חטאת so that they may, as the principal agents in the performance of the rite, take away or remove the people's עון , so making atonement.[61]

3. The Israelites in the wilderness : Num. 14:34

[62] תשאו את-עונתיכם

Zimmerli in his article[63] refers to this case only in a footnote and without explanation, as an example of נשא עון in the sense of vicarious punishment or suffering. It is not difficult to show that this is not the case.

Numbers 14 follows the story of the sending of spies from the wilderness of Paran to spy out the land of Canaan and bring back an account of the land, its inhabitants and its cities (chapter 13). The spies return and make their report (13:25-29). After some discussion the people, terrified by the report of the gigantic stature of the inhabitants of Canaan, rebel against Moses and Aaron. Chapter 14 narrates this rebellion and its consequences.

Both chapters 13 and 14 contain a number of repetitions and discrepancies, and it is generally agreed that there are two main sources here, ascribed to JE and P respectively. In chapter 14 the sections attributed to P are verses 1-2, 5 - 7, 10, 26 - 38, and it is with this source that we are concerned here. The consequence of the rebellion of the people against Moses and Aaron is the appearance of the glory of Yahweh at the tent of meeting (verse 10). Yahweh then speaks to Moses and Aaron, declaring his anger at the rebellion (verses 26-27) and commanding them to deliver to the people his judgement upon them. This judgement, which is recorded in verses 27-34, is cast in the form of a direct address to the people in which Yahweh condemns them, with the exception of those under the age of twenty years (and also of Caleb and Joshua) to remain in the wilderness for the remainder of their lives and never to enter the land of Canaan. Those under the age of twenty will also have to remain in the wilderness until the last of their elders has died. The number of years envisaged is forty.

Although the affinities of verses 27-34 are clearly with P rather than with JE, they contain repetitions and variations in vocabulary[64] which show that they are not a literary unity. One example of these inconsistencies is relevant to the present discussion. In verse 34 the people, presumably including the older and the younger generation since no distinction is made, are told: "*You shall bear your sins* (תשאו את-עונתיכם) for forty years". On the other hand in verse 33 they (presumably the same people, since no change of audience is mentioned) are told: "*Your children* will be shepherds in the wilderness for forty years and will bear your fornications (ונשאו את-זנותיכם) until the last of your dead bodies falls in the wilderness". Both the similarities and the differences between these two statements suggest the possibility that one is intended as an interpretation of the other. It is therefore necessary to consider the meaning of verse 33 before passing on to the example of נשא עון in verse 34.

In verse 33, although the word עון does not occur, it is certainly the case that one group of people (the children) are to suffer the consequences of the sins of others (the parents). This is true whatever may be the critical decision reached about the difficult word זנותיכם:[65] the reference is clearly to some kind of sin. But[66] there is no question here of a *vicarious* punishment: although the innocent children suffer a punishment incurred by their guilty parents (that is, the necessity of remaining in the wilderness for forty years before entering the land of Canaan), the parents do not escape the punishment: indeed, theirs is the greater punishment, since they are to be totally excluded from the land for ever, while the children will be able to enter it once all their elders are dead. This is then a case of the innocent suffering the consequences of the sins of others, which is not the same as vicarious suffering.

Verse 34 refers only to that part of the punishment which consists of the people being compelled to remain in the wilderness for forty years. As in verse 33 this punishment is to fall on the whole people, parents and children alike, for, as Gray pointed out,[67] if it referred to the parents only, "the whole sentence would then imply that these died all together at the end of the forty years". The people is addressed as a whole.[68] Consequently "you shall bear your עון" involves, by implication, the innocent children in their parents' punishment exactly as in verse 33. But here also the suffering of the children in being forced to remain in the wilderness for forty years is not vicarious: they simply share during those forty years in the punishment justly meted out to their parents.

4. The Scapegoat: Lev. 16:22

ונשא השעיר עליו את-כל-עונתם אל-ארץ גזרה [69]

This is the only passage in the Old Testament in which the phrase נשא עון is used with an animal as the subject of the verb. As has already been pointed out,[70] it is nowhere stated that an animal slaughtered in sacrifice "bears the guilt" of the person(s) for whom the sacrifice is offered.

It is universally agreed that Lev. 16, the ritual for the Day of Atonement, is composite; and there is wide agreement that its various strands cannot with complete success be separated by the methods of literary criticism, since part at least of the history of its composition belongs to a pre-literary stage which to some extent defies analysis. It may, however, be regarded as probable[71] that the ritual concerning the two goats forms a distinct element in the chapter, and that in the most ancient form discernible to us it consisted of verses 5, 7-10, 15, 20-22 and perhaps 26.

According to these verses Aaron was to take two male goats (verse 5).[72] He was to cast lots upon the two goats, "one lot for Yahweh and the other lot for Azazel" (verse 8). It is then explained that the first goat is to be offered as a חטאת while the other is to be presented alive before Yahweh (verse 10).[73] The second goat is to be "sent away into the wilderness to Azazel". These general instructions are then amplified. After the offering of the first goat as a חטאת , and the performance of the atoning ritual with its blood (verse 15), the ritual with the second goat is to be performed (verses 20b-22) as foreseen in verse 10, except that the reference to Azazel has now mysteriously disappeared and does not reappear. Otherwise the ritual is now described in greater detail. Aaron is to "bring near" (הקריב) the goat and to put

(ונתן) all the sins (עונת) of the people on its head by laying his hands on it and "confessing" them (התודה) over it. The goat is then to be sent away into the wilderness. This statement is then further expanded in verse 22, which says that the goat "will carry upon itself all their sins (ונשא השעיר עליו את-כל-עונתם) to a solitary (or, desert) land (אל-ארץ גזרה)".

It is not necessary here to discuss many of the controversial questions concerning this account such as the origins of the ritual, the meaning of Azazel, and the reason why Azazel appears only in the early part of the account. Our sole concern is the meaning of ונשא ... את-כל-עונתם in verse 22. There are overwhelming reasons for believing that נשא here means "carry away" rather than "bear" in the sense of "suffer". One of these is the adverbial clause "to a solitary land", which necessarily gives the verb the character of a verb of motion. A second reason is that nothing is said about the suffering or death of the second goat. It is not a sufficient counter-argument to say that such passages describing rituals in the legal sections of the Old Testament do not mention every detail, and that it may have been taken for granted that the goat was killed. If the goat was in fact killed, this would have been a significant element, if not the most significant one, in the ritual, and certainly would not have been omitted.[74]

We can only conclude that the ritual with the goat sent into the wilderness represents an entirely different concept of the removal of the people's sin from that of the propitiatory sacrifice, and that the essence of this ritual is that the sins (or guilt) are placed upon the goat, which then removes them to such a distance that they cannot return. It is probable that the juxtaposition of this concept with that of propitiatory sacrifice in Lev. 16 is a relatively late development. The ritual of the scapegoat reflects a concept of sin as something menacingly close to the sinner which terrifies or threatens to destroy him by weighing upon him, a state which can only be relieved by its being taken away and removed to a distance. So in Ps. 51:5 (EVV 3) the psalmist complains that his sin is ever-present (נגדי), and in Ps. 38:5 (EVV 4) another psalmist laments that his sins (עונתי) have "gone over" (עברו) his head and are a burden too heavy for him to bear. Other passages speak of the removal of sin far away, using the verb רחק in the Hiphil or Piel. This may be achieved by repenting and turning from one's sin (Job 11:14; 22:23; Ezek. 43:9) or by the action of God himself, who removes a man's transgressions (הרחיק ... את-פשעינו) from him as far as the east is from the west (Ps. 103:12), or may be asked to remove from him (הרחק ממני) falsehood and lying (Prov. 30:8). The ritual of the sending away of the goat may thus be seen as a symbolic action, or dramatization, of this definitive removal of sin, in this case from the whole people. There is no "suffering" or "punishment" imposed upon the goat that could in any way be said to be vicarious.

5. Ezek. 4:4-8

(verse 4)[75]   תשא את-עונם

(verse 5)[76]   ונשאת עון בית-ישראל

(verse 6)[77]   ונשאת את-עון בית יהודה

Ezek. 4:4-8 relates Yahweh's command to Ezekiel to lie on his left side for 390 days and then on his right side for 40 days, bound by Yahweh with "cords". He is then to turn his face towards the city of Jerusalem and prophesy against it. An explanation is given of these actions: in lying first on one side and then on the other he will "bear the punishment" (נשא עון) of the house of Israel and the house of Judah respectively.

The passage is difficult and raises many questions which have been thoroughly discussed, some of which are relevant to the present purpose. The actions which Ezekiel is commanded to perform belong to the category described by modern scholars as "symbolic actions". This passage belongs to a section of the book (3:16 − 5:17) in which a number of such symbolic actions are recorded. There is evidence of considerable expansion and editorial activity throughout these chapters, and 4:4-8 have almost certainly undergone considerable expansion and may also have been misplaced from another context. Possibly only part of verse 4 is original: some commentators[78] regard the whole passage as an invention of Ezekiel's disciples, differing from the neighbouring symbolic actions in being purely literary in character and not intended to be carried out. Our present concern, however, is with the meaning of the phrase נשא עון in the passage as it now stands.[79]

The nature and function of the symbolic action in the prophetical literature have been widely discussed[80]. It is agreed that it has something of the character of the prophetic divine word in that it is a dramatized threat (or promise). In other words, it symbolizes an action or state of affairs which Yahweh will bring about in the future. The main point of disagreement between contemporary scholars concerns the relationship between the symbol and the thing symbolized. Does the prophet's action bring about or help to bring about the action or state which it symbolizes, in a way analogous to (even though in important respects distinct from) the practice of sympathetic magic, or is it merely a dramatized threat whose form (i.e. action rather than speech) has been chosen simply to bring home the reality of their situation to the prophet's audience with especial vividness? The matter cannot be discussed here; but the probability seems to lie with those who hold the former view[81]. If this is so it follows that there must be some kind of identification between the prophet and the role which he plays.

In view of this, and since Ezekiel in performing these extraordinary actions would inevitably experience some degree of actual suffering, a further question must be asked: does he, in performing the symbolic actions described in 4:4-8, represent God, or the inhabitants of Jerusalem? The other symbolic actions described in the immediate context illustrate both possibilities. When in 4:1-3 Ezekiel is commanded to mime the siege of the city of Jerusalem and to "set his face against it", he plays the part of Yahweh himself: it is Yahweh who has set his face against Jerusalem and who is the true power behind the armies of Nebuchadnezzar. On the other hand, when in 4:9ff. Ezekiel is commanded to mime the actions of a person suffering from famine, it is not Yahweh whose part he plays but the besieged inhabitants of Jerusalem whom Yahweh has brought to this state (verses 16-17). Yet once again in 5:1-4, when the prophet is commanded to shave his hair and beard, to divide the hair into three parts and to destroy these respectively by burning, striking with the sword and scattering, he once again plays the part of Yahweh who will do these things against the inhabitants of Jerusalem. The immediate context, therefore, provides no clue to the interpretation of 4:4-8 in this respect.

4:4-8, unlike these neighbouring passages, refers – at least in its present form – almost certainly not to the suffering of the inhabitants of Jerusalem during the coming siege, but to the suffering which is to follow the capture of Jerusalem: the long suffering of their Exile.[82] In spite of the evidence that 4:4-8 was not originally connected with 4:1-3 it has been argued[83] that in the former as in the latter it is Yahweh who is symbolized by the prophet. According to this view the symbolic action indeed foreshadows the real suffering which Yahweh will bring upon the people of Jerusalem because of their guilt (עון), but, although he has been forced to become their enemy, he himself first suffers the sorrow caused by this cruel necessity. He thus shares the consequences of his people's guilt; and the prophet's suffering, described as "bearing punishment" (נשא עון), symbolizes the suffering of God as much as it symbolizes the future suffering of the people.

It is extremely unlikely that this interpretation is correct. In the symbolic action described in 4:4-8, in contrast with the neighbouring symbolic actions, there are not one but two persons involved: Yahweh and Ezekiel. It is Yahweh who acts ("I assign to you", verses 5, 6; "I will put cords upon you", verse 8; possibly "I will lay the עון ... upon you", verse 4).[84] Ezekiel is the one who suffers the consequences of the action and so represents the people in exile. Moreover, the notion that Yahweh should suffer the עון of his own people would be a concept unique in the Old Testament.[85]

In this symbolic action, then, the prophet does not represent Yahweh. His action – or rather, his enforced inactivity or paralysis – is undertaken at Yahweh's bidding, and it is specifically said that he plays the part of the nation in "bearing its punishment" (נשא עון). It must now be asked in what sense he does this.

It is generally agreed that this symbolic action points forward[86] to the Exile which will follow the fall of Jerusalem, here interpreted as the punishment to be imposed on the nation by Yahweh for their sins.[87] A similar use of עון is found in Lam. 5:7, where סבל עון is used in referring to the actual sufferings of the population which remained in Palestine after 587 B.C.[88] As in the case of other prophetic symbolic actions the prophetic activity or experience points to and helps to bring about another action or experience in the future: the Exile. This future experience will, when it occurs, be an objective reality. The fact that it has been prefigured in the symbolic action does not make it any the less so: on the contrary, the symbolic action is concerned to emphasize the inescapable reality of what it symbolizes. It cannot therefore be maintained, as is usually done, that the action or experience of Ezekiel is in any sense vicarious. He prefigures and helps to bring about the future punishment which the people have deserved, and is "identified" with it in the same way as any symbolic action is "identified" with what it symbolizes, but he does not bear it *instead* of them: his suffering does not in any way take away or lessen theirs.[89] Indeed, his "suffering" through paralysis is not really the point of the symbolic action at all. As in the other symbolic actions which he performs — and indeed in the symbolic actions performed by other prophets — the action performed has no significance in itself. Its only significance lies in its relationship to the thing symbolized. It is, to use the word employed to describe the previous symbolic action (verse 3), a "sign" (אות). The prophet's immobilization or paralysis for a certain number of days is a "sign" that the nation will be "paralyzed" for a certain number of years, in exactly the same way as — for example — his actions in 5:1-4, when he cut off his hair and divided it into three parts, are a "sign" of what God will do to the inhabitants of Jerusalem when the city is captured. Ezekiel "bears the punishment" (נשא עון) of the people only in the same sense that he can be said to "besiege the city" (וצרת עליה) in the symbolic action of the iron plate in 4:3. His "bearing the punishment" is the thing symbolized by his paralysis, not the symbol. The symbol, which is the state of paralysis, signifies that the inhabitants of Jerusalem will in the future themselves bear their עון , which they have fully deserved.

6. Ezek. 18:19-20

(verse 19)[90] מדע לא-נשא הבן בעון האב

(verse 20)[91] בן לא ישא בעון האב ואב לא ישא בעון הבן

Ezekiel 18 is, as is generally agreed, a disputation in which the prophet, speaking in the name of Yahweh, attacks an attitude of disillusionment current among his fellow-exiles to which they are giving expression in the proverb "The fathers have eaten sour grapes, and the children's teeth are set on edge" (verse 2).[92] Although Yahweh is not mentioned by name in this proverb, it contains an implicit accusation that he is unjust (cf. verse 25). In the verses which follow Yahweh defends himself against this accusation.

After swearing that from henceforth there will be no more occasion to use this proverb (verse 3), Yahweh categorically asserts that each human person belongs individually to him, and that he will see to it that any person who sins will die (verse 4). The meaning of this assertion is then made clear in a series of hypothetical examples of its application (verses 5-9, 10-13, 14-18) in which Yahweh gives an assurance that his treatment of each individual – in assigning to him life or death – will be based solely on his own conduct and will be unaffected by the conduct of his father.[93]

Verses 19, 20, in which the three occurrences of the phrase נשא בעון are to be found, may be regarded either as a brief summary of Yahweh's previous speech or as a further stage in the disputation. Yahweh alleges that a question has been put to him (ואמרתם , "Yet you say"), which he now answers. The question repeats in different words the charge expressed in verse 2, prefaced by the word "Why?": "Why does not the son bear the punishment of the father?" (מדע לא-נשא הבן בעון האב). The answer (verses 19b, 20) reiterates the answer already given, partly repeating phraseology already used there but also picking up that of the objectors, including the phrase נשא בעון .

This disputation raises a number of problems. These occur in the proverb (verse 2) and in the second reply in verses 19b-20 with which we are concerned here. The interpretation of the disputation as a whole can best be undertaken by an examination of the meaning of the first reply (verses 4-18), which presents no major difficulties.

It should first be noted that, in order to answer the accusation made about his treatment of the nation as a whole, Yahweh picks up the words "fathers" and "sons" from the proverb and individualizes them. He takes his examples, however, not from the practice of criminal law in which a verdict of guilty or not guilty is pronounced and the accused consequently either set free or executed, but from the sacral sphere, in which God's judgement, pronounced by the priest, operates directly upon the accused person without human intervention.[94] Since every person belongs to Yahweh, Yahweh himself will deal directly with every person.

In this context of direct divine action three cases are then cited: those of the righteous man, his wicked son and his righteous grandson. Yahweh will in each case take into account only the actions of the particular person. The deeds of his father will be considered totally irrelevant. Thus the wicked son will not share in the "life" granted to his righteous father (verses 10-13), nor will *his* righteous son share in the punishment of his wicked father (verses 14-18).

It should be noted that nothing is said in these verses about the question of vicarious punishment (or vicarious reward). The question at issue is not whether a man should be punished (or rewarded) *in the place* of his father, but whether children should *share* in the fate of their fathers. Such vicarious punishment is never envisaged even in the traditional sacral law: the principle expressed in the words "I Yahweh your God am a jealous God, visiting the iniquity of the fathers upon the children to the third and fourth generation of those that hate me" (Exod. 20:5; cf. Exod. 34:7) certainly does not mean that the first generation, that is, those who committed the sin, should escape the consequences of their deeds while their descendants would suffer instead of them. This is made entirely clear in the comparable statement in Num. 14:18, where it is again said that the sins of the fathers would be visited on the children "upon the third and fourth generation", but where this formula is preceded by the phrase "he will by no means clear the guilty" (ונקה לא ינקה).

With the principles enunciated in Ezek. 18:4-18 in mind we turn to the interpretation of the proverb in verse 2 which is the starting-point for the succeeding disputation. Taken by itself[95] it is ambiguous: the metaphor of the grapes certainly means that the younger generation is being punished for sins which not they but their fathers committed, but there is no indication whether it merely shares in the punishment of the older generation, or whether the complaint is that the fathers have escaped punishment for their sins, which is now being borne by the children. It is in the nature of a proverb to be allusive rather than precise, and it is probably unwise to over-interpret this proverb and to enquire precisely what is meant by "the fathers". If the "fathers" are to be understood as earlier generations of pre-exilic Judah such as the wicked Manasseh, who escaped punishment for his sins,[96] then it might be said that the later generation did suffer vicariously for the sins of its ancestors, who died without experiencing the destruction of the Judaean state. But it is unlikely that such a precise meaning was intended.[97] If the proverb were intended to express a complaint that the present generation of exiles was suffering vicariously for the sins of its ancestors, we should expect this complaint to have been specifically dealt with in Yahweh's reply in verses 4-18. But in fact these verses are wholly concerned with restricting the effect of the punishment to the sinner, and not with the question of the sinner's escaping punishment because it has been transferred to his descendants.

The proverb and the first answer to it must be kept in mind when we interpret the question in verse 19a and the answer to it in verses 19b, 20.[98]

There is nothing new in the substance of this second answer, which simply summarizes previous statements in language taken from the previous answer and also picks up the words of the question, denying their truth. The only new element is the introduction of the phrase נשא בעון . This expression occurs nowhere else in the Old Testament. It cannot be explained as a stylistic peculiarity of Ezekiel, since elsewhere (4:4-6) he uses the normal phrase נשא עון . It is therefore reasonable to suppose that its meaning is different from the latter. But the peculiarity of the syntax has baffled the commentators.

The insertion of the preposition ב after a transitive verb and before the noun which would otherwise be its object is rare. Presumably some modification of the relationship between verb and object is intended which leaves the noun something other than simply the direct object of the verb. Zimmerli suggests, though with hesitation, that the preposition is the *beth pretii*. But this is improbable. Not only would "at the cost of" make no sense, but this interpretation would leave the transitive verb נשא without an object. The same arguments apply to the interpretation of ב as instrumental. It seems clear that the phrase only makes sense if עון remains the object of נשא in some sense, if only in a modified one.

There are instances where we find ב apparently expressing the object of a verb, e.g. פרש בידים , "spread the hands" (Lam. 1:17); פער בפה , "open wide the mouth" (Job 16:10); קרא בשם , "call out a name" (Gen. 12:8).[99] But in these cases an element of instrumentality is involved: e.g. the hands are the object of the verb "spread", but they are also the instrument with which the action is performed. There is thus in these expressions a combination of two relationships of the noun to the verb, viz. those of object and instrument. This is not true of נשא בעון .

There are only two true syntactical parallels to נשא בעון , Num. 11:17 and Job 7:13; and it is significant that in each case the verb in question is the same: נשא in the sense of "bear (a burden)". The more interesting of these cases is Num. 11:17. In Num. 11:14 Moses had complained to Yahweh that he was unable to bear alone the burden of dealing with the people. Yahweh therefore commanded him to assemble seventy of the elders so that (verse 17) he might place upon them some of the spirit which was upon himself (מן–הרוח אשר עליך), "and they shall share with you the burden of the people (ונשאו אתך במשא העם) and you will not bear it alone".[100] Only in these three cases (Ezek. 18:19-20; Num. 11:17; [probably] Job 7:13) does the word נשא , "bear", occur followed by a noun preceded by ב which is in some sense its object. In the case of Num. 11:17 (and probably also Job 7:13) the function of ב is clear: it is partitive. The status of the noun as the object of the verb is modified by ב to indicate that the "burden" (משא) is only *partially* borne by the elders. Moses continues to bear the burden; but it is *shared* with the elders.[101]

55

There are thus good reasons for interpreting נשא בעון in Ezek. 18:19f. as meaning "to bear some of the punishment", i.e. "to share the punishment". The objectors' question in verse 19a should then be translated by "Why does not the son share the punishment of the father?", and in reply Yahweh, having repeated his earlier statements that the righteous man will live and the wicked man die, then adds: "The son shall not share the punishment of the father, and the father shall not share the punishment of the son". This interpretation is entirely in accordance with the meaning of the proverb and with the first answer to it. There is no question of vicarious punishment: the only question asked and answered is whether punishment justly meted out to one man should or should not be extended to members of his family.

7. Conclusion

All the passages in which the phrases נשא עון and נשא בעון have been or could be interpreted as referring to vicarious suffering or punishment borne by one person (or, in one case, by an animal) on behalf of another person or persons have now been reviewed, and it has been shown in each case that this is not the correct interpretation. The following modification of Zimmerli's classification[102] is therefore proposed.

a. Zimmerli's first category, in which נשא עון is a priestly verdict declaring that the commission of certain kinds of sin will bring divine punishment on the person who commits them, stands. But it should be enlarged by the addition of Num. 18:1 and 18:23.[103]

b. Zimmerli's second and third categories, in which נשא עון refers respectively to vicarious punishment and to a simple assumption of responsibility, must be deleted as erroneous.

c. Five new categories should be added.

i. נשא עון in a sense similar to that of the priestly verdict formula, but used more loosely and in somewhat different contexts. In Num. 14:34[104] the priestly formula (תשאו את-עונתיכם) is employed, but in a narrative context, not as a divine warning of what will happen if a certain sin is committed, but as a divine judgement on a sin already committed. A further difference is that the phrase is applied not to an individual but to the whole people without distinction between guilty and innocent. It is also in this category that the occurrences in Ezek. 4:4-6 must be placed: here the phrase has been adapted to refer to the punishment of the whole people by the destruction of the state and consequent exile, and this punishment is foreshadowed in a symbolic action performed by Ezekiel: the prophet acts out in advance Israel's punishment for its own sins.[105]

ii. נשא עון in the sense of "taking away guilt". In Lev. 10:17 it refers to the removal of guilt by the performance of an atoning sacrifice.[106] Compare the use of the phrase with God as subject to denote the divine forgiveness of sins.[107]

iii. נשא עון as the physical act of removal of guilt. In Lev. 16:22 נשא is a verb of motion: the scapegoat literally "removes" the people's guilt to a distant place in the wilderness.[108]

iv. נשא בעון in the sense of "participate in, share, punishment": Ezek. 18:19, 20.[109]

v. נשא עון in the rather specialized sense of carrying (into the sanctuary) an object which represents the people's guilt: Exod. 28:38.[110]

The phrase נשא עון , as has already been mentioned, does not occur in Isaiah 53 at all. Nevertheless, as has already been noted,[111] it is sometimes used interchangeably with נשא חטא , which occurs in Isa. 53:12. The above study of the meaning of נשא עון , therefore, has been necessary in order to show that the phrase והוא חטא-רבים נשא in that verse, like ועונתם הוא יסבל in verse 11,[112] refers not to the vicarious suffering of the Servant, but to his sharing, in a greater measure, the suffering of his fellow-exiles.[113]

C. Supposed References to Vicarious Suffering
(continued from **A**)

c.   אכן חלינו הוא נשא ומכאבינו סבלם   (verse 4a)[114]

These statements are similar in meaning to ועונתם הוא יסבל in
verse 11 and והוא חטא־רבים נשא in verse 12. The words חלינו
and מכאבינו refer back to verse 3, where the Servant is said by the speakers
to have been in the past a "man of pains" (איש מכאבות) and "acquainted
with[115] sickness" (וידוע חלי). Both מכאב and חלי can be used in
either a literal or a metaphorical sense. The statements in verse 3 occur in a
context which is most naturally interpreted literally: the speakers confess that
the Servant's physical appearance or condition[116] had repelled them (verses
2, 3b), and the reference to sickness and pain accord with this.   איש
מכאבות , then, means a man consumed by pain to such an extent that it
seemed to have become his distinguishing feature; ידוע חלי , whether it
means that he was accustomed to physical weakness or ravaged by it,[117] has
a similar connotation.

The speakers' confession in verse 4 that the Servant has borne their sick-
nesses and pains must then be a confession that they, who had previously
misunderstood the cause of his sufferings, have now (אכן) realized what that
cause is. It is really, they say, *our* diseases and *our* pains by which he has been
smitten. But this statement is capable of more than one interpretation.

The very emphatic word-order in verse 4a, stressing the contrast between
"he" and "we", has led to the view that it is a vicarious suffering which is
referred to here: the Servant has borne vicariously the pain which ought
rightly to have been borne by the speakers. But this interpretation is made
untenable by a fact already referred to elsewhere,[118] that the speakers are
the fellow-exiles of the Servant-prophet and therefore themselves by no means
free from the afflictions of divine punishment. What could be the additional
sins, additional to those of the nation for which punishment was already being
suffered by *all* the exiles, for which the Servant was vicariously suffering?
There is nothing in the chapter to suggest that there were any such additional
sins in the mind of the author.

The clue to the interpretation of this text is to be found in the double
meaning of the words חלי and מכאב . Both words, literally interpreted,
appropriately describe the actual bodily state of the Servant. But they also
have a metaphorical meaning which makes them eminently suitable to express

the broken state of the nation after the destruction of Jerusalem in 587 B.C.
Isaiah at the time of the Assyrian invasions had used the word חלי of the
condition of Judah in a descriptive passage (Isa. 1:5f.) which uses the imagery
of a sick man in a way distinctly reminiscent of the way in which the Servant
is described in Isa. 53:2f. Jeremiah also uses חלי of the state of internal
dissension in Jerusalem (Jer. 6:7). מכאב is used in Ps. 38:18 (EVV 17) and
Jer. 30:15 of punishment incurred through sin. Even more significantly,
מכאב is used three times in Lamentations (Lam. 1:12 [twice], 18) in a
passage where a personified Jerusalem complains of the punishment which
Yahweh has brought upon her through the Babylonians. Both words, then,
are extremely suitable for use by the speakers in Isa. 53 to describe their fate
as exiles, and the passage in Lamentations may suggest that they were so used
as stock expressions in lamentations composed during the exilic period. There
is abundant evidence in Deutero-Isaiah that such lamentations were used not
only by those who had remained in Palestine but also by the exiles in Babylonia.

In verses 3 and 4 the speakers are using the words חלי and מכאב in both
the literal and the metaphorical senses. In verse 4 they use them to refer to
the sufferings of exile: they are "*our* diseases" and "*our* pains", sufferings
which are real enough. But at the same time they have now come to realize
that the actual bodily diseases and pains undergone by the Servant (verse 3)
are closely related to these. This relationship they express by a double use of
חלי and מכאב . The Servant, then, is not suffering instead of them; but,
because of his special vocation, he is suffering more intensely than they, and
in a more literal sense.

What were these sufferings undergone by the Servant? The common view
that verse 3 refers to the earlier life and condition of the Servant as hideous
and riddled with disease makes little sense. It is more probable that the verse
refers to more recent events: to his arrest and ill-treatment by the Babylonian
authorities because of the message which he had proclaimed as a prophet.
These events had not at first led to his being honoured by his fellow-Jews,
who had simply despised him and judged his ill fortune to be a well merited
punishment due to some sins which he had committed (verse 4b). But now
the speakers realize that his physical torture and pain were totally unmerited,
and were a more intense form of their own sufferings: he bore *their* suffering,
but he bore it in a far more intense form.

This interpretation is supported by the interpretation given above of סבל
עון and נשא חטא in verses 11 and 12.[119] Indeed, the structure of the
chapter itself confirms it: there is an *inclusio* here. In their confession of their
new understanding of the work and suffering of the Servant, the speakers
begin (verse 4a) and end (verses 11b, 12b) with essentially identical statements,

the first of which uses the words חלי and מכאב in a metaphorical sense in order to make a play on words which links verses 3 and 4 together in order to bring out their own unworthy behaviour, and conclude with a statement in plain, non-metaphorical language. Between these two statements is set the main section of the chapter which describes the Servant's experiences in greater detail.

d. ויהוה הפגיע בו את עון כלנו (verse 6b)[120]

The context here is again one which emphasizes the contrast between "we", the speakers, who have deserved their punishment, and the Servant who has suffered innocently. That he alone is innocent is emphasized by כלנו , "us all", with which the verse begins and ends.

Modern translations seem to go out of their way to suggest the presence here of the notion of vicarious suffering.[121] Phrases like "laid on him" suggest some kind of transference of guilt such as is usually — but wrongly —[122] associated with expiatory sacrifices and with the ceremony of the scapegoat.

The phrase הפגיע עון which occurs in this verse is entirely unique. The Hiphil of the verb פגע itself is rare. Of the five other occurrences in the Old Testament, one (Job 36:32) is of doubtful interpretation and may be corrupt.[123] Of the remaining four, two (Jer. 15:11; 36:25) have the meaning "urge, plead with, entreat" (with the preposition ב preceding the person entreated) and one "intervene" (Isa. 59:16). In the fifth, Isa. 53:12, it is the first of these senses which is the more probable.[124] But here in Isa. 53:6 neither of these two meanings is possible, and it must be concluded that הפגיע here is to be taken as expressing the causative of the verb פגע in its meaning of "touch, meet". Yahweh caused the Servant to meet, that is, caused him to suffer, the punishment deserved by "all of us"(כלנו).

It is interesting here to observe that in making the statement that Yahweh afflicted the Servant with a punishment which he did not deserve but his compatriots did deserve, the author avoided the use of language which might suggest a connection with sacrificial rites but used a phrase which is unique and, as far as we can judge, not associated with any other Israelite tradition. The reason for his choice of language may be the predilection for word-play which is found in the poems of Deutero-Isaiah himself: the Hiphil of פגע is used again later on in the chapter (verse 12) but in an entirely different sense and with the Servant as the subject: Yahweh imposed (הפגיע) upon the Servant a punishment which he did not deserve (verse 6), whereas the Servant יפגיע (interceded) for the sinners (verse 12). The word play is intended to bring out the contrast between the behaviour of the Servant and his fellows.

The question still remains whether the thought here could be one of

60

vicarious suffering or punishment. As elsewhere in the chapter the statement that the Servant, unlike his companions in exile, did not deserve punishment but nevertheless received it (and, by implication, in greater measure than they) certainly does not in itself imply that their punishment was transferred to him. Once more the historical situation has to be kept in mind: the speakers in this chapter are members of – and perhaps regard themselves as representatives of – the community of Jewish exiles in Babylonia. They are all suffering a "term of imprisonment" (סבא) which is a punishment imposed by Yahweh for their sins (40:2). No person has relieved them, or could relieve them, of this suffering by suffering for them. What the speakers in chapter 53 are saying is that the Servant, who deserved no punishment, has, as a result of *their* sins, which had necessitated his dangerous and fateful prophetical ministry, received the largest share of it. This is not vicarious suffering. This conclusion is completely supported by the demonstration already made[125] that the phrases נשא/סבל עון/חטא do not, as is commonly believed, have such a connotation, and by the fact that the idea of vicarious suffering occurs nowhere else in the Old Testament.

2. Statements that the Servant was wounded for the sake of others

והוא מחלל מפשעינו (verse 5a)[126]

מדכא מעונתינו (verse 5a)[127]

מפשע עמי נגע למו (verse 8b)[128]

These three phrases, of which the first two stand in parallel clauses, are similarly constructed. The Servant's fate is described in each case by a passive participle or equivalent expression: נגע למו; מדכא; מחלל .[129] This fate is in each case related to "our" sins (מפשע; מעונתינו; מפשעינו; עמי), the relationship being expressed in each case by the preposition מן -.

It is frequently assumed that this preposition here denotes a kind of exchange or vicariousness: the punishment of the Servant was accepted by Yahweh as a kind of equivalent of that due to be paid by the sinners. This view is illustrated by the use of the word "for" in English translations: "he was wounded for our transgressions", etc. But Orlinsky has rightly pointed out[130] that if such a sense were intended it would most naturally be expressed not by מן - but by ב in its sense of *beth pretii*. This view is supported by the lexica and grammars, none of which allows the sense of "in exchange for, in payment for" as one of the meanings of מן -. On the other hand it is interesting to observe that where Deutero-Isaiah himself wishes to speak of a punishment accepted for sin (though not, of course, in a vicarious sense) he uses the *beth pretii*: in 40:2 the prophet states that the exiles ("Jerusalem") have received from Yahweh's hand "double *for* all her sins" (לקחה מיד יהוה כפלים בכל-חטאתיה). There can be little doubt that this is the *beth pretii*; and if the suggestion of von Rad is accepted that כפלים here means not "double" but "equivalent",[131] this interpretation is further confirmed.[132]

There is therefore every reason to suppose that מן – in these three phrases is used in the sense of "in consequence of, as the result of". This brings them into line with the meaning of the other phrases already considered: if Israel had not sinned, the Servant would not have had to suffer; but he did not suffer in the place of others to allow them to escape from the consequences of their sin.[133]

3. Statements relating the suffering of the Servant to the healing of others

מוסר שלומנו עליו (verse 5b)[134]

ובחברתו נרפא-לנו (verse 5b)[135]

These statements associate the suffering (חברה, מוסר) of the Servant with a restoration of the exiles, represented by the speakers, to a state of well-being (שלומנו, נרפא-לנו). שלום is a state of wholeness: the word is clearly intended to form a contrast with the present broken state of the exiles. Its meaning for them is well illustrated by its use in 54:10, where the prophet looks forward to a future ברית שלום , "covenant of שלום ", for God's people, and 55:12, where in another prophecy of the future it is associated with paroxysms of joy. The verb רפא , "heal", which does not occur elsewhere in Deutero-Isaiah, is used in a similar sense by other prophets of Yahweh's restoration of his sinful people.[136] Correspondingly the cry "Who can heal you?" (Lam. 2:13) reflects a state of affairs in which the speaker has lost faith in such a possibility.

This healing activity of Yahweh and this bringing of שלום are intimately related to the prophetic message. It is the prophet who announces שלום in 54:10; 55:12. It is equally a prophet who pronounces Yahweh's promise to heal in Jer. 30:17; 33:6. In Jer. 3:22 the healing is dependent on repentance, but it is again the prophet who preaches the repentance on which the promise of healing depends. Similarly in Isa. 6:10 the astonishing command given to Isaiah that he is to deliver a message which will make the people *unable* to "turn and be healed" serves to emphasize the normal concept of the prophetic function which is here reversed.

That the sufferings of Old Testament prophets were intimately connected with their vocation needs no proof. This relationship is, apart from the case of Deutero-Isaiah, perhaps most clearly seen in the ministry of Jeremiah, the prophet who was "like a gentle lamb led to the slaughter" (Jer. 11:19), of whom there may be a direct reminiscence in verse 7 of this chapter. It is also seen in the lives of some other Old Testament prophets.[137] In the case of all these prophets the message and the suffering are inseparable; but in the case of Deutero-Isaiah, the Servant of this chapter, there is a feature which distinguished him from either Jeremiah or his other prophetic predecessors: his message was *entirely* one of hope and promise. He was entirely a prophet who announced שלום and healing. Yet it was precisely this healing and restoring activity which led to his suffering at the hands of the Babylonians. Without his ministry there would have been no שלום and no healing, for the speaking of the prophetic word was an essential element in this process. Of this fact he himself testifies in his teaching about the prophetic word in 55:10-11.

It is in this sense that the speakers in this chapter, having arrived belatedly at a full understanding of the Servant's function, are able to say that the Servant's divinely permitted chastisement was a necessary part of Yahweh's plan for his people's future restoration to wholeness (מוסר שלומנו עליו), and that the healing which formed the burden of his message would be achieved through (ב) the ill-treatment which he had received (בחברתו נרפא-לנו).[138] In the context of verses 4-6 as they have been interpreted in this study these statements can have no other meaning. Although the phrases under consideration may be capable of bearing a vicarious interpretation, the context, as well as the general considerations urged above concerning the inherent improbability of such a thought in ancient Israel, render this interpretation highly improbable. These lines express the feeling of gratitude which the speakers have towards the man who, by persisting in the proclamation of his politically dangerous message prophesying the immediate overthrow of the Babylonian state by the God of the Jewish exiles, had ensured the fulfilment of those promises.

4.   אשם in verse 10

אם תשים אשם נפשו [139]

If the text is correct, this phrase may theoretically be construed in one of two ways: either by taking חשׂים as 2nd pers. masc., presumably referring to Yahweh: "If you make him" (or, "his life"–נפשׂו) "a guilt-offering (אשׂם)"; or as 3rd pers. fem., with נפשׂו as the subject: "if he (נפשׂו) makes (חשׂים) an אשׂם ". The first of these is extremely improbable since Yahweh is not otherwise addressed in the immediate context, and is rejected by most modern commentators.

But the second possibility is also beset with difficulties. It is generally agreed that the substitution of נפשׂ with a pronominal suffix (נפשׂי/ך/ם etc.) for the personal pronoun in cases where a particularly strong emotion is to be expressed is a regular idiom in biblical Hebrew. But its use as the subject of an active verb having no intrinsic emotional content is extremely rare. In almost every case this idiom is used only with verbs expressing (and not merely implying) emotions or psychological[140] and occasionally moral states.[141] On the few occasions when it is used with a verb denoting positive and specific action it still carries a special intensity of feeling.[142] There is in fact only one clear example in the Old Testament (repeated four times in the same passage) of נפשׂ with a pronominal suffix and a third person verb occurring as a substitute for the verb in the appropriate person without an explicit reference to some strong emotion: the references to the blessing given by Isaac in Gen. 27.[143] Here also a strong emotion may be implied; but more probably this case should be regarded as a peculiar idiom.

In the case of Isa. 53:10 it might be argued that there is in the context an emotional tone intense enough to explain the use of נפשׂ in this sense as the subject of the predicate "make an אשׂם ". This is a matter for individual judgement; but it can hardly be maintained that this usage is commonly to be found in the Old Testament.

There are, however, more weighty arguments against taking נפשׂו here as the subject of the verb. The first of these concerns the meaning of the verb שׂים/שׂום here. If נפשׂו were the object of the verb, the verb could be understood as having the frequently attested sense of "transform into" or "treat as". It might be said that someone (whoever is the subject) makes the Servant's life into, or regards it as, an אשׂם . But if נפשׂו is the subject of the verb, the only sense which can be given to the verb is that of "make, establish, appoint": the phrase would mean that the Servant makes or establishes an אשׂם . What this could mean, however, is not clear.

The verb שׂים/שׂום never occurs elsewhere in the Old Testament with the name of a sacrifice (whether an אשׂם or not) as its object. The phrase is unique. It cannot be said to be in any way an example of priestly or sacrificial terminology; and to take it for granted that it means "offer a guilt-offering" is to make an unwarrantable assumption. But there is a further difficulty: even if it were granted that it could have this meaning, the line as now interpreted fails to state who or what the victim. The victim certainly cannot be the Servant, for נפשו is not the object but the subject of the verb. Nothing more is said than that the Servant "makes" a guilt-offering. There are no grounds here for a vicarious interpretation.[144]

Before passing from the linguistic to the theological difficulties of this passage it is necessary to draw attention to the question of the meaning of the imperfect or jussive preceded by the particle אם in the phrase אם-תשים. Although there are cases in the Old Testament where אם appears to have a temporal rather than a conditional sense ("when" rather than "if"), and although recent research into the meanings of the Hebrew "tenses" (perfect and imperfect) has confirmed the view that in classical Hebrew these primarily indicate "aspect" rather than temporal succession, there is as far as is known to the present writer no case in which אם with the imperfect refers to a past event.[145] The only meaning which can plausibly be given to אם-תשים here is a present or future one.

But to put the supposed "guilt-offering" of the Servant in the future or present, as an event which has not yet taken place or is at least not yet completed, is to make nonsense of the thought of the passage.[146] Whatever it is that the Servant, according to this chapter, does for those who call themselves "we", it has already been done and belongs to the past. Only from the next line onwards (from יראה זרע) are future events referred to: the Servant will receive his reward. But the whole context makes it clear that this reward will be not for some possible action of the Servant in the future but for those actions which have already been described earlier in the chapter. If there was an אשם offered, it was offered then. To say[147] that the offering is past but its effects are not yet complete is to twist the natural sense of the words.

So we come to the theological or religious aspect of the question. If the traditional interpretation were to be accepted that the Servant is here said to have become (whether by his own volition or by the decision of God) an אשם, this would be a statement entirely unique in the Old Testament. That אשם here must, if it is to be retained as part of the text, mean that particular kind of expiatory sacrifice generally so called may be regarded as certain.[148] But as has already been said, the idea of the acceptance by Yahweh of a human life as an offering for sin is entirely foreign to the Yahwistic tradition, and indeed the idea of human sacrifice was entirely abhorrent to all true Yahwists. It would have been unthinkable for them to interpret the sufferings or death of the Servant, whether by execution or any other cause, as being in effect an example of such a sacrifice, commanded by, or at least accepted by, Yahweh.

It is also important to note that, even according to the Priestly law, the efficacy of the אשם sacrifice was in any case extremely limited and was ineffective to atone for those who had sinned "with a high hand" (Num. 15:30), a phrase which is interpreted as denoting contempt for the word of Yahweh and the breaking of his commandments (Num. 15:31). The sins of Israel which had led to the punishment of the Exile were certainly of this kind. Certainly there is no passage in the Old Testament which would suggest that any form of sacrifice could atone for Israel's wanton rejection of God. That such a notion should be found in the prophetic literature would be, if possible, even more unimaginable. And it is indeed the essence of the message of Deutero-Isaiah himself that only God's unconditional grace can bring about forgiveness and restoration to favour with him.

It is with all these considerations in mind that the occurrence of the word אשם in Isa. 53:10 must be viewed. Linguistic and grammatical impossibilities, the consensus of critical opinion that the entire immediate context is corrupt, the uniqueness of the supposed idea that the Servant in some way became a guilt-offering and the abhorrence of the idea of human sacrifice to the true Yahwist combine to cast the gravest of doubts upon the correctness of the text as regards the word אשם.

On the other hand it would clearly be unwise to rely on any of the emendations which have been proposed, and concerning which no unanimity of critical opinion has begun to emerge. The whole line (ויהוה חפץ דכאו החלי אם־תשים אשם נפשו) presents many difficulties, and many emendations presuppose that the corruptions extend throughout its length and beyond. Some of these proposals remove אשם entirely from the text, either through emendation of the existing text or on the hypothesis that it is an interpolation.[149] It is sufficient to conclude, especially in view of the remarkable possibilities of metathesis, haplography and dittography which this sequence of letters must have presented to a succession of scribes,[150] that the text is so uncertain that 53:10 cannot properly be used to support any theory of the vicarious suffering of the Servant.[151]

5. צדיק in verse 11b

יצדיק צדיק עבדי לרבים [152]

Although this line, together with the preceding words יראה ישבע בדעתו , is frequently regarded as corrupt, most commentators retain צדיק . If this is correct, עבדי , "my servant", is clearly its subject, and לרבים either is its direct object or stands in some more indirect relationship to it:

66

"for the many" or "with regard to the many".[153]

The meaning of יצדיק here is a crucial question for the present study.[154] According to traditional interpreters and some modern commentators it is an external causative Hiphil denoting an action performed by the Servant which in some way transforms the many or alters their status.[155] Taken with the following line ועונתם הוא יסבל as usually interpreted[156] this action is then seen in vicarious terms. Other modern commentators interpret יצדיק quite differently: "dispense justice";[157] "show oneself to be right-eous" (internal Hiphil).[158]

הצדיק , the Hiphil of צדק , occurs twelve times in the Old Testament. It is most frequently used to denote a judicial function. In three passages (Deut. 25:1; I Kings 8:32 = 2 Chron. 6:23) it refers to one of the functions of a judge, whether human or divine, in rendering justice. In all these passages it occurs in the expression הצדיק (את-ה)צדיק , associated with the corresponding phrase הרשיע (את-ה)רשע . Its meaning is "to acquit", that is, to pronounce the innocent party to be innocent, while הרשיע רשע means "to convict (the guilty)". There is no question of הצדיק meaning to "let off" a guilty party. In I Kings 8:32 this is made clear beyond any doubt by the addition of the phrase לתת לו כצדקתו , "rendering to him according to his innocence (or righteousness)", with a similar phrase in the case of the conviction of the guilty party.

In two other cases (Isa. 5:23; Prov. 17:15) the case of the dishonest judge is considered. His actions are described by reversing the terms of the two phrases considered above: the unjust judge acquits the guilty (הצדיק רשע) and convicts the innocent (הרשיע צדיק , Prov. 17:15) or denies justice to him (וצדקת צדיקים יסירו ממנו , Isa. 5:23). In a sixth passage, Exod. 23:7, Yahweh is the judge, and gives warning that he will not acquit the wicked.[159] It is to be noted that the crime of acquitting the guilty is regarded as being especially heinous, being included in a series of solemn "woes" in Isa. 5:23 and described as "abomination to Yahweh" (תועבת יהוה) in Prov. 17:15.

There is, then, in these six juridical passages no suggestion that the acquitting of the guilty can ever be anything other than a heinous sin, and it is clear that such an action would never be performed or approved by God.

Of the five remaining passages (apart from Isa. 53:11) Isa. 50:8 uses הצדיק in a similar juridical sense: the Servant is speaking, and he asserts his willingness to appear before his accusers, knowing that he is innocent, and that Yahweh will acquit or vindicate him (קרוב מצדיקי).

In 2 Sam. 15:4 and Ps. 82:3 הצדיק has a slightly different, though still juridical, sense. In 2 Sam. 15:4 Absalom expresses the wish that he were judge in the land: if he were, he would hear the legal pleas of anyone who had

a case (ריב) to bring, and see to it that he obtained justice (והצדקתיו).
This is an assurance not of acquittal but of justice, with the implication that
at present justice was not to be had by those who had no influence. Nevertheless the use of the word here is in line with the cases considered above:
judgement will be given in favour of the party which is in the right. There is
certainly no suggestion that a judgement might be given in favour of a party
which is at fault; rather the reverse.

In Ps. 82:3 the emphasis is on the necessity of giving impartial justice to
those who are unable to defend themselves against the powerful. The
command to do so is addressed by Yahweh to the gods (אלהים), but the
principle is the same as that required in dispensing human justice. The gods
are commanded: שפטו-דל ויתום עני ורש הצדיקו . Here הצדיק is
parallel with שפט , "judge", and as in 2 Sam. 15:4 means to administer true
justice. Here again there is no idea that the poor and weak should receive
special treatment or be let off their crimes. They are to be given justice,
which previously they have not been able to obtain, but no more than that.

Job. 27:5 is somewhat different from the preceding examples in that
הצדיק does not denote the function of a judge but the action of a partici-
pant in a dispute or lawsuit who concedes the case, declaring his opponents
or accusers to be in the right. Job, who has never conceded that he was other
than in the right (cf. the use of צדק in the Qal in 9:15; 11:2; 13:18), now
goes further, asserting with an oath that he will never do so (חלילה לי
אם-אצדיק אתכם).

In all the cases considered above הצדיק expresses or implies an exact
apportionment of justice: the declaration of the innocence of the innocent
and the guilt of the guilty, the upholding of the right in a civil case, or the
carrying out of the process whereby the rights of a case may be brought to
light. The only passages which speak of the giving of judgement in favour of
the guilty or against the innocent make it clear that this is a heinous offence
against God as well as man. It must be concluded that הצדיק would be
totally inappropriate as a term equivalent to the forgiving of a sinner.

Dan. 12:3 falls into quite a different category. It speaks of a class of
persons known as the משכלים , "the wise", who at the end of time, when
"many" will rise from the dead (verse 2), will "shine like the brightness of the
firmament". The parallel clause states that the מצדיקי הרבים will also
shine like the stars for ever and ever. The commentators are agreed that the
משכלים and the מצדיקי הרבים are intended by the author to refer
to the same group of people.[160] It is therefore legitimate to seek elucidation
of the phrase מצדיקי הרבים by examining the function of the
משכ(י)לים in other passages of the book of Daniel.

In the narrative section of the book the verb השכיל , including the
participle משכיל , is used of wisdom or learning in general (1: 4, 17). In

the prayer of Daniel in 9:4-19 it is used in a religious sense, of understanding God's truth or his faithfulness (אמת). In 9:22, 25, however, it has a more restricted sense: the comprehension of the apocalyptic mysteries of the End which God gives to Daniel. It is in this restricted sense that the participle משכילים should be understood in 11:33, 35; 12:3, 10. The משכ(י)לים, "wise", here are the leaders of the people in the time of its affliction, whose function it is to instruct the people in the apocalyptic mysteries and so to enable them to endure to the end.[161] They can therefore be called משכלי עם, the wisest among the people, who give understanding to the many (יבינו לרבים) during the blasphemous and murderous assault of the "contemptible person" (11:33), enabling them to stand firm (יחזקו) and to be a people which knows its God (עם ידעי אלהיו .), resisting those who try to persuade them to be breakers of the covenant (מרשיעי ברית, verse 32). They are able to do this because they understand (יבינו) that the limit to this period of distress has been fixed and that the End is near (12:10).

In what sense can these משכילים be said to be מצדיקי הרבים ? Some commentators on this passage[162] have suggested that the phrase מצדיקי הרבים refers not to their instruction of the people only, but also to their martyrdom and its effects upon the people. They point out that 11:33 clearly implies that the משכילים will be martyred. This is so; but there is nothing in the text of the book of Daniel to suggest that their martyrdom is directly related to their function as מצדיקי הרבים . This conclusion has been dictated by the resemblance of the phrase מצדיקי הרבים to צדיק ... לרבים in Isa. 53:11, on the supposition that the former is a conscious reminiscence of the latter.[163] This supposition is probably correct. It is not surprising that an apocalyptic writer living during the crisis of the persecution of the Jews by Antiochus Epiphanes should have found in the figure of the Servant in Deutero-Isaiah a model for the spiritual leaders of the persecuted Jews of his own time. But this does not prove that he saw a vicarious element in the sufferings of the Servant.[164]

There is, then, no reason to suppose that the phrase מצדיקי הרבים in Dan. 12:3 has any other reference than to the function of instructing the people with which the משכילים are credited in 11:33. This means, however, that הצדיק here does not have the juridical sense which it has in the passages so far discussed. It has not a declarative but a causative or factitive sense which does not appear in the earlier literature (excluding for the present Isa. 53:11): the משכילים through their teaching bring צדק/צדקה to the "many". This might be interpreted in a moral sense: they persuade them to become righteous. More probably, however, the צדק or צדקה in question is a "state of salvation".

This meaning of צדקה is found in a number of passages in the Psalms.

where it is something which will be given by Yahweh to those who truly worship and obey him. Thus in Ps. 24:5 it is the man who is pure and upright who "will receive blessing (ברכה) from Yahweh and צדקה from the God of his salvation (ישעו)". Ps. 36:11 (EVV 36:10) prays God to "continue thy חסד to those who know thee (לידעיך , cf. ידעי אלהיו in Dan. 11:32) and thy צדקה to the upright of heart". According to Ps. 103:17f. "the חסד of Yahweh is . . . upon those who fear him, and his צדקה . . . to those who keep his covenant (שמרי בריתו)": contrast מרשיעי ברית in Dan. 11:32.[165] In the context of Dan. 11 – 12 it would appear that the משכילים by their instruction persuade the hesitant "many" to decide for the covenant and for knowing and obeying God and to take a stand against the pressures exerted upon them to become apostate in order to save their lives. In this way they "bring many to salvation".

The exact meaning of הצדיק here — whether in terms of moral conversion or of taking a stand for God — may remain in doubt. But it may in any case be affirmed that it was by their teaching, and not by their being "suffering servants", that the משכילים are said to have fulfilled their task as מצדיקי הרבים . It may well be that their own sufferings played a part in the conversion of the "many"; but the sufferings were not vicarious: the "many" received salvation because, persuaded by the משכילים , they themselves became worthy to receive it.

From the above discussion it must be concluded that none of the senses of הצדיק to be found in other passages of the Old Testament is capable of yielding a vicarious meaning to the action of the Servant described in the phrase יצדיק . . . עבדי לרבים in Isa. 53:11. It cannot mean that the Servant in this way brought about the acquittal of the many, since the many are constantly described in the chapter as guilty, and the examples of הצדיק in this juridical sense indicate that to acquit the guilty is a heinous sin and abhorrent to God. Similarly it cannot mean that the Servant thus obtained justice for the many, for to do so would be to convict rather than to acquit them. The sense of "concede the adversary to be in the right" (Job 27:5) is equally out of the question. Dan. 12:3, in which the משכילים bring צדקה to the many, at first seems capable of supporting a vicarious meaning for the work of the Servant; but — apart from the fact that this meaning of הצדיק is not attested before Daniel, which was written almost three centuries later than Deutero-Isaiah — there is really no evidence that the משכילים achieved this through their suffering or death. They achieved it through their teaching.

The range of meanings attested for הצדיק elsewhere in the Old Testament offers two possible alternative interpretations of יצדיק in Isa. 53:11. One possibility is that it should be taken as in Dan. 12:3.[166] The Servant, in other words, brought "salvation" to his fellow exiles through his teaching as a prophet. If the previous word בדעתו , "by his knowledge", could be shown to be a correct reading and to have been intended to be taken with צדיק rather than with the preceding line, this interpretation would be considerably strengthened: it was by his knowledge that the Servant was able so effectively to teach the people. There is no difficulty in taking "knowledge" here to mean knowledge of God or God-given knowledge, and Deutero-Isaiah was above all a prophet who proclaimed the imminent arrival of God's צדקה/צדק , and so might be said to have been the instrument of the bringing of this salvation to his fellow-exiles.[167] But the textual authenticity, meaning and syntactical connections of בדעתו are all in doubt;[168] and without this support this interpretation is perhaps somewhat unlikely, since it is the only explicit reference to the Servant's teaching in the chapter, and stands in a context which refers rather to his sufferings. It also fails to account for the word צדיק , which immediately follows יצדיק .

The second alternative proposal is a more probable one. It was suggested by Mowinckel,[169] followed by Westermann, that יצדיק here is an "internal causative Hiphil",[170] and that יצדיק צדיק עבדי לרבים should be translated by "My Servant will show himself to be righteous (and so stand) as righteous before the many". This suggestion may be defended by analogy with some other verbs denoting moral qualities or actions[171] such as יטב , which in the Hiphil can have the meaning "do right" or perhaps even "be good".[172]

This interpretation has the advantage that it makes it possible to retain צדיק , which many commentators wish to remove as a dittography or to displace. צדיק would then belong to the class of "adverbial accusatives"[173] which in a variety of ways qualify the verb which precedes them; but it is distinguished from most other examples in that its function is to strengthen the force of the verb rather than to define its scope more closely, and also in that it is derived from the same root as the verb.[174] There are however at least two examples of a similar usage: Isa. 22:18 and 24:22.[175] The phrase may, then, be translated, "My Servant being guiltless acted righteously", that is, he acted in every respect like a righteous man. This interpretation of צדיק would not be possible if יצדיק had the sense of "brought to salvation".[176]

Between these two interpretations of יצדיק here it is difficult to decide. But whether the Servant brought salvation to the many through his teaching, or acted righteously with regard to the many, his action has nothing to do with vicarious suffering.

6. ולפשעים יפגיע (verse 12c)[177]

It is maintained by many commentators that יפגיע here means that the Servant "intervened" or "made intercession" for the transgressors through his suffering and death: for example, Westermann says, "This does not mean

... that he made prayers of intercession for them, but that with his life, his suffering and his death, he took their place and underwent punishment in their stead."[178] This view has been strongly influenced by traditional Christian interpretation, which regards the whole chapter as a prefiguration of the passion and atoning death of Jesus. It is not supported by the text.

As has already been stated, the Hiphil of פגע occurs with certainty only five times in the Old Testament;[179] and – leaving Isa. 53:12 aside – these passages attest its use in no less than three distinct senses:

a. Cause to meet, i.e. cause to experience or suffer (Isa. 53:6).
b. Urge, plead with, entreat with words (Jer. 36:25; possibly also Jer. 15:11).[180]
c. Interpose oneself, intervene physically on behalf of another person (Isa. 59:16).

Of these three meanings, only the second and third are possible in 53:12. It could be said of the Servant here that he entreated Yahweh on behalf of the "sinners" (פשעים) (that is, that he offered intercessory prayer for them), or that he interposed himself or intervened with God in some more concrete way on their behalf (though, if this is the case, the text does not explain in what way this was done). The choice between these two meanings is not a simple one, because the notions of verbal intercession and more active intervention, though distinct, have much in common, and the extant examples of the use of the word are too few to permit a full understanding of its possible nuances. It might well be that the action of the Servant here would not correspond exactly to that described in either Isa. 59:16 or Jer. 36:25.

We first examine the view that the Servant is said in Isa. 53:12 to have interposed his life between Yahweh and the "sinners", thus himself bearing the punishment which Yahweh intended to impose upon them. Can לפשעים יפגיע have such a meaning? The only passage where it has the sense of someone's interposing himself or intervening other than with words on behalf of another party is Isa. 59:16.

In this passage it is Yahweh who acts. The situation of his people was desperate because they had "no man" (אין איש) to act as a מפגיע, "one who intervenes, a champion". Therefore Yahweh himself intervened on their behalf: he appeared as a warrior and himself alone defeated their enemies. It was he who became their מפגיע.

But the difference between Yahweh's action in Isa. 59:16 and that supposedly attributed to the Servant in Isa. 53:12 can hardly be exaggerated. The most informative account in the Old Testament of the role of such a "champion" (though he is not there called a מפגיע) is the story of David's fight against Goliath in I Sam. 17.[181] The situation is so similar, *mutatis mutandis*, to that of Isa. 59:16 that it seems possible that the author of the latter had the former in mind. In both cases the protagonist saw that Israel had no champion to fight for them and took that role upon himself. In Isa. 59:16, in the expression ויֹרא כי-אין איש , the word איש (parallel with מפגיע) appears to mean "champion". It occurs also in this sense in the taunts of Goliath in 1 Sam. 17: ברו-לכם איש וירד אלי , "choose for yourselves a champion, that he may come down to me" (verse 8); תנו-לי איש ונלחמה יחד, "provide me with a champion, that we may fight together" (verse 10); and probably also in the remarks of the Israelites in verses 25, 26, 27. Goliath is the "champion" of the Philistines,[182] and David offers himself as the corresponding "champion" on behalf of Israel.[183]

It is clear from Isa. 59:16 and the fuller account in 1 Sam. 17 that, while the champion undoubtedly exposed his life to danger on behalf of others, his success in that role depended entirely on his killing his adversary. To be killed himself, or to be humiliated, would make him a total failure as a champion, and would have the effect not of saving his people but of delivering them into the hands of their enemies: when Goliath was killed, the Philistines fled and were slaughtered by Israel. It is of course theoretically possible that הפגיע possessed a more profound connotation which might embrace the idea of giving one's life for others, but this would be pure speculation: the only relevant text which we have is Isa. 59:16, and this gives no support to the idea. As far as our knowledge goes, the verb הפגיע would not convey to those who heard it the idea of a man who obtained deliverance for his people not by victory over the enemy but by being himself defeated and wounded or killed.

The alternative view which is open to us on the precarious basis of our limited knowledge of the meanings of הפגיע is to take יפגיע in Isa. 53:12 in a sense similar to that which it has in Jer. 36:25 and perhaps also in Jer. 15:11: that of verbal entreaty.[184] In Jer. 36:25 the king's advisers try to prevent Jehoiakim from burning the scroll containing Jeremiah's prophecies: הפגעו במלך לבלתי שרף את-המגלה . That their intervention is purely verbal is made clear by the words which follow: "he would not listen to them" (ולא שמע אליהם). If הפגיע can denote an entreaty made to men, it can obviously equally be used of similar entreaty to God, that is, of intercessory prayer, and indeed פגע in the Qal has this meaning.[185]

There has been much recent discussion of the question whether intercessory prayer was one of the functions of the Old Testament prophets. While the more extreme advocates of this view, who regard it as a kind of sacral "office" to which prophets were called,[186] have probably overstated the case, it cannot be denied that some prophets did intercede with God on behalf of Israel.[187]

In the case of Deutero-Isaiah, however, it might be argued that such intercession would have been out of place and unnecessary, since it was now too late to prevent punishment from falling on his people, and the main burden of his message was that Yahweh had already freely forgiven them and was now promising an immediate release from their sufferings. But this is to fail to take into account the character of Deutero-Isaiah's oracles of salvation, through which this forgiveness and release were made available to them. Von Waldow has drawn attention to the importance of the role of the prophet in pronouncing salvation-oracles in response to the people's lamentation.[188] In the process of prayer and answer to prayer (lamentation and oracle of salvation) it is reasonable to suppose that the role of the prophet was not restricted to representing God to the people, but that he also represented the people to God in bringing their complaints before him. The existence of the salvation-oracles is proof that he was successful in this role. Whether this prophetic function is best described as intercessory or in a deeper sense as mediatorial, the word הפגיע is eminently suited to express it.

But it must be emphasized that there is nothing in our text to suggest that this prophetic role was identified with or directly related to Deutero-Isaiah's sufferings. It has been supposed that this is so because of the context in which the phrase stands, especially the immediately preceding statement that the Servant "bore the sin of the many" (והוא חטא־רבים נשא). But the two phrases are intended to express a poignant contrast rather than a parallelism of thought: the Servant suffered a punishment which others and not he deserved; yet it was he who had always interceded (and successfully!) with God for those very people.[189]

The intercessory activity of the Servant finds an analogy not only in the work of Deutero-Isaiah's prophetic predecessors but also in that of Moses[190] and Samuel.[191] Both of these earlier leaders are credited with intercessory prayer on behalf of sinful Israel, but their prayers were accepted not because of any vicarious suffering but because of their special relationship with God. This was the case with the Servant of Yahweh in Deutero-Isaiah also; and he saw his prayers accepted.[192]

D. Conclusion

The individual phrases examined in the previous discussion must now be placed in the context of the poem as a whole.[193] Two moods are dominant: that of penitence, which the author expresses on behalf of his fellows ("we") for having in the past failed to understand the nature of the Servant's work which had led him into such suffering for the sake of those who deserved it so much more than he; and that of joy that Yahweh had now delivered him and would fully restore him to health and prosperity.[194] The second of these motifs is virtually confined to verses 1, 10-12b. The penitential motif, however, is expressed again and again, often in similar language, throughout the poem. The penitent mood of the author leads him to introduce the theme of the undeserved suffering of the Servant with its causes and its effects on the community not only into the main confession (verses 4-6), but also into a secondary confession attached to the account of the Servant's sufferings (verse 8), into Yahweh's oracle of salvation in verses 11-12b, and into the final summing up in verse 12c.[195]

It has been demonstrated that, quite apart from the inherent improbability of such a notion in the Old Testament, none of these expressions individually can properly be interpreted as referring to vicarious suffering. Nor can their constant recurrence make such an interpretation more probable. To a casual reader the constant reiteration in different words of the theme "he has borne our sins" may well give the impression that some event of stupendous religious significance is being stated with great emphasis. Such an impression, however, is due to ignorance of the category to which the poem belongs: that of the individual thanksgiving.[196] In that type of psalm there is frequently an overlapping and repetition of themes within a fairly constant structure. Repetition does not add to the meaning of what is being repeated; and what is being repeated is not a statement about vicarious atonement.

If then it has been established that the concept of vicarious suffering is not to be found in Isa. 53, the question arises why it has seemed self-evident to so many Christian theologians and exegetes of past and present that it is. The answer lies in the history of Christian doctrine and in the tendency of traditional Christian exegesis to interpret the Old Testament christologically wherever possible. Once the idea had arisen in the early Church that Jesus was the Servant of whom the second half of the book of Isaiah speaks, it was but a further step to interpret Isa. 53 as foretelling or prefiguring the atoning sufferings of Jesus. The theme of vicarious suffering was thus read back into Isa. 53 from the Christian theology of the atonement.

The history of this line of exegesis up to modern times seems not to have been fully investigated, and such an investigation would lie outside the scope of the present enquiry. A recent investigation of the theme of the Servant in early Jewish and Christian literature by Morna Hooker is, however, illuminating.[197] After noting the absence of the idea of vicarious suffering or atonement in Jewish literature up to the end of the first century A.D.,[198] she pursues her investigation of early Christian interpretation, concluding that "the traditional belief that Jesus saw himself as the 'Suffering Servant' not only lacks any sufficient evidence in the New Testament, but is based on an incorrect interpretation of the Jewish concept".[199] Not until the time of Origen in the third century A.D. can it be said that the relevance of Isa. 53, "not only to the facts of the Passion Story, but also to their significance . . .

was well established."[200] With regard to the later development of the idea she suggests that "once this comparison has been made . . . it is easy to imagine hints at the Servant concept in the New Testament where none is intended."[201] She does not pursue further the history of this belief. But she is quite clear about the error made by modern scholarship: "Modern scholarship, in over-estimating the importance of the concept for Jesus and the early Church, has also inevitably exaggerated the part played by the same concept in contemporary Judaism. Consequently, too much emphasis has been placed . . . upon his" (the Servant's) "experience of suffering."

It is of course the exponents of Christian "modern scholarship" who are the authors of most commentaries and other learned works not only on the New Testament but also on the Old, in which the view that vicarious suffering is to be found in Isa. 53 is too often taken for granted rather than impartially investigated.[202]

Whatever may have been the subsequent history of the idea in later theology, the fact that there appears to have been a gap of several centuries between the composition of Isa. 53 and its interpretation in terms of vicarious atonement is significant. It is indeed clear that once the Servant is seen as prefiguring Jesus it is not difficult to find detailed references to his atoning death in the chapter. But it is equally certain that the Hebrew text itself, interpreted without preconceived ideas and inherited convictions, does not permit that conclusion.

In the discussion so far the question whether Isa. 53 speaks not only of the Servant's sufferings but also of his death has not been raised. This must be the next stage of the investigation.

Part II. Was the Servant Dead?

PART II. WAS THE SERVANT DEAD?

Introduction

Most interpreters of Isaiah 53 are agreed that a significant change of theme and mood occurs at verse 10. Verses 2-10a speak of things which have already occurred: of the Servant's past experiences.[1] The textual difficulties of the first part of verse 10 make it uncertain at exactly what point the change to a future perspective occurs; but at least from "he shall see" (יראה) it is clear that the author is speaking of the future.[2] This impression is confirmed by the use of Hebrew tenses: after a long and almost unbroken sequence of perfect tenses in verses 2-10a there follows a completely unbroken series of imperfect tenses in verses 10b-12a (up to and including "and he shall divide [the] spoil with the strong [חלק ירצומים שלל] ואת-עצומים יחלק שלל).[3]

The events referred to in verses 2-10a have generally been taken to describe not only the Servant's sufferings but also his death. Verses 10b-12a, however, speak of him as alive. If this interpretation of verses 2-10a is correct, it follows that verses 10b-12a must presuppose or describe the restoration to life of one who had previously died. The miraculous and unexpected character of this divine act of restoration would then account for the astonishment expressed by the speakers in verse 1.

The questions of the death of the Servant and of his restoration to life are interrelated. If verses 10b-12a can only be interpreted as speaking of the restoration to life of a dead person, the view that verses 2-10a refer to the Servant's death as well as to his suffering is thereby confirmed. If they may be but need not be so interpreted, they neither confirm nor exclude that view. But if they cannot be so interpreted, the case for the death of the Servant is seriously weakened.

Before considering the question of the death of the Servant, therefore, it may be convenient to turn to the interpretation of verses 10b-12a.

A. The Servant's Supposed Resurrection

The phrases which speak of the Servant's being alive in the present or future are the following:

1. יראה זרע יאריך ימים   (verse 10b)[4]

The expression האריך ימים , literally "lengthen (one's) days", is a frequent one in the Old Testament, and signifies "to live a long life".[5] To speak of seeing one's children or grandchildren (the phrase ראה זרע itself does not occur except here), that is, to live long enough to see one's descendants, is another way of referring to longevity; here the concept of a life that is not only long but also happy and honoured, which is only implicit in the former expression, is made explicit, since the knowledge that one's family would continue for generations to come was counted one of the greatest of blessings. The two concepts of longevity and an assured line of descendants are closely linked, as is well illustrated by Gen. 50:22-26, where it is said that Joseph lived to be 110 years old and that (verse 23) he "saw Ephraim's children of the third generation" (וירא יוסף לאפרים בני שלשים), that is, probably his own great-grandchildren, and Job 42:16, where Job is said to have lived 140 years after his rehabilitation and to have seen three (or four)[6] generations of descendants.[7]

Critical opinions differ concerning the syntactical relationship between the two phrases יראה זרע and יאריך ימים . Most interpreters regard them as parallel and asyndetic: "he will see his descendants (and) he will live long". Others[8] regard יאריך ימים as a relative clause: "he will see off-spring which will live long", that is, "he will live to see his descendants living to a great age". The second of these two interpretations is the more probable.[9] "He will see seed" is hardly satisfactory: although there are no exact parallels to this expression we should expect זרעו , "*his* seed"; the suffix would not, however, be necessary if זרע were followed by a relative clause. Moreover, if these were parallel clauses, the logical order would be the reverse of the present one: we should expect first the statement about the Servant's longevity and then that about his seeing his descendants. Finally a statement that the Servant will live long enough only to see the birth of his own children would seem to be inadequate in a passage which is evidently in a superlative mood: it would be expected that the author should have matched the statements about Joseph and Job mentioned above, which may be taken to reflect traditional modes of speech.

We have here, then, a statement, expressed in traditional language, that the Servant's life in the future will be exceptionally blessed in that he will live to see his own children live to a ripe old age. One further question must be asked: is this statement to be taken literally or figuratively? Some interpreters[10] maintained that the "descendants" of the Servant here are "spiritual" descendants: they are the future generations of Israel who have received and enjoy the benefits achieved by the work of the Servant.[11] But there is a grave objection to this view: the word זרע , "seed" in its derived sense of "progeny" is never used in the Old Testament in any other than a physical and literal sense.[12]

There are then no grounds whatever for interpreting this statement about the Servant's longevity other than literally. It is a plain statement that the Servant can look forward to an ordinary earthly existence, but one which will be especially blessed as regards longevity and progeny. There is no suggestion at all that he has been or will be raised from the dead.[13]

2. וחפץ יהוה בידו יצלח (verse 10b)[14]

This phrase speaks of the successful accomplishment of Yahweh's will or
purpose in the future through the agency of the Servant. It is not specifically
stated which aspect of that purpose the author has particularly in mind, nor
in what way the Servant will carry it out. But it may be supposed that what
is referred to is Yahweh's plan for the restoration of his people through
imminent historical events, since this is the central theme of all Deutero-
Isaiah's prophecies. This is the case with the other three references in Deutero-
Isaiah to the accomplishment of Yahweh's חפץ : 44:28; 46:10; 48:14. In all
these cases the appointed agent is not the prophet-Servant but Cyrus. But the
functions of Cyrus and of the prophet are clearly complementary: Deutero-
Isaiah's prophetic announcement of what Yahweh will do is no less essential
than Cyrus' obedient transformation of that announcement into concrete
historical reality.

Two further considerations suggest that what is referred to is the Servant's
prophetic activity. The first is the employment of the expression ביד . Although this is frequently used in the Old Testament of human agency in a
general sense, it is used with especial frequency in both the priestly and the
Deuteronomic literature — literature composed at a time not far removed
from that of Deutero-Isaiah's prophecies — of the action of prophets and
other persons in speaking the word which Yahweh has given them to speak.[15]
Yahweh addresses his people through the agency (ביד) of his prophets.

The second consideration concerns the passage on the nature of the prophetic word in 55:10-11, where the verb הצליח and the root חפץ (this time
as a verb, חפצתי "I have purposed") once more occur together (verse 11).
As in 53:10b it is asserted here that Yahweh's purpose will assuredly be
accomplished. But the means by which it will be accomplished are here
clearly defined: it will be accomplished by the word of prophecy. The passage
might almost be a commentary on וחפץ יהוה בידו יצלח

The allusiveness of the language in 53:10b makes it impossible to be quite
precise; but its most natural interpretation is as a promise that the Servant's
earlier career, interrupted by the events described in verses 2-10a, will now
be resumed and brought to a successful conclusion.

3. מעמל נפשו יראה (verse 11a)[16]

It is now agreed by most commentators[17] that מעמל נפשו means
something like "after his terrible experiences", - מן having a temporal sense.
This interpretation neither implies nor excludes the view that these experiences led to the Servant's death.

There is, however, less agreement about יראה . The opinion that the line
should be emended by the addition of the word אור, "light", a reading

81

found in 1QIs[a] and 1QIs[b] and presupposed by LXX,[18] is almost, though not quite, unanimous;[19] but although the most obvious rendering of יראה אור would be "he shall see light", it is argued by G.R. Driver[20] and D.W. Thomas[21] that יראה here is derived not from ראה "to see" but from a verb ראה which is a by-form of רוה , "to be drenched, sated".[22] This, in the view of Driver, who accepts the addition of אור, suggests the translation "he shall be flooded with light"; for Thomas, on the other hand, the addition of אור is unnecessary: רוה/ראה means "drink deep" and has no direct object.[23]

There are therefore three ways in which the whole phrase has been rendered by recent scholars. Thomas' translation, "When he shall have drunk deep of his anguish", contains no reference at all to the servant's possible re-habilitation. Driver's "he shall be flooded with light", a phrase which in the Hebrew occurs nowhere else in the Old Testament, and in which both noun and verb are understood as separate metaphors, is too vague to yield any certain information about this rehabilitation. It may be questioned, however, whether there is any real justification for the view that יראה here is derived from רוה/ראה , "be drenched, saturated" rather than from ראה, "see". The main argument in its favour seems to be that it makes a satisfactory parallelism with the following word ישבע , "will be sated, satisfied"; but this argument is not sufficiently compelling to dislodge the third, most widely supported, and most natural interpretation: "he shall see light".

But what is meant by saying that "after his terrible experiences he will see light"? The word אור , "light", is used in a number of derived or meta-phorical senses in the Old Testament. In a number of passages[24] it is a synonym for "life"; and, like the word חיים , "life", its meaning is frequently further extended to denote a special kind of life: life in its fullest and most positive sense, attended by happiness and prosperity, and particularly by God's favour, blessing or salvation.[25]

Of the eight passages in which the phrase ראה אור [26] occurs, three use the word אור in a literal sense.[27] In all the five remaining passages it has the meaning of "life". In Job 3:16; 33:28; Ps. 49:20 (EVV 19) this is life in the purely physical sense.

In Job 3:16, Job, expressing the wish that he had never been born, asks why he was not "hidden like an untimely birth, or like infants who never saw the light (לא-ראו אור)". The phrase ראה אור here might in theory mean "to be born (alive)" rather than "to live"; but the other two examples do not support this meaning. In 33:28 the same writer represents a man as praising God for preserving his life in the words "and my life[28] shall see the light (באור תראה)." Here it is clearly the continuation of the man's present life which is meant. In Ps. 49:20 (19) not to see the light means to have died: "He will go to join the company of his fathers, who are for ever dead (עד-נצח לא יראו-אור)". There is no reference here to speculations about a possible rebirth. The point is that the dead remain dead: they are in an eternal state of not living (לא יראו-אור).

In the final two passages – Ps. 36:10 (EVV 9) and (probably) Isa. 9:1 (EVV 2) – the word אור, "life", has the extended meaning referred to above: it refers to people already alive in the physical sense who obtain from Yahweh a fuller kind of life: a life of greater happiness or prosperity.

יראה אור in Isa. 53:11, then, certainly does not refer to the renewal of life of one who has been dead. There is no allusion to resurrection or anything of the kind. In view of the context (verses 10b-12a), which speaks of a future joy and happiness reserved for the Servant, the phrase is most naturally translated as promising a full and happy life which is about to begin for the Servant: "he will enjoy the fullness of life".

4. ישבע בדעתו (verse 11a)[29]

This text, which some interpreters[30] regard as impenetrably obscure, adds little or nothing, on the basis of any of the interpretations so far offered, to the evidence concerning a supposed restoration to life of a dead Servant. Leaving aside various proposed emendations of בדעתו which have now been generally abandoned by modern commentators, the interpretations of these two words by recent scholars may be divided into two main groups: those that follow the Massoretic accentuation and link ישבע with the immediately preceding (אור) יראה, taking בדעתו with the phrase which follows; and those that make a major break after יראה (אור) and take ישבע בדעתו either as an independent statement or as the beginning of a statement which is continued in the phrase יצדיק צדיק עבדי לרבים.

Those who take ישבע with the phrase which precedes it[31] regard ישבע as concomitant with or immediately consequent upon the Servant's "seeing (light)": he will derive satisfaction or contentment either from the cessation of his sufferings or from the result which has been achieved through them. ישבע in itself cannot in any way be interpreted as implying a restoration to life. בדעתו, according to this type of interpretation, is then part of the following statement about the Servant's activity with regard to the רבים.[32]

Those who take ישבע and בדעתו together are by no means united in their interpretations, as the following table, incomplete but representative, shows:[33]

a. דעת = "knowledge"; text unemended

   i. "will be sated/satisfied by (his) knowledge" (Kaiser, Lindblom)

   ii. "will have fullness of knowledge" (North)

b. דעת = "knowledge"; emendation by the addition of צדיק, transferred from after יצדיק to follow בדעתו.

"will be satisfied in knowing himself true" (Torrey)

c. רַעַת = "humiliation";[34] text unemended
"will receive full measure of humiliation" (Thomas)

d. רַעַת = "humiliation"; text emended as in b. above with the additional
emendation of צֶדֶק to צדיק
"will win full justification through his humiliation" (Driver)

Once again none of these renderings either implies or excludes the view that
the Servant died and was restored to life.

5. לכן אֲחַלֶּק-לוֹ ברבים ואת-עצומים יְחַלֵּק שלל (verse 12a)[35]

These statements form a parallel couplet or poetical line. Together they
constitute a further statement, this time made by Yahweh himself, concerning
the reward which will be given to the Servant after the sufferings which he has
undeservedly borne. That the reward is given in recompense for the suffering
is indicated by the use of the particle לכן, "therefore". The nature of the
reward is stated in metaphorical terms, through the figure of the distribution
of captured booty after a military victory.[36]

There are several ambiguities here which can hardly be solved by grammatical or philological means, and these have led to a wide diversity of interpretation.

a. The verb חלק both in the Piel (as here, in both occurrences) and in the
Qal, whose meanings differ very little from those of the Piel, can mean either
"share out, distribute, allot (to others)"[37] or "share out (mutually)", "participate in sharing out".[38] Consequently in Isa. 53:12, although the addition
of לו, "to him" makes it certain that אחלק-לו can only mean "I will allot
to him", יחלק, the second occurrence of the verb, may mean either "he will
allot (to others)" or "he will participate (with others) in sharing out".[39]

b. Both רבים and עצומים can mean either "many" or "great ones",
"strong ones".

c. Both the ב in ברבים and the את in את-עצומים are ambiguous.
ברבים may mean "among (i.e. as one of) the many/strong ones" (compare
Prov. 17:2, ובתוך אחים יַחֲלֹק נחלה), or, as in Job 39:17 (ולא-חָלַק
לה בבינה , "and he did not give her a share of understanding"), it may
indicate that רבים is in some (partial) sense the object of אחלק. Similarly
את in ואת-עצומים may mean either "with, among" as in Prov. 16:19
(מֵחַלֵּק שלל את-גאים , "(than) sharing out spoil with the proud")[40] or
it may denote the direct object, making עצומים the object of יחלק, in
which case שלל would mean "as spoil".

84

In spite of these divergences of interpretation in detail there is agreement among the commentators on the main thrust of the assertion made in this line. Through the metaphor of military victory and the realization of its rewards the Servant is presented as a victor. He is to receive a share of the spoils of victory (שלל) and/or to share out spoils to others. These "spoils" are either undefined (if ב and את mean "with, among") or they are defined as "(the) great" or "(the) many".

What do these statements tell us about the future life of the Servant? Simply that the Servant is a victor. He will emerge victorious from his trials. But there is nothing here to suggest that this victory is a victory over death. The author of the poem has chosen a military metaphor to describe the future triumph of the Servant. Some kind of "battle", therefore, has been fought and won by the Servant: it has been won because it was fought with the support of Yahweh. That is all we can conclude from this line.

6. We may summarize the results of the above investigation in the follow-ing way: in verse 10b יראה זרע יאריך ימים states that the Servant will now enjoy a long and happy life. וחפץ יהוה בידו יצלח promises a successful conclusion to his career. In verse 11a מעמל נפשו יראה (אור) states that after his suffering he will enjoy life to the full. The mean-ing of ישבע בדעתו is uncertain, but these words speak in some way about his satisfaction at the outcome of his sufferings, or they may speak about the sufferings themselves. Verse 12a promises him a reward which will be a re-compense for those sufferings. Neither these statements nor any other phrases in verses 10-12 in themselves offer any grounds for supposing that the happy recipient of all these blessings has died and has been or will be restored to life.

B. Individual Resurrection from Death in the Old Testament

Any uncertainties which may remain about the interpretation of Isa. 53: 10-12 in terms of a restoration of the Servant from death to life must be further tested by another question: is it conceivable that a writer of the sixth century B.C. such as the author of Isa. 53 could have believed that the Servant, having died, could be so restored to life?[41]

We must first take note of the fact that the phrases "resurrection" and "restoration to life" cover a number of concepts which must be distinguished from one another. In the Old Testament there are three such concepts: 1. the restoration of a dead person to ordinary life, that is to mortal life, which will eventually be ended by a second death (as in the case of persons restored to life by Elijah and Elisha); 2. the bodily removal of a person to, presumably, eternal life with God or in heaven without his having experienced death in the usual sense of that word (as with Enoch and Elijah); and 3. the gift of eternal life after death (Dan. 12:2). If the Servant is a historical figure and if he has just died, only the first of these concepts is relevant to Isa. 53. As has been shown above,[42] there is nothing in the statements about his future in verses 10-12 which suggests that anything other than ordinary mortal human life is intended, nor anything in the statements in the chapter about his past experiences which suggest that he was bodily removed by God from this world.[43]

It is generally agreed that such *ideas* as those of the resuscitation of corpses, life after death, and the exceptional removal of certain persons from this world by God were familiar to the ancient Israelites, and are to be found in the Old Testament. The question to be asked is whether for the Israelite of the sixth century B.C. these ideas were associated only with the realms of fantasy, poetry, myth and the like, or whether he could seriously have en-visaged restoration to life by God as a practical possibility for someone whom he had himself known, and known to be a man like himself.

The passages in which some kind of belief in resurrection, restoration of life after death or similar phenomena has been thought to be present may tentatively be classified in the following way:[44]

1. **Passages in which a belief in a general resurrection, not restricted to special, extraordinary cases, of ordinary individuals to eternal life after death is clearly stated**: Dan. 12:2, perhaps also Isa. 26:19. It is universally agreed that these passages were written much later than Isa. 53 and they consequent-ly provide no information about beliefs held by Israelites in the sixth century B.C.

2. **Specific and exceptional cases of resurrection or translation recorded in traditional stories**. These are of two kinds:

a. The "translations" of Enoch, who walked with God, and "was seen no more, for God took him away" (ואיננו כי-לקח אתו אלהים , Gen. 5:24), and Elijah, who "went up in a whirlwind to heaven" (ויעל אליהו בסערה שמים) and was seen no more (2 Kings 2:11), of whom also it is said that God "took (לקח)" him (2 Kings 2:3, 5). Both these incidents, one from the "primaeval" traditions about legendary figures from the remote past, and the other from a collection of popular prophetic legends about prophets which in other incidents also attribute miraculous and quasi-magical powers to their heroes,[45] are narrated precisely because of their totally exceptional and mysterious character. They no more provide evidence about contemporary beliefs concerning the fate of ordinary individuals than do modern fairy-tales. Moreover such "translations" have nothing in common with any beliefs which the author of Isa. 53 might have held about the fate of the Servant, who, whatever may have happened to him, was certainly not bodily translated.

   b. Prophetic stories about persons restored to life by Elijah and Elisha: Elijah's resuscitation of the widow's son (1 Kings 17:17-24); Elisha's resuscitation of the Shunammite's son (2 Kings 4:18-37); and the revival of the dead man whose corpse was thrown into Elisha's grave (2 Kings 13:20-21). In all these cases the resurrection in question was a restoration to ordinary mortal life. Like the "translations" of Enoch and Elijah considered above, however, they all occur in collections of popular stories or legends, and are told solely to illustrate the extraordinary powers of these two prophets. The first two show how Elijah and Elisha respectively were "men of God" to whom God granted extraordinary gifts; the third is pure hagiology bordering on the magical. None of the persons so resuscitated was himself in any way remarkable or deserving of such special treatment. Once again there is no reason whatever to believe that those who invented, transmitted or recorded these stories believed that such resuscitations were possible in ordinary life.

   3. Passages which use the theme of restoration to life by Yahweh in metaphors or parables expressing hope of the "revival" of a community which is in some way regarded as "dead" ("spiritually" dead or near to extinction): Ezek. 37:10; Hos. 6:2.

   Ezek. 37:10 occurs in the vision of the valley of dry bones (Ezek. 37:1-14). All the commentators are agreed that this vision, in which the "whole house of Israel" is pictured as a collection of dry bones, the corpses of an   army killed in battle, which Yahweh then resuscitates, cannot in itself be taken to be a prophecy of the resurrection of individuals from the dead. Its function is entirely metaphorical. Nevertheless it may be asked whether the use of such a metaphor reflects a belief of this kind which was familiar to the prophet. Zimmerli denies this quite categorically:[46] he regards the passage as absolutely unique, describing the rescue of the exiled people of Israel by Yahweh as a single, once-for-all event shortly to take place, expressed in terms not of individual resurrection but of a new creation. The source of the metaphor is the traditional belief in the original creation of the world such as is found in Gen. 2, and not that of the abode of the dead, Sheol, from which Yahweh is, amazingly, now about to release its inhabitants. Some exegetes, however, have suggested that the passage does in fact reflect the beginnings of a belief in individual resurrection.[47] It is difficult to sustain this view. Even if the passage does show that Ezekiel knew of some tradition of a miraculous

87

revival of persons who were not only dead and buried but also totally de-
composed so that only their bones remained — and there is no evidence elsewhere in the Old Testament of such a tradition except in what may perhaps
be inferred from Isa. 26:19 and Dan. 12:2 — there is no proof that the tradition which he knew took the form of a belief that resurrection from the dead
could be the fate of ordinary men and women living in his own day. He can
only have known it, if at all, in the form of myths[48] or legends of the remote
past. Moreover, as has been pointed out by a number of commentators, the
prophet's reply, "O Lord God, thou knowest", to Yahweh's question "Son of
man, can these bones live?" (verse 3), strongly suggests that he knew nothing
of such a tradition, though he recognized that the power to give life lay
entirely in Yahweh's hands.

Hos. 6:2 also speaks of a restoration of the people of Israel in terms which
have been supposed by some commentators to reflect some kind of belief in
individual resurrection from the dead. It occurs in a penitential prayer in
which the speakers express the hope that Yahweh (or some other god) will
accept their penitence and "revive" them. The expectation is thus corporate,
not individual; and the form of expression is clearly metaphorical. It may be
asked, however, whether the motif is borrowed from some more literal and
personal belief. Although most commentators now reject this view, it still has
some supporters.[49]

The imagery of Hos. 6:2 has been derived by some modern scholars from
a cultic source: that of a supposed cult of a dying and rising vegetation god
which was held to have been widely practised in the ancient Near East and
may be supposed to have been familiar to Israelites in a Canaanite form.[50]
But apart from the facts that our knowledge of Canaanite cults is almost entirely inferential and hypothetical, and that the evidence for cults of dying
and rising gods even in some other parts of the ancient Near East such as
Babylon is now seen to be very precarious if not non-existent,[51] there seem
to be insufficient grounds for holding that the phraseology of Hos. 6:2 is in
fact derived from sources of this kind.[52]

Further, there is no explicit reference to death in this passage (Hos. 6:1-3).
The only two words which might be so interpreted are יחינו , "he will
revive us", and יקמנו , "he will raise us up" (both in verse 2). Both of these
expressions, however, may be used of the restoration of a sick man to health,
and this is the most natural interpretation in view of וירפאנו , "and he will
heal us", and ויחבשנו , "and he will bind us up", in verse 1. The passage is
using metaphors derived from the idea of the healing by God of a sick man
rather than from that of the restoration to life of a dead one.[53]

Neither Ezek. 37:10 nor Hos. 6:2, therefore, provides evidence of a belief
in the resurrection of the individual from death.[54] Neither passage does more
than to assert the belief that Yahweh has absolute power over life as well as

over.death. This belief, although it goes further than some Old Testament passages which seem to suggest that in dying men pass into a realm over which Yahweh has no control,[55] and although it is an essential pre-requisite to a doctrine of the individual's resurrection from the dead, does not in any way require as its corollary a belief that individual men expect that they will in fact be resurrected.

4. Passages in psalms, mainly of lamentation or thanksgiving, in which the psalmist states that Yahweh has delivered or will deliver him from death.[56]

Recent studies[57] have shown conclusively that these passages speak neither of a real death nor of a real resurrection. For the ancient Israelite as for other peoples of the ancient Near East the concept of death was more fluid and wider than the modern western concept, and included states of extreme physical sickness or misery in which the sufferer or victim felt himself to be in the grip of death. These statements about rescue from death are therefore expressions of confidence or of thanksgiving for Yahweh's rescue of the speaker from such states, which we should describe rather as states of danger from death. There is consequently no expression here of a belief in the resuscitation of individuals from beyond the grave.

5. Passages expressing confidence in God as protector, vindicator or companion.

The four most notable of these passages are Job 19:25-27; Ps. 16:9-11; 49:16 (EVV 49:15); 73:23-28. Since the possibility cannot be excluded that they are as early as or earlier than Isa. 53, the question arises whether they imply an eternal relationship with God which could be interpreted as life after death in some sense for the individual.

Job in 19:25-27 expresses confidence that his righteousness will eventually be vindicated by God; but this is the only point on which commentators are agreed in interpreting this passage, which is one of the most difficult in the Old Testament. There is no clear statement here concerning when, where or how Job will receive his vindication. His assertion in verse 26 that he will "see God מבשרי " continues to receive two quite diametrically opposed interpretations, since מבשר י may be translated either by "from my flesh" or by "without my flesh". Some modern commentators[58] hold that the vision of God will take place before Job's death, while others believe that it is to take place after death. Of the latter, some[59] think of it as a brief momentary vision which does not in any way imply a belief in a continuous and eternal life after death, or think that[60] it will simply be a moment of awareness by Job in Sheol itself which is not in any way inconsistent with the statements elsewhere in the book that there is no return from death. The vagueness of the belief expressed by Job has also been pointed out.[61] Job may feel confident that God will vindicate him after death, but does not formulate any precise notion how this will be done.

Any interpretation of this passage must take account of the fact that Job himself in other speeches in the dialogue specifically asserts that there is no return for men from beyond the grave.[62] Although there are other instances of such changes of mood and self-contradictions in Job's speeches, it is clear that Job, if indeed he is speaking in 19:25-27 of experiences after death, is not expressing a fully formulated belief but at most a tentative hope. No modern commentator goes beyond this in his interpretation of the passage.[63]

In Ps. 16:9-11 also the speaker expresses confidence in God. The only verse, however, which might require to be interpreted as referring to life after death is verse 10: "For thou dost not give me up to Sheol, or let thy godly one see the Pit." The question is whether this means that God will protect the psalmist from sudden or premature death, or whether it means that he will, at his death, save him from the gloomy half-existence of Sheol and confer on him eternal life in the divine presence. There is certainly here, as in Job 19:25-27, no precise formulation of such a belief; and although some interpreters[64] hold that the psalmist is thinking, however vaguely, of a divine protection which will extend beyond death, there can be no doubt that the view of Barth[65] and Kraus[66] is correct that the similarity of the style and phraseology of the passage to those of the psalms of lamentation and thanksgiving show that the thought here is of deliverance in the present life from the danger of death rather than of the ultimate avoidance by the psalmist of the descent into Sheol.

On Ps. 49:16 opinions are again divided. Whereas Barth[67] interprets the verse in the same way as Ps. 16:9-11, as an expression of confidence that Yahweh will rescue the psalmist from premature death, permitting him to continue his ordinary life, some interpreters[68] see here a belief that those who trust in God will, in contrast with the wicked, be rescued by God after death from Sheol to eternal life. In favour of this view are supposedly the use of פדה, "ransom", in both verses 8 and 16 (EVV 7 and 15), which makes it possible for these verses to be understood together as meaning that while man cannot buy off death, God can redeem him from its effects, and the occurrence of the word יקחני , "he will take me". It is supposed that the word לקח , which in earlier times had been used in the special cases of Enoch and Elijah in Gen. 5:24; 2 Kings 2:3, 5,[69] was later – as in this psalm – taken up again in a somewhat different sense of the gift of life *after* death.

This hypothesis of an ancient technical term re-used in a different sense is, however, no more than a supposition. It is easier to suppose that לקח here has no such technical meaning but simply refers to the action of God in "carrying off" the psalmist from the brink of death, "snatching" him back in the nick of time. The word פדה can also be interpreted in a similar way.

There is a similar ambiguity with regard to the interpretation of Ps. 73: 23-28.[70] Here again the psalmist expresses his confidence in the eventual vindication by God of those who are "pure in heart" (ברי לבב , verse 1) in contrast with the punishment which will be meted out to the wicked. The only phrase which seriously invites an interpretation in terms of a life after death is verse 24b: ואחר כבוד תקחני , "and afterwards thou wilt take me away to glory". As Kraus points out, אחר ("afterwards") refers back to the אחרית , "end", of the wicked in verse 17, which is described in verses 18-20 in terms of sudden destruction. In verses 23-28 the psalmist expresses his confidence that such a terrible end will be spared him: Yahweh will guide him throughout his life and eventually relieve him from his present miserable state, referred to in verses 2f., 14, and give him "glory" (כבוד). While it is possible to interpret אחר as "after this life", תקחני as "thou wilt carry me off to life after death" and כבוד as "eternal life", it is more natural to translate the line as meaning that Yahweh will bestow on the psalmist in his old age a life of honour and prosperity (a very frequent meaning of כבוד), in contrast with the wicked who will lose all their possessions and reputation and suffer a premature death.

With regard to both Ps. 49:16 and 73:23-28, then, while these passages *may* express an aspiration (though hardly an established doctrine) concerning a happy existence after this life, this cannot by any means be regarded as a certainty. As several commentators have remarked,[71] both psalmists are concerned mainly to testify to their experience of the reality of their communion with God in the present and their complete trust in him, and this experienced reality is so much in the centre of their thoughts that they fail to proceed in any but the most general terms to formulate a corollary concerning the inability of death to put an end to it.[72]

From the above survey of texts it must be concluded that there is no evidence in the Old Testament until much later than the time when Isa. 53 was written of a doctrine of the resuscitation of individuals from death to renewed life on earth or to eternal life. While some of the passages considered in the final section above may indicate the growth of a conviction that the intimate communion with God enjoyed by the faithful in life is a state of blessedness which nothing can disrupt, there is no attempt there to relate this conviction specifically to the universal phenomenon of death. It is possible that the ambiguity of some of the language used in Ps. 49:16; 73:23-28 reflects the vagueness of the psalmist's expectations.

In Isa. 53, however, the confident statements about the Servant's future in verses 10-12 form the climax of the poem. The Servant's vindication is to be complete. This is no meditative or speculative poem but a positive, declaratory one. If the author's intention had been to say that the Servant's reward was to be given to him beyond the grave or after recall from the grave, it would have been necessary for him to say so unequivocally, since this would have been a revolutionary and startling assertion in the sixth century B.C. But he does not do so. On the contrary, he speaks of the Servant's future in language whose most obvious reference is to the continuation of ordinary life under happier circumstances than heretofore.

Those commentators, therefore, who interpret Isa. 53:10-12 as evidence that the Servant was believed by the author of the poem to be about to rise from the dead are attempting to explain a text which does not naturally yield this meaning in terms of a belief which did not exist when the text was written.

C. Supposed References to the Servant's Death

Throughout chapter 53 there are statements about the past sufferings and humiliations inflicted on the Servant. Not all of these have been interpreted as referring directly to his death, though they have all played their part in the building up of the conventional picture of the Servant as a martyr.

1. Statements that the Servant was unprepossessing, isolated and despised.

These statements occur principally in verses 2-3, to which must be added 52:14b (אדם ... כן-משחת), which originally stood after 53:2. Although there has been some difference of opinion among the commentators about the meaning or implications of some phrases,[73] there is a general consensus of opinion that these verses speak of the physical state of the Servant and the impression which he made on others at some time during his lifetime. There is no reference to his death.[74]

One feature of these verses, however, needs to be pointed out which will have an important bearing on the subsequent discussion. This is the similarity of some of the language used here to describe the Servant's state to that used in the psalms of lamentation and related literature (psalms of thanksgiving, psalms of confidence and some similar passages in the book of Job).[75]

a. ויעל כיונק לפניו וכשרש מארץ ציה (verse 2a)[76]

The image of the plant doomed to wither because of the inadequacy of the parched soil to sustain it is found frequently in the Old Testament in passages which speak of the fate of the wicked. It is in this sense that the phrase ארץ ציה is used in Hos. 2:5 (EVV 3); Joel 2:20; Ezek. 19:13. But it is also used in an individual lamentation (or song of confidence) (Ps. 63:2 [EVV 1]) to express the psalmist's sense of his need for Yahweh's support and strength when hard pressed by his adversaries.

92

b. ‏ותארו מבני אדם‎ (verse 2b);[77] ‏לא-תאר לו ולא הדר‎ b.
(52:14b)[78]

‏תֹּאַר‎ occurs in Lam. 4, a corporate lamentation, in a passage describing the appearance of Judaean survivors who are near starvation: they are unrecognizable, and "their appearance (‏תארם‎) is blacker than soot" (verse 8). ‏הדר‎ , "dignity", is said in Lam. 1:6, formally an individual lamentation, to have been lost by the "daughter of Zion".

c. ‏נבזה‎ (verse 3a, b)[79]

The verb ‏בזה‎ , "despise", occurs in an individual lamentation (Ps. 22:7 [EVV 6]), where the psalmist complains that he is "despised by the people" (‏בזוי עם‎). Later in the same psalm the psalmist thanks Yahweh for not despising him (verse 25 [EVV 24]). The verb also occurs in Ps. 119:141 in an expression of confidence that Yahweh will defend the psalmist, despised though he is.[80]

d. ‏חדל אישים‎ (verse 3a)[81]

The commentators are divided on the interpretation of this phrase. It is uncertain whether it means "rejected by men" or "avoiding men". The theme of the loneliness of the afflicted man, deserted even by his friends, is a commonplace of the individual psalms of lamentation, e.g. Ps. 38:12 (EVV 11). In Job 19:14, Job similarly complains of being abandoned by his friends (‏חדלו ממני‎). On the other hand Job in his misery asks to be left in peace by God (‏חדל ממני‎ , 7:16; 10:20). In all these cases the isolation from others, whether voluntary or not, is the result of the dreadful change which has come upon the sufferer, and which is normally interpreted by others as a sign of punishment for sin.

e. ‏איש מכאבות וידוע חלי‎ (verse 3a)[82]

The individual lamentations abound with descriptions of the state of sickness into which the supplicant has fallen. ‏מכאב‎ , "pain", is used a number of times in this connection: Ps. 38:18 (EVV 17); 69:27 (EVV 26); Lam. 1:12, 18 (where the complainant is the personified "Zion" of the exilic period); and Job 33:19, where, although the state of nearness to death is said to be characteristic of the human condition in general, the language is once more taken from the lamentation.

f. ‏וכמסתר פנים ממנו‎ (verse 3b)[83]

. The meaning of this phrase is disputed. The majority of commentators consider that it means "as one from whom men hide their faces". If this is correct, it is simply a further statement that the Servant was regarded by his contemporaries as horrible in appearance or despicable. An alternative theory is that the Servant hides his face from men. But it has also been argued[84] that it is God who hides his face from the Servant: "and as if Yahweh were hiding his face from him". This is also the interpretation of Targ. and Aq. The motif of God's hiding his face from the suppliant in the time of his distress is found very frequently in the psalms of individual lamentation (Ps. 13:2 [EVV 1]; 27:9; 30:8 [EVV 7]; 69:18 [EVV 17]; 88:15 [EVV 14]; 102:3 [EVV 2]), where the request is made that God will not do so or the question asked why he has done so, and also occurs in a psalm of thanksgiving, where God is thanked for not doing so (Ps. 22:25 [EVV 24]).

g. כן-משחת מאיש מראהו ותארו מבני אדם   (52:14b)[85]

This statement, which suggests that the Servant was so disfigured as to be barely recognizable as human, is strongly reminiscent of Ps. 22:7 (EVV 6), "But I am a worm and not a man, the scorn of men and despised by the people" (ואנכי תולעת ולא-איש חרפת אדם ובזוי עם).

The description of the former condition of the Servant in Isa. 53:2f. corresponds, then, both in general content and to a large extent in the words and phrases employed, to the descriptions given by the suppliant about himself in the individual lamentations referred to above and in a number of similiar individual lamentations in the book of Psalms. This, combined with other examples of the same kind which will be pointed out below in considering other parts of this chapter, creates a strong probability that the author of Isa. 53 was using conventional language and imagery taken from that type of psalm. It is generally agreed that the psalms of lamentation are not "private" psalms but compositions available for use by those who came to the Temple to make a lamentation in a cultic setting.[86] The descriptive passages in these psalms are therefore not precise descriptions of the state of any worshipper in particular, and it may indeed be assumed that they overstate rather than understate the actual condition of at least the majority of those who used them, since their purpose is to make as strong an appeal as possible to Yahweh to intervene and save his distressed servant.

This raises the question whether in the case of Isa. 53, where the same conventional language is used, the description of the Servant's former pitiable state should be taken literally. The speakers undoubtedly confess in verses 2-3 that the Servant has had the appearance of one whom God had in some way afflicted. Like the speaker in the individual psalms of thanksgiving who overstates the intensity of his former distress in order to throw into relief the wonder of God's subsequent rescue of him,[87] they present his former state in the darkest possible terms in order to stress the wonder of his subsequent transformation. It is therefore quite wrong to interpret these verses, as did Duhm,[88] as referring to the ravages of a disease which proved to be fatal.

2. Statements that he has in some way "borne the sins" of the speakers.

These statements are identified and discussed in Part I of this study,[89] where it is argued that they refer to the sufferings which the Servant shared with his fellow-exiles, though with two differences: that his were more intense than theirs (probably, in fact, arrest and imprisonment), and that they were undeserved. Once it has been recognized that there is no reference here to vicarious suffering there is no reason to interpret them as meaning that the Servant died in consequence of them.[90] The same is true of the other statements and phrases (verses 5, 10 (אשם), 11 (יצדיק), 12 (יפגיע) which have been similarly interpreted.[91]

3. Phrases used to describe his sufferings and humiliation.

These are:

נגוע, "smitten" (verse 4b), together with the textually suspect phrase נגע למו, "a blow to them"(?), verse 8b

מכה אלהים , "struck by God" (verse 4b)

מענה, "afflicted" (verse 4b), together with נענה , "making no resistance" (?), verse 7a

מחלל, "pierced" (verse 5a)

מדכא "crushed" (verse 5a), together with דכאו , "to crush him" (verse 10a)

מוסר, "discipline" (verse 5b)

חברתו, "his wound" (verse 5b)

נגש, "he was ill-treated" (verse 7)[92]

This group of words conveys a quite different impression from those discussed in section 1 above. Unlike the latter, these words do not appear in general to have formed part of the stock vocabulary of the individual lamentation. Only ענה (in the Piel) occurs three times in lamentations: in Ps. 88:8 (EVV 7); 102:24 (EVV 23) the psalmist complains that God (not his enemies) has afflicted him, and in Ps. 94:5 a complaint is made against national enemies. The Piel of דכא is twice so used, once of national oppression (Ps. 94:5, parallel with ענה) and once in an individual lamentation (Ps. 143:3). Ps. 73:14 uses נגוע (the only other occurrence of the Qal passive participle of this verb) of the psalmist's disciplining by God; and the Hiphil is used once in a lamentation describing the suffering of the man who "waits for" and seeks God (Lam. 3:30). חַבּוּרָה (חַבֻּרָה) occurs once in an individual lamentation (Ps. 38:6 [EVV 5]). These few examples, most of which are not complaints of individuals against oppression by human assailants, cannot be said to constitute a regular stock of vocabulary. The other words in the group are not used at all in the lamentations for this purpose.

Unlike the words used in verses 2-3 to describe the Servant's unprepossessing appearance and despised status, therefore, these words are not generalized or formalized expressions. There is no reason to doubt that they refer to actual events in which the Servant was involved. But what were these events? There is certainly no possibility that they refer to his death. On the other hand, they almost certainly refer to acts of violence perpetrated against his person. Each of them, even when considered separately and apart from its context, frequently refers to violent action, some of them almost exclusively so.

נגע, properly "to touch", is very frequently used in the sense of "do harm"; and frequently this harm is of a violent and deliberate kind inflicted either on a people or an individual.[93]

נכה, used in the Hiphil, means "to strike". The Hophal, of which מֻכֵּה is the participle construct, expresses the corresponding passive meaning. The sense of striking another person deliberately in order to injure him is a very frequent one. In several passages[94] it has the more specific meaning of "flog": punishment by beating with rods. This meaning may be difficult to sustain here if מכה אלהים is to be taken as meaning "struck by God",[95] but there may be grounds for thinking that אלהים here does not refer to the Deity, but has the force of a superlative: "horribly beaten".[96]

ענה in the Piel primarily refers to ill treatment of the weak by the strong. The Pual, of which מְעֻנֶּה is the participle, expresses the corresponding passive meaning. Like the other words in this verse this verb may be used with reference to the actions of God against men, but it is very frequently used of human oppression and harsh treatment. It is therefore entirely appropriate as an expression of the Servant's harsh treatment by his enemies or captors. This verb also occurs in verse 7a in the Niphal in the expression נהוא נענה which follows נגש, "he was ill-treated". The Niphal of this verb occurs only in one other passage in the Old Testament (Exod. 10:3), where it means "to humble oneself". Here it is probably to be understood as a *Niphal tolerativum*. The phrase is a circumstantial clause referring to the circumstances attending the action of the previous verb: "he was ill-treated, while (although) he all the time was accepting his ill treatment" (i.e. making no resistance). This interpretation is supported by the words which follow: ולא יפתח פיו , "and he did not open his mouth".

The three words discussed above form a triad of expressions intended to describe what happened to the Servant. As has been shown, they are all frequently used in a similar sense elsewhere in the Old Testament, differing only in the degree of their precision of meaning. Their juxtaposition here suggests that the author's intention was not to describe three different actions but to emphasize the degree of the Servant's suffering by piling one upon another. Between them they strongly suggest that the Servant was subjected to severe physical ill treatment.

חלל . This is a rare verb, occurring at most only seven times in the Old Testament,[97] though the adjective חָלָל , "pierced, slain", which is closely associated with it, occurs frequently. מחלל is the Poal participle and the only occurrence of the Poal. Apart from two passages where it is used metaphorically[98] it has the literal meaning "to pierce". Whether it necessarily carries the implication that the action is a fatal one will be discussed below.[99] Its meaning here should be determined in the light of the parallel word מדכא and the immediate context, especially the second half of this verse. But it will not be contested that its most natural interpretation is one which denotes some kind of physical violence.[100]

דכא , used in the Piel, has a meaning similar to that of ענה, and the two words are used in parallel clauses in a corporate lamentation referring to the oppression of the poor and helpless in Ps. 94:5. The primary meaning is "to crush". מְדֻכָּא is the Pual, that is, passive, participle. דַּכְּאוֹ , in verse 10a, if the text is correct, is the Piel infinitive: "(It was the will of Yahweh) to crush him". The meaning would then be, as frequently in the Old Testament, that the Servant's ill treatment, though inflicted by men, was in fact instigated by God.[101]

מוסר is a noun which appears originally to have belonged to the vocabulary of the education of children. Outside this context, in which it appears frequently in Proverbs, it is used primarily to denote the discipline or punishment imposed on Israel by God. In view of the parallel word חברה , "wound", it is most probable that it refers here to physical "discipline", that is, beating with a rod, as in Prov. 13:24; 22:15; 23:13, where it refers to corporal punishment.[102]

חברה (elsewhere חבורה) occurs five times in the Old Testament. In three of these passages (Gen. 4:23; Exod. 21:25; Prov. 20:30) it means either a physical blow or an injury caused by such blows inflicted by others. In Isa. 1:6 it is used metaphorically in a description of the pitiable state of Judah caused by the physical assaults of its enemies. In Ps. 38:6 (EVV 5) it has a somewhat different meaning: it refers to sores caused by illness, in a psalm of lamentation in which the sufferer describes his physical state in some detail. Here, in view of the parallel מוסר and the general context, it clearly refers to physical violence against the person of the Servant.

נגש in the Qal always denotes the application of pressure, often physical, by the strong on the weak or helpless, and may generally be translated by "to oppress". The context here shows clearly that the perfect Niphal נגש , "he was oppressed", refers to physical assaults on the Servant: he received these assaults meekly (והוא נענה), and, like a lamb brought to be slaughtered or a sheep to be shorn, remained silent.

The characteristic which all these words have in common is that they all include within their range of meanings that of physical violence committed by human beings against other human beings; for some of them this is their most common meaning. Taken together within the same short passage and referring as they do to one person as the recipient of this treatment, there can be no doubt that they speak of severe suffering deliberately inflicted on him. They do not, as some commentators have maintained,[103] belong as a whole or in any significant degree to the vocabulary of the individual lamentation, and consequently it is most improbable that they are merely stylized expressions. They refer to actual individual acts of violence.[104]

But it is equally the case that these words do not speak of the Servant as having been killed. Six of them (חברה, מוסר, דכא, ענה, נגע, נגש) either never or very rarely have that connotation.[105] נכה can mean "kill", but very frequently only means "strike, beat" with no connotation of fatal consequences. Only חלל , "pierce", normally denotes an act of violence ending in the death of the victim. Of the four other occurrences of this verb in a literal sense[106] two (Job 26:13; Isa. 51:9) refer to God's slaying of the dragon or "fleeing serpent"; a third (Ezek. 28:9) speaks of the imminent death of the prince of Tyre (חלל is here paralleled by הרג , "kill"); and the fourth (Ezek. 32:26) refers to those slain by the sword who have been consigned to the abode of the dead. However, G.R. Driver[107] has pointed out the strange fact that in Isa. 53:5 only one of the ancient Versions (Pesh.) translates מחלל by "killed".[108] He concludes that "Neither מחולל (sic!) nor מדכא per se imports the death of the victim; indeed, the whole context suggests that these and other expressions used to describe the sufferings of the Servant refer to physical ill-treatment and not to his death at the hands of his fellow-men".[109] Certainly "pierce" is the proper meaning of the verb,[110] and "kill" (as in the case of נכה) a purely secondary development. When מחלל in verse 5 is considered as one in a series of words of which the others do not imply that the Servant died from his ill treatment, Driver's judgement would appear to be incontestable.[111]

4. Phrases which have been held to refer specifically to the Servant's death or burial.

a.   כשה לטבח יובל וכרחל לפני גזזיה נאלמה   (verse 7b)[112]

This line makes no direct statements at all about the Servant's actions or afflictions, but consists simply of two comparisons. The Servant's silence before his captors or tormentors referred to in the previous line is compared with the way in which a sheep quietly submits, whether to being driven off to the slaughter-house or to the shearer: "and he did not open his mouth, just like a sheep that is led to the slaughter, or like a ewe that is dumb in the presence of its shearers".[113] לפני גזזיה נאלמה and יובל לטבח are relative clauses expressed, as frequently in poetry, by simple co-ordination without the use of the particle אשר. To take יובל and נאלמה as main verbs — "He was led away like a sheep to the slaughter; he was silent like a ewe before its shearers" — is an unnecessarily complicated operation and, in the case of the latter verb, involves either the emendation of the feminine נאלמה to the masculine נאלם [114] or the acceptance of the improbable view that נאלמה is an archaic masculine form.[115] The traditional interpretation of the line is quite satisfactory, and none of the arguments against it has any real substance.[116]

The comparison of the Servant with a sheep led to the slaughter thus in no way suggests that he himself was killed.[117] It is indeed surprising that this view should have been held at all. Such an interpretation ignores the fact that there are two parallel comparisons here, of which the second refers to nothing more drastic than sheep-shearing. Further, the very similar phrase in Jer. 11:19 "But I was like a trustful lamb led to the slaughter" (ואני ככבש אלוף יובל לטבוח), in which Jeremiah refers to his own experience, shows that this kind of comparison carried no suggestion that the person so depicted was dead. The point of comparison in the two cases is admittedly different: in Jer. 11:19 it is ignorance or lack of suspicion of what is in store for the one so so described, while in Isa. 53:7 it is the silence of the one who has fallen into the hands of others. Probably the comparison was a familiar one which could be used in more than one way.[118]

b. מעצר וממשפט לקח (verse 8a)[119]

Skinner, in commenting on this phrase, quite correctly observed: "Every word here is ambiguous". The meanings of עֹצֶר and משפט here have been exhaustively discussed by the commentators. עצר occurs in only two other passages (Ps. 107:39; Prov. 30:16), in each of which its meaning is uncertain. משפט is notoriously a word of many meanings. In view of the context of Isa. 53:8, in which the Servant is a helpless captive, and having regard to the fact that the Qal of the verb עָצַר regularly means "hold back, detain" and is also specifically used of imprisonment or arrest (2 Kings 17:4; Jer. 33:1; 39:15), the most probable meaning of the phrase is "From (after) imprisonment (arrest) and trial he was taken away". It may be that the particle מן – occasionally has the meaning of "without" (in the sense of absence),[120] but

in connection with the verb לקח, "take, take away" the sense "from" for
מן - is by far the most probable. The two are frequently found in combination in the Qal, and even more frequently (proportionately) in the passive
Qal, which is the form employed here. Of the fourteen occurrences of the
passive Qal לֻקַּח (apart from Isa. 53:8) in the Old Testament, the verb is
followed or preceded by מן -, "from", in eight.[121] מן - never has any other
sense in connection with לֻקַּח. Moreover, one of these occurrences is in
Deutero-Isaiah itself: 49:24 = 49:25.

But does לֻקַּח mean simply "taken away" here? Two other meanings have
been proposed. The first is that the Servant was removed from this world by
God without having died.[122] There is one example of the use of the passive
Qal לֻקַּח in this sense in the Old Testament: 2 Kings 2:10, where Elijah
speaks to Elisha of his being "taken" from him (אם-תראה אתי לֻקָּח
מאתך, "If you see me taken from you"). לקח is also used in this sense in
the active Qal in Gen. 5:24, where God "took" Enoch to himself (לֻקַח אתו
אלהים). But there is no evidence whatever that this is the meaning here.[123]
The second, and much more frequently advocated, proposal is that לֻקַּח here
means "he was led away to execution". There is equally no foundation for
this view. The phrase לְקֻחִים למות , "those who are led away to death",
in Prov. 24:11 has been cited in its support;[124] but Prov. 24:11 in fact
strengthens the case *against* this meaning of לקח *by itself.* Far more relevant
is the evidence from within Deutero-Isaiah itself. Of the three occurrences of
the passive Qal of לקח in Deutero-Isaiah apart from the case under consideration, two (one) have the simple neutral meaning "be taken",[125] while the
third (52:5), where the verb is used absolutely as in 53:8, refers to the taking
of a people into captivity: "My people are carried off (לֻקָּח) for nothing".
This meaning, applied to the individual Servant, is the most obvious one in
53:8 also: the Servant was led away under guard to prison as a (?convicted)
criminal.[126] Finally it may be noted that, like the corresponding passive, the
active Qal also never means "kill". There is therefore no justification for
interpreting לֻקַּח in Isa. 53:8 as referring to the Servant's death.

c.   כי נגזר מארץ חיים (verse 8b)[127]

This phrase has frequently been taken as an unequivocal statement that
the Servant was killed. It is true that in a number of passages[128] ארץ
(ה)חיים , "the world of living creatures", appears at first sight to be used
simply to refer to the state of being alive: the phrase itself looks like the
counterpart of the ארץ תַּחְתִּית or ארץ תַּחְתִּיות , the underworld which
is the world of the dead.[129] To be removed, uprooted, cut off from the ארץ
חיים would seem to be synonymous with dying.[130]

Yet there are grounds for questioning this identification of ארץ חיים
simply with a state of animation, removal from which is death. In Ps. 27:13,

in an individual lamentation where the psalmist, hard pressed by enemies, expresses his confidence that he will "look on the goodness of Yahweh in the land of the living", it seems to be the quality or circumstances of a happy life to which he looks forward, rather than simply deliverance from the danger of death: a life enriched by God's goodness (טוב). The same is true of Ps. 142:6 (EVV 5), where the psalmist exclaims that God is his "portion" (חלק) in the land of the living. But there are also passages where ארץ חיים appears to refer to a particular human aspect of life: its social aspect. In Job 28:13, where the poet states that wisdom is "not found in the land of the living", the parallel phrase "Man does not know the way to it" suggests a reference to human society: it is there, where it might be expected to be found, that wisdom is lacking. Such an interpretation is even more probable in Ezek. 32:23-27, 32, where it is stated that various nations (Assyria, Elam, Meshech and Tubal, Egypt) had, during their time of power, "spread their terror in the land of the living".[131] Though this expression, unattested elsewhere in the Old Testament, may have been chosen in this case in order to point the contrast between this world and the underworld to which these nations have now been consigned, it is unlikely that this completely accounts for the phrase. The "land of the living" here seems to refer to human society or to human communities: the places where human beings live peaceably together unless disturbed by hostile attacks. (This may also explain the use of the plural "lands of the living" in Ps. 116:9, a passage which is frequently emended, following some of the Versions, to the singular.)[132]

Such was the view of G.R. Driver, who translated ארץ חיים in Isa. 53:8 by "the world of living men" but made his meaning clear by commenting that the phrase בגזר מארץ חיים "may refer only to solitary confinement away from the society of men".[133] It may be noted that solitary confinement or other forms of total isolation from one's fellow-men would in all probability have been regarded in the ancient world as constituting a state not far removed from death itself; but it does not follow that phrases which speak of removal from the land of the living actually in themselves refer specifically to death.[134]

It is further necessary to elucidate, as far as that may be possible, the exact meaning of the verb גזר. This word occurs infrequently in the Old Testament.[135] In the Qal, where it occurs six times, its primary meaning is "cut, sever, cut down" in a literal sense.[136] In the Niphal (where it occurs seven times including Isa. 53:8) the notion of severance may be applied to human beings without the thought of death being present: in 2 Chron. 26:21 the verb is used of the exclusion of the leprous king Uzziah from the Temple (נגזר מן -). It also, however, occurs four times in the Niphal in expressions of lamentation: in a despairing speech made by the people of Israel in Ezek. 37:11 (אבדה תקותנו נגזרנו לנו , "our hope has

101

perished, we are cut off"); in Ps. 31:23 (EVV 22), referring to the sufferer's mood of despair before he knew that Yahweh had heard his prayer (ואני אמרתי..., "I said ..., I am cut off from thy נגזרתי מנגד עיניך sight"); in Ps. 88:6 (EVV 5), where the sufferer compares himself with the dead, who are "cut off" from Yahweh's effective power (מידך נגזרו); in Lam. 3:54, in which the psalmist, brought near to death by the attacks of his enemies, says simply, "I am cut off!" (נגזרתי). From these examples it is clear that the Niphal of גזר can be used in connection with death, but that this is not necessarily the case. Combined with the expression מארץ חיים in Isa. 53:8, however, a reference to death would appear at first sight to be probable; and this interpretation would seem to be strengthened by the reference in verse 9 to the preparation of the Servant's grave.[137]

Recently, however, J.A. Soggin[138] has pointed out some significant facts about the use of גזר in the Old Testament which make this interpretation less than certain. This verb is never used in prose texts either in the Qal or the Niphal of death or putting to death; only in the case of the four lamentations cited above can it be argued that it has some specific connection with death. Soggin has pointed out the existence of a clear distinction in this respect between גזר and the much more frequent כרת, "cut, cut off", which is used regularly in the Niphal in the legal texts of P with reference to the death penalty, in such phrases as "He shall be cut off from his people",[139] and also in the Hiphil in the sense of "destroy, kill". כרת is also used in Jer. 11:19 in connection with the phrase ארץ חיים : "Let us cut him off from the land of the living" (נכרתנו מארץ חיים). Here it is clearly the death of Jeremiah which is being plotted. Apart from Isa. 53:8, however, there is in the Old Testament no corresponding phrase using גזר rather than כרת. Soggin argues that there is a distinction between the meanings of the two verbs: while כרת refers to concrete instances of actual physical death, גזר refers not to death itself but to situations of apparent hopelessness from which, however, Yahweh is believed to be able to rescue the victim. In the case of the lamentations mentioned above we may perhaps interpret this, in view of 2 Chron. 26:21, where גזר simply means "exclude", as meaning that the sufferer felt, before his confidence in Yahweh overcame his fears, that he was already (as good as) separated either from this life or from Yahweh's power to give life.[140] If this is so, נגזר even in those passages does not denote death itself but a state of separation, which *in these particular contexts* is a separation from life and so tantamount to death. But if in Isa. 53:8, as has been suggested above, ארץ חיים does not mean "life" but "human society", it is possible that G.R. Driver may be right in his view that the whole phrase means simply that the Servant was "cut off, i.e. removed, from human society by imprisonment".[141] This would, then, entail rendering ארץ חיים here by "human society".

Whether this be the correct interpretation or not, the fact that in many parts of the poem language is used which is drawn from the vocabulary of the individual lamentation leaves a substantial doubt whether the phrase under discussion refers specifically to death. Driver, though he admits that its meaning is "not clear",[142] and that taken in isolation it might refer to execution, came to the conclusion[143] that in the absence, as it seemed to him, of any other evidence that the Servant is regarded in the poem as having died, the phrase must refer to imprisonment rather than death.[144] The final decision must therefore wait on the conclusion of the present investigation of the various phrases which have been interpreted as speaking of death. The fact, referred to above, that both ארץ חיים and גזר occur, though not together, in individual lamentations should be noted.

d. כומתו [145]   ואת-עשיר [146]   את-רשעים קברו   ויתן   (verse 9a)[147]

It should hardly be necessary now to argue that this line does not necessarily imply that the Servant had died and been buried. C.C. Torrey's comment on it, long ignored by most commentators, is still valid in all essential respects:

> It is certain that where "death" is spoken of in these verses, it is either in hyperbole or else (as in the present case) in the description of what the onlooking Gentiles[148] *expected.* They did not *dig* his grave; they "assigned" it, a signification of the verb used here which is very common. They were all ready to bury him with the criminals, as soon as the last spark of life should be gone. He was "as good as dead". But of course the whole significance of the poem rests on the fact that the Servant did *not* die, but lived to be brought to triumph.[149]

This has recently, but belatedly, been recognized by a number of scholars.[150] Torrey was also correct in seeing the image (though his interpretation was a metaphorical one, the Servant being identified with Israel) as descriptive in character rather than simply as hyperbole. It is true that in the lamentation/thanksgiving psalms of the Old Testament the speaker not infrequently states that he is or has been in the toils of Sheol, or like those who lie in the grave, or the like,[151] but the image here is somewhat different: it refers to the preparation of the grave by others in anticipation of the Servant's imminent death.[152] This image does not occur elsewhere in the Old Testament,[153] but it is to be found in literature of a similar character in other parts of the Semitic world. So in the Babylonian "Poem of the Righteous Sufferer" (*Ludlul bēl nēmeqi*), II 114f., the speaker, towards the end of a long description of his pitiable state which has many similarities with the individual lamentations in the Old Testament, complains:

My grave was waiting, and my funerary paraphernalia ready,
Before I had died lamentation for me was finished.[154]

The theme of anticipation of and preparation for the funeral before the
sufferer is dead – though in this case there is no reference to the grave[155] –
is also to be found in an Akkadian poem from Ugarit, where in a similar
situation the speaker complains:

My family was assembled to bow (the head) before the time,
My kin were at hand, were present for the grief.[156]

It is consequently reasonable to suppose either that Isa. 53:9a means literally
that the Servant had been expected to die as a result of his ill treatment and
that the place of his burial had already been designated in a plot reserved for
criminals, or that it is more generally a way of saying that he has had a narrow
escape from death. It does not state that he had died, nor indeed would it
be an appropriate way of saying this.

e. הערה למות נפשו ואת-פשעים נמנה   (verse 12b)[157]

The meaning of the second half of this line is not in doubt. The problems
occur in the first half, with regard to the meaning of the two words הערה
and למות .

Reference has already been made,[158] in connection with the proposed
emendation of למו to למות in verse 8, to the theory that מות was sometimes used in biblical Hebrew without any connotation of death, as a way of
denoting the superlative.[159] Several scholars have held the view that this is
so here in verse 12.[160] By no means all the examples which they cite[161] are
convincing, though in two cases, both of which refer to extreme anger or
impatience,[162] this interpretation has considerable probability. It should
probably be allowed as a possibility in Isa. 53:12, though since there is no
real parallel elsewhere in the Old Testament to the use of a verb such as
הערה in connection with למות it cannot be regarded as certain.

However, the question whether the phrase הערה למות נפשו implies
that the Servant died does not depend on the interpretation of למות . The
meaning of the verb הערה also requires investigation. There are two
questions here: the meaning of the verb taken by itself and its interpretation
in the context of the whole phrase. All except the most recent translations
render the phrase by "he poured out his soul to death" (with slight variations).[163]

The meaning of הערה here is not easy to determine. Of the 14 probable
occurrences of the verb ערה in the Old Testament[164] the text of four[165] is
in doubt, and these will be discounted in the following discussion. In the
Piel it can mean either "pour out" or "empty" (a vessel or container) (Gen.

104

24:20; 2 Chron. 24:11) or "lay bare, make naked" (Isa. 3:17). The two meanings are clearly closely connected: to empty a container is to lay it bare. The former meaning is also found in the Niphal, used metaphorically of the "pouring out" of the Spirit (Isa. 32:15), and the latter in the Hiphil (Lev. 20: 18, 19, "make naked") and the Hithpael (Lam. 4:21, "make oneself naked").

Did the Servant in Isa. 53:12 "pour out" or "empty" his life (phrases which would most naturally be understood to imply the extinction of that life), or did he in some sense "lay it bare"? The latter metaphor may most plausibly be understood in a sense similar to that which the Piel of this verb has in Ps. 137:7, where the Edomites are alleged to have called for the destruction of Jerusalem, crying "Lay it bare, lay it bare (ערו ערו), even to its foundations!", that is, to have called for the destruction of its fortifications, leaving it defenceless.[166]

A meaning of this kind, applied to the life of an individual person, seems to be present in the only other passage in the Old Testament in which the verb ערה (in the Piel) is found with נפש as its object: Ps. 141:8. Here, in an individual lamentation, the speaker, having stated that he has come to God to seek refuge (בכה חסיתי , "in thee have I sought refuge"), immediately adds אל-תער נפשי . Here the modern translations agree in rendering the phrase by "leave me not defenceless!" and similar expressions.[167] As G.R. Driver has pointed out,[168] there is no mention in this psalm of the possibility of the speaker's being killed by his enemies.

There is then ample justification for regarding הערה ... נפשו in Isa. 53:12 as meaning that the Servant "exposed" himself or left himself defenceless, in other words that he consciously put himself in a position in which he was at the mercy of his enemies or persecutors. It is therefore virtually irrelevant whether למות means "to death" or "to the uttermost": indeed, in this context they have virtually the same meaning. There is on the other hand no evidence which would support the interpretation of this phrase as "pour out one's life" in the sense of "die".

It is therefore extremely probable that the phrase הערה למות נפשו means that the Servant risked death rather than that he died. This interpretation receives some support from the following and parallel phrase ואת-פשעים נמנה "he was reckoned as one of the rebels", which would be an anti-climax after a statement that he had died. It is also perhaps relevant to point out, with G.R. Driver,[169] that Saadia translated the phrase by "he laid bare his soul to death", which Driver takes as referring to danger of death but not to death itself.

D.   Conclusion

Of the very large number of words and phrases in Isa. 53 which refer to the sufferings and humiliations of the Servant, none refers unequivocally to his death, and only one (נגזר מארץ חיים , verse 8b) might reasonably, in other contexts, be so interpreted. Of two others — the reference to the grave in verse 9a, and the phrase הערה למות נפשו in verse 12b — it has been shown that the traditional interpretation is mistaken. Two verbs used about the Servant — נכה (verse 4b) and חלל (verse 5a) are capable of meaning "kill" and are often so used, but are equally capable of a non-fatal connotation ("wound", "pierce"). Only if the whole context called for the former interpretation would it be justifiable. But this is not the case. The mass of statements in the poem about the Servant, taken together, make it quite clear that he was subjected to violence and humiliation, but that these stopped short of his death.

This conclusion is made even more inescapable by verses 10-12. If the earlier part of the poem spoke of the Servant's having died, verses 10-12 would necessarily have to refer to his expected resurrection. But, as has been demonstrated above,[170] this is impossible: the concept of the resurrection of the individual either in this life or beyond the grave was not current in Israel in the sixth century B.C., and there is nothing in these verses to suggest that the author expected such an unheard of occurrence: they simply anticipate that the Servant, whose life has hitherto been so wretched, will at last receive the due reward for his faithfulness in the form of an honoured and prosperous old age.

Part III. The Interpretation of Isaiah 53

PART III. THE INTERPRETATION OF ISAIAH 53

A. The Contents and Structure of the Poem

If the Servant is not represented in Isaiah 53 as having died, the questions regarding the nature, purpose and detailed interpretation of the chapter must be examined afresh.[1] The first task is to set out its general structure. This may be done in the following way:

1. An anonymous expression of astonishment and satisfaction at news just received about some manifestation of God's power towards some unnamed person (verse 1)
   - a. The reception of the news
   - b. The contents of the news

2. The earlier miserable state of this person (verses 2-3)
   - c. He was unprepossessing
   - d. He was stricken in health
   - e. He was despised
   - f. He was rejected by his fellowmen as loathsome
   - g. He appeared to be one from whom God had turned away his face[2]

3. A group of persons declare that this person did not deserve his misfortune and confess that they are the guilty ones (verses 4-6)
   - h. He bore the punishment which only they deserved
   - i. They had previously thought of him as deserving his punishment

4. Description of this person's persecution and sufferings (verses 7-9)
   - j. Ill treatment
   - k. Conviction as a criminal
   - l. Nearness to death
   - m. Silence before his persecutors
   - n. Innocence

5. Promise of an honoured and happy future, expressed partly in a divine oracle which concludes the poem (verses 10-12)[3]
   - o. The person in question will enjoy a long life and see his children doing the same
   - p. He will have the satisfaction of knowing that his mission is completely accomplished
   - q. He (now designated by Yahweh as "my Servant" [עבדי]) will take his place among the great

r.   A summary statement of the sacrifice which he
      made, justifying the reward which he will receive

Fundamentally the poem is a narrative poem into which the speakers have interpolated their interpretation of the events which they describe, and their reactions to them. The events described comprise a chronological sequence in two parts: 1. the dark past and 2. the rescue from that past with its certain promise of a bright future. Interwoven into the narrative are the speakers' comments. These are to be found to some extent in the mainly narrative sections (sections 2 and 4 in the above analysis), but particularly in sections 1, 3 and 5. Section 1 refers to the astonishment, clearly joyful astonishment, with which the speakers have received the news of the afflicted person's rescue by God; section 3 is at one and the same time a declaration of his innocence and a confession of the speakers' guilt. Section 5 draws conclusions from the divine act of rescue: it is a proof of God's intention to confer upon the rescued person every blessing in his future life. These conclusions are confirmed by a final divine oracle.

These, then, are the main elements in the poem: joyful astonishment at God's intervention to rescue his Servant; description of his past affliction; declaration of innocence/confession of guilt; anticipation of a bright future under God's blessing; a divine oracle. The predominating mood – in spite of the fact that this is not specifically expressed in words – is one of thanksgiving to God who has performed this great wonder.

B.   The Literary Type

Does this pattern, and do these elements, correspond to any literary type or *Gattung* to be found elsewhere in the Old Testament? There can be no doubt that – with certain modifications which will receive consideration below – they do. They correspond to that type of psalm which Gunkel designated "Das Danklied des Einzelnen"– the "individual psalm of thanksgiving".

The affinities of Isa. 53 (or rather, according to most interpreters, Isa. 52: 13–53:12 regarded as a single unit) with the individual thanksgiving have been noted by other scholars. According to Begrich[4] the poem is the work of the prophet himself, who in 53:1-11a uses the first person plural style and speaks about himself in the third person, prophesying his own death and resurrection and explaining their necessity and meaning: his death would be the consequence of his fellow-exiles' rejection of him and his message. But God's plan could not and would not be frustrated by this: he would use the death of his Servant-prophet as a means of bringing atonement to the exiles. The Servant's resurrection, which would then follow, would open the eyes of the exiles to their guilt and at the same time cause them at last to accept the

Servant as God's messenger and instrument. So God's will for his people's good which the prophet had proclaimed throughout his ministry would be carried out in spite of the people's sin. This theme of the distressed Servant of God rescued and vindicated found its most effective expression, according to Begrich, in the form of the individual psalm of thanksgiving. The purpose of the divine oracles preceding and following this (52:13-15; 53:11b-12) was to give authority to it and to convince those who heard it that it was a true prophecy.

In Begrich's view, then, the thanksgiving psalm in Isa. 53 was a literary device through which the prophet spoke about the future, and not a genuine cultic psalm giving thanks for an actual past event. His theory — leaving aside his interpretation of the chapter as referring to the Servant's death and resurrection — is too complicated to carry conviction. He fails to explain adequately why the prophet chose the form of the individual thanksgiving to convey his message: it is not enough to say that the themes of that type of psalm were germane to what he wanted to say. There is nothing in Isa. 53 or its context to prepare the reader for the mental effort required to grasp the fact that the prophet is using the unique and complex device of an imaginary future thanksgiving ceremony at which thanks are given for events which have not in fact yet occurred, and all this in order to convey a message which could have been conveyed more plainly by the use of more normal and familiar forms of prophetic utterance. Moreover Begrich fails to explain adequately another unusual aspect of the poem: the use of the third person by the prophet in speaking about himself. This is in itself an unusual form for the individual thanksgiving, though Begrich provides an explanation of this along lines which will be followed later in the present study.[5] But it becomes inexplicable when it is supposed that it was used by the speaker to refer to himself as if he were someone else. Begrich's explanation of this feature, that this mode of speech was necessary if the prophet was to make his meaning clear to his audience,[6] is itself far from clear.

Kaiser[7] also regards the chapter — or part of it — as an individual thanksgiving. For him the poem as a whole (i.e. 52:13—53:12) is a *Heilsorakel* ("oracle of salvation") in which the individual thanksgiving (53:1-6) plays a secondary role. The Servant is identified with Israel or the exiles, and the oracle is a genuine cultic oracle given by Yahweh and addressed through the prophet to the Servant (עליך , 52:14) as an answer to an actual lamentation made by the people. The thanksgiving in verses 1-6 is intended to strengthen the force of the oracle by explaining the meaning of the people's suffering (there is no reference to death) and so leading them to accept it. The main thrust of the passage thus resides in the oracle itself, which promises the future elevation of the Servant-Israel. Thus although Kaiser sees the passage as a genuine cultic oracle, the thanksgiving element in it is, as in Begrich's theory, not understood by him to be an independent and actual cultic thanks-giving, but is a literary borrowing of the thanksgiving form to serve a different purpose (in this case that of the *Heilsorakel*).

Kaiser's theory is as unsatisfactory as that of Begrich. He is unable to give any other examples of the thanksgiving form used in this way elsewhere in the Old Testament, and also fails to explain why this form should be effective, or even appropriate, for the purpose which he assigns to it. He also fails to give an adequate explanation of verses 7-10, which according to him belong neither to the oracle form nor to that of the thanksgiving. He misses the fact, for which evidence will be given below,[8] that the whole chapter (though not including 52:13-15) has the character of an individual thanksgiving psalm and is to be understood as such.[9]

Before demonstrating this proposition, however, it may be useful to con-sider some other attempts which have been made to identify the *Gattung* of Isa. 53. On the whole, commentators, in so far as they have been interested in form-critical questions, have been unwilling to classify it, regarding it as unique in both form and content; but some attempts to do so may briefly be referred to.

Several scholars have defined the chapter as a "prophetic liturgy",[10] that is, as a literary imitation by the prophet of a type of complex liturgical com-position originally used in the Israelite cult which is characterized by the combination of different types of speech (*Gattungen*), each sung or spoken by a different person or group of persons.[11] In general it must be said that when in the prophetical books of the Old Testament a passage is described as a prophetic liturgy this is often tantamount to an acknowledgment that attempts to achieve a more precise understanding of its structure and mean-ing have failed. Although it is now recognized on the one hand that there are some psalms which are properly to be described as liturgies,[12] and also on the other hand that cultic forms were utilized by some of the prophets, the term "prophetic *liturgy*" should be used with caution. Isa. 52:13 – 53:12 as a whole does not resemble any of the liturgies in the Psalter, nor does it correspond to any series of cultic actions known to have been practised in Israel.[13] On the other hand, as will be shown below, chapter 53 *by itself*, without 52:13-15, does correspond, not indeed to a *liturgy* involving several speakers, but to a single known *liturgical moment* or action in the cult, namely that at which the friends of the person offering his individual thanks-giving to God add their own voices of praise for his deliverance.[14] If that is what is meant by a "prophetic liturgy" the term may be accepted for Isa. 53, but in that case the question must be asked[15] why it should be regarded as a literary imitation by the prophet of a cultic form rather than as a psalm actually used in worship in a concrete situation.

J. Lindblom[16] sees Isa. 53:2-12 as "a prophetic revelation in the form of a vision"[17] and as "a symbolic narrative, an allegorical picture".[18] Together with 52:13—53:1 these verses form a single composition, the first part being a declaration by Yahweh concerning a distressed person whom he will greatly exalt, and the second expressing the same thought in parabolic or allegorical language. The person thus portrayed symbolizes Israel, although Lindblom lays great stress on the difference between symbol and identity. The Servant figure was used to portray symbolically the present and the future *situation* of Israel — the exaltation from humiliation to triumph — and its mission to the world rather than to follow the *history* either of the nation or of an individual in concrete detail. Lindblom maintains that this "allegory" has parallels in other allegorical passages in the Old Testament, though he does not say to which of these he is referring.[19] His theory — which has not been widely accepted — raises a number of problems which would, if pursued, take the present discussion too far afield; but it may be remarked that the differences between Isa. 53:2-12 and other parabolic or allegorical passages in the Old Testament are very great indeed: so great that the passage would in fact have to be regarded as an example so exceptional as to make the comparison valueless.[20] The theory — which Lindblom applies not merely to the Fourth Song but to the other three as well — was elaborated, as the subtitle of the work indicates, in order to "solve an old problem", i.e. the problem of the identity of the Servant: if these compositions can be classified as allegories or (more properly) parables, the problem of identification disappears, since in parables[21] such identification is not to be looked for. In other respects, however, the theory raises more problems than it solves.[22]

C. Isaiah 53 and the Individual Thanksgiving

Gunkel's identification and analysis of the form of the individual thanksgiving and also of the other types of psalm which have themes in common with it or are otherwise related to it[23] remains the classic study. Numerous contributions to the study of both the individual lamentations and the individual thanksgivings have however been published since the appearance of his pioneering work.[24] With regard to the individual thanksgiving, the main topics which have received attention are 1. the identification of the genre and its independence as a distinct genre; 2. its origin and history within the period of the Old Testament; 3. the identification of those psalms which belong to it; 4. its form; 5. its function and *Sitz im Leben.* In spite of some

major differences of opinion on some of these topics – in particular Westermann's denial of the existence of the genre as an independent one and the
discussion generated by this, and the varying opinions on the question which
psalms are to be included within it – there is a general consensus of opinion
on two major points which are relevant to the present discussion: it is agreed
that this type of psalm was composed for recital by individuals in a cultic
context in thanksgiving for their rescue by God from their former distress;
and there is general agreement about its formal features in its classical form,
based on an analysis of those psalms which are universally or almost universally held to be examples of it, especially Ps. 18; 30; 32; 34; 40; 66; 116; 118;
138.

The form and structure of the individual psalm of thanksgiving are more
flexible than in any other type of psalm.[25] No two examples contain exactly
the same elements or present them in precisely the same order, and in some
cases these divergences are substantial. When a formal comparison is made
with Isa. 53, therefore, the main questions to be considered are 1. whether
Isa. 53 contains the basic elements of the thanksgiving psalm – i.e. those
elements which are common to all or nearly all of them; and 2. whether it
contains a substantial number of lesser motifs and of elements of vocabulary
in common with them.

The main constituents of the individual thanksgiving are 1. the narrative
by the worshipper of his experiences and 2. an act of recognition or confession of his debt to Yahweh for his deliverance. The narrative section
usually contains three elements: a. description of former distress; b. a reference to the worshipper's prayer to God for deliverance; c. a description
of Yahweh's act of deliverance in answer to the prayer. These three elements
may occur in any order.

To this basic structure some other elements are usually added, but none
of these is essential, and some of them occur only rarely: an introductory
statement of an intention to praise God, or a call to others to do so; a similar
statement or call at the end of the psalm; a reference to the making of a
sacrifice of thanksgiving.

The narrative section usually refers to Yahweh in the third person, being
addressed to the friends or congregation who are present at the ceremony.
In the other sections Yahweh may be, and usually is, addressed directly at
some point, but there is at least one case, namely Ps. 34, where he is not
addressed at all.[26]

We may now proceed to a more detailed comparison of the individual
thanksgiving psalms with Isa. 53. But one remark must first be made with
regard to method. This concerns the fact, pointed out by Gunkel himself [27]
and now universally accepted, that the description of former distress in the
individual thanksgiving, which often occupies a substantial part of the psalm,

often closely resembles, even in small details, the corresponding description of *present* distress which is an equally prominent feature of the individual *psalm of lamentation.* It is therefore legitimate to use such material from the psalms of lamentation – as has often been done[28] – to illuminate the relationship between the psalms of thanksgiving and Isa. 53. The legitimacy of this procedure depends upon the universally admitted fact that lamentation and thanksgiving are really two parts of the same series of events: the thanksgiving psalms, indeed, frequently actually refer to the earlier lamentation which the worshipper made when they state that he called upon God to come to his aid [29]

1. The Narrative Section

The following are characteristics of the narrative section of the psalm of thanksgiving: it is an essential element which is never lacking; its position within the psalm is variable, and it often appears more than once in different parts of the psalm; it often occupies a very substantial part of the psalm and sometimes almost the whole of it; it refers mainly to Yahweh in the third person; its chief characteristic is one of joy at Yahweh's deliverance of the worshipper from intense distress to happiness and fullness of life; the contrast between the past and present states of the worshipper is very marked; the description of distress is mainly expressed in fixed, generalized formulae without many concrete details.

Each of these features has its counterpart in Isa. 53.

i. The narrative section is extremely prominent in Isa. 53, occupying verses 2-11a.

ii. Although verses 4-6 to some extent have a narrative character they also contain non-narrative elements (reflection on the events, confession of sin on the part of the speakers), so dividing the narrative proper into two sections. Verses 7-11b to some extent repeat what has already been said in verses 4-6 about the suffering of the Servant, as is the case in several of the psalms of lamentation.

iii. Yahweh is referred to throughout this section in the third person.[30]

iv. The mood throughout is one of joy at the Servant's rescue.

v. There is a very marked contrast between the past and present (and future) states of the Servant.

vi. Although it is probable that verses 4-9 contain some concrete details of the Servant's sufferings, at least verses 2-3 are expressed in a style which closely resembles that of the lamentations/thanksgivings, especially the former.[31]

We now turn to a more detailed consideration of the three parts which make up the narrative section in the psalms of thanksgiving.

a. The Narrative of Former Distress

i. *Reference to bodily sickness or weakness.* This is a frequent theme in both the individual lamentation and the individual thanksgiving.[32] As in Isa. 53:3, 4 this is sometimes indicated by the use of the words "sickness" (חלי) or "pain" (מכאוב).[33]

ii. *The attitude and behaviour of others towards the sufferer*

This is also frequently referred to:[34] enemies and bystanders scoff and taunt, even familiar friends despise the sufferer or stand aloof from him in horror or disgust. In this connection we may especially note two phrases in Ps. 22, a psalm in which an individual lamentation (verses 2-22) is followed by an individual thanksgiving (verses 23-30): in the lamentation section the sufferer, in complaining of his treatment by others, uses the words "But I am a worm, and no man" (ואנכי תולעת ולא-איש) (verse 7 [EVV 6]), a phrase strongly reminiscent of "his appearance was ravaged so that he no longer seemed to be a man" (כן-משחת מאיש מראהו) in Isa. 52:14b; and in the same verse he says that he is "despised by the people" (בזוי עם), corresponding to the "he was despised" (נבזה) of Isa. 53:3. Indeed, this verb בזה and its byform בוז , both of which mean "despise", are characteristic of this type of psalm: they are frequently employed in statements that enemies, bystanders and others despise the sufferer,[35] and the sufferer elsewhere expresses his confidence that Yahweh, in whom he puts his trust, will not do so.[36]

These attitudes are fully expressed in Isa. 53, where the speakers are presumably, as are the persons referred to in several of the passages mentioned above, the friends and acquaintances of the Servant. It is there stated that he was disfigured in such a way as to cause revulsion or contempt (52:14b; 53:2b-3), that he was despised and rejected by them (53:3), thought to have been smitten by God (53:4b) and the victim of general indifference or neglect (53:8b).

iii. *The turning away of God's face*

The complaint that God has forgotten the sufferer, forsaken him or hidden himself from him is a particularly frequent theme in the lamentation/thanksgiving literature.[37] The sufferer also frequently calls on God not to do so; and in some of the thanksgivings he praises him for having, in the end, not done so (Ps. 22:25 [EVV 24]) or for having relented after doing so (Ps. 30:8-12 [EVV 7-11]). It is clear that the speakers in Isa. 53 also believed that God had forsaken his Servant: this is implicit throughout the poem, and accounts for their astonishment (verse 1) when they realize that God has rescued him. There may also be a verbal parallel here between Isa. 53 and the lamentations and thanksgivings. Reference has been made earlier[38] to the possibility that the phrase וכמסתר פנים ממנו in verse 3 may refer not to the turning of human faces away from the Servant, but to God's turning his face away from him, a symbol of rejection of the Servant by God. The phrase "turn away the face" (הסתיר פנים) is frequently used in the lamentations and thanksgivings in this connection.[39]

iv. *The confession of sin / declaration of innocence*

In many of the lamentations and some thanksgiving psalms the speaker makes either a *confession of sin* or a *declaration of innocence*: that is, he admits that his distressed state is or was due to his sin, and asks God to forgive it or thanks him for having done so; or on the other hand he asserts his innocence as a reason why God should come to his help, or praises God for having at last recognized his innocence and vindicated him.[40] These confessions and declarations are often closely connected with the narrative section of the psalm.

In Isa. 53 also there is a confession of sin and a declaration of innocence, equally closely connected with the narrative section. The roles played by these are, however, different from the roles which they play in the usual thanksgiving psalm or lamentation.[41] It is others who declare the innocence of the sufferer, and these same speakers confess their own sin. Nevertheless there is reason to suppose that the phenomenon is basically the same. There are in fact considerable similarities between the confession made by the speakers in Isa. 53:4-6 and the confessions in the psalms. In verse 4 they use the terms חלי and מכאוב of the sufferings borne by the Servant, and confess that it was they who deserved these afflictions.[42] The similar confession in verse 5 that the Servant's physical ill-treatment was caused by sins (פשעים) and iniquities (עונת) which they and not he had committed uses vocabulary which is found in the majority of the confessions in the individual lamentations and in the two confessions in the individual thanksgivings (Ps. 32:1; 40:13 [EVV 12]). In verse 6a the speakers make a formal confession: "All we like sheep have gone astray" (כלנו כצאן תעינו). The similarity of this to Ps. 119:176, where in a section having the form of an individual lamentation (verses 169-176) the author confesses "I have gone astray like a lost sheep" (תעיתי כשה אבד) is striking. The verb תעה " to wander, go astray" in the sense of sinning against God also occurs in another section of the same psalm (verses 105-112) in which the author makes a declaration of innocence: "And I have not gone astray from thy precepts" (ומפקודיך לא תעיתי) (verse 110).

The *declarations* made by the speakers in Isa. 53 that the Servant is

117

wholly *innocent* of the sins with which they had previously credited him (verses 4-9), which amount to a portrait of his character as one who trusted in God for his vindication, are reminiscent of similar declarations of innocence in the individual psalms of lamentation (e.g. Ps. 26) in which the sufferer appeals to God for his vindication. Here again some remarkable similarities of phraseology may be noted. The statement in Isa. 53:7 that the Servant did not open his mouth (ולא יפתח-פיו) when ill-treated closely parallels the statement by the sufferer in Ps. 38 that in spite of his persecution he is "like a dumb man who does not open his mouth" (וכאלם לא יפתח-פיו , verse 14 [EVV 13]), because, as the next verse states, he waits upon God. Ps. 39:10 (EVV 9) resembles Isa. 53:7 even more closely: the words נאלמה ולא יפתח פיו of the latter are almost identical with those spoken by the sufferer in the former when he says "I am dumb; I do not open my mouth" (נאלמתי לא אפתח-פי).[43] Again, the statement in Isa. 53:9 about the Servant that "there was no deceit in his mouth" (ולא מרמה בפיו) is paralleled by the claim of the sufferer in Ps. 17:1 that he is one whose lips are free from deceit (בלא שפתי מרמה).

v. *The account of ill treatment by enemies and persecutors*

Reference has already been made[44] to the *accounts of ill treatment* by enemies and persecutors which figure so prominently in the lamentation literature, and to the fact that the language used there is usually rather general and to a large extent stylized and conventional. The use of conventional language does not of course mean that the sufferings about which the speakers complained were not genuine sufferings; but it to a large extent makes it impossible to know in detail what these were. It has been suggested, however, that the language used in Isa. 53:4-9, which has few parallels with that of the lamentation literature, is less conventional than that used in verses 2-3 and permits the conclusion that the Servant was subjected to physical ill treatment, trial and imprisonment.

In these circumstances verbal parallels are hardly to be looked for in the lamentation literature. It may however be significant that in at least two passages in that literature there are references to trial and/or imprisonment. In Psalm 37, which although primarily a "wisdom" psalm also contains elements derived from the individual lamentation,[45] the author expresses his confidence that the wicked man who seeks to slay the righteous man (verse 32) will not succeed, because "Yahweh will not abandon him to his power, or let him be condemned when he is brought to trial (ולא ירשיענו בהשפטו)" (verse 33). The view that the author is referring to actual trials at which innocent persons were in danger of conviction and execution as a result of false accusations gives the most natural interpretation

118

to the legal language (הרשיע), "condemn"; נשפט , "be tried in court". In
Ps. 142, an individual psalm of lamentation, there is a reference in verse 8
(EVV 7) to the supplicant's being in prison (מסגר). Having besought God
to save him from his persecutors who have overpowered him, he continues:
"Release me from prison, so that I may praise thy name!" (הוציאה
ממסגר נפשי להודות את-שמך).[46] While it is not certain that the reference to the prison is to be taken literally, this interpretation has been
accepted by a number of commentators.[47] Another passage in which a specific
reference to prison has been supposed is Ps. 118:5, where the psalmist proclaims that Yahweh has released him, when he called on him, מן-המצר .
Schmidt interpreted this as meaning "from imprisonment".[48] This interpretation has not, however, been generally accepted. But it should be noted that
Schmidt's interpretation was made in the context of a much more far-reaching
theory embracing a large number of Psalms: that many of what Gunkel
classified as "psalms of lamentation" are in fact prayers made by an accused
man awaiting trial by ordeal.[49]

The circumstances of the Servant described in Isa. 53, if they refer to
imprisonment, were of course quite different from those of the speakers in
the psalms referred to above. The prison would be a Babylonian one, and
there would be no question of a trial conducted in accordance with Israelite
custom. And indeed, the chapter is not a psalm of lamentation. But the
references to imprisonment and trial in these psalms, if a literal interpretation is correct in some instances, provide a plausible setting for the use of
Isa. 53 as a thanksgiving psalm. They show at least that the ordeal of unjust
imprisonment was a recognized form of distress, release from which would be
attributed to the intervention of God and might be celebrated by a psalm of
thanksgiving in a cultic ceremony at which the released prisoner and his
friends would gather. It is to such a thanksgiving ceremony that the speaker
in Ps. 142:7 looks forward, and in which he promises to participate, when he
says, "Bring me out of prison, that I may give thanks to thy name!"

An element in the individual thanksgivings which is, however, completely
absent from Isa. 53 is a direct reference to the enemies who have caused the
sufferings described, and to their hatred of their victim. This element is
usually less fully developed in the thanksgivings than in the psalms of lamentation, where the sufferer attempts to strengthen his appeal to God by
depicting his persecutors and their attacks upon him in a vivid and spectacular
manner; it is nevertheless a regular feature of them,[50] except in those psalms
where the sufferings are recognized as having been sent by Yahweh without
recourse to a human agency. The speaker rejoices and praises God that his
enemies have been defeated or thwarted, or prays for vengeance to be taken
on them. In Isa. 53, on the other hand, there is not a single direct allusion to
those responsible for the Servant's sufferings. The nearest that the author

comes to a direct reference to them is when he says that "they" (or "someone") assigned (וְיִתֵּן) his grave among the criminals (verse 9). Otherwise the sufferings which he underwent are referred to in a curiously neutral way. One of the most remarkable features of the chapter is the use of passive verbs: no less than twelve or thirteen times is a passive verb (participle, perfect or imperfect) used in this connection.[51] Elsewhere the Servant is simply made the subject of a verb denoting suffering.[52] Once it is Yahweh who is said to be the author of the sufferings.[53] The sufferings are also described by the use of nouns with no indication of the agent.[54]

The reason for this reticence is not clear. It may be due to the absence of a spirit of revenge, or to a need for caution in view of possible reprisals, or to some other cause.[55] It constitutes what may be a significant departure from the usual pattern of the individual thanksgiving, but not one sufficiently great to remove Isa. 53 from that category.

vi. *The reference to the speaker's nearness to death*

In both the individual thanksgivings and the individual lamentations there are frequent references to the speaker's *nearness to death.*[56] The speaker in the latter complains that he has been brought close to death, either through the attacks of his enemies or through sickness or some other cause, and beseeches God to help him. Sometimes he even claims that he is (virtually) dead.[57] In the thanksgivings he either recalls that experience in the narrative section, or in other sections of the psalm praises God for delivering him. The fact that the speakers in Isa. 53 speak of the Servant's former state in the same way has already been discussed,[58] with some references to the — very few — verbal similarities. Even without such verbal similarities, however, the appearance of this theme in Isa. 53 constitutes an important further piece of evidence for the view that the chapter is in the form of an individual thanksgiving.

b. The reference to the worshipper's prayer for deliverance.

This theme is characteristic of the individual thanksgiving; yet it is not always present. It does not occur, for example, in Ps. 9[59] or in Ps. 92.[60] The speaker in these psalms is presumably so engrossed in the wonder of what has happened to him that all other thoughts are driven from his mind. In Isa. 53 also there is no reference whatever to such a prayer, although the Servant is represented as supremely a man of God. There are a number of possible reasons for this apart from that suggested in the case of the psalms mentioned above. It must be remembered that the prayers in question — prayers of a man driven close to despair — are not particularly an indication of the sufferer's piety, showing him to be a "man of prayer" in the modern sense.

They do, it is true, show him to be a man who trusts God sufficiently to believe that God will answer his appeal for help. The Servant in Isa. 53, however, is represented not just as a man in deep trouble but as a person who bore his suffering silently: perhaps a man whose confidence in God was so great that such a cry for help was unnecessary. Or it may be that his prayer is not referred to because it was not, and could not be, in the circumstances, the formal prayer for help in a cultic setting which is, we may presume, the prayer to which the majority of the individual thanksgivings refer: the cultic individual lamentation. It must also be borne in mind that Isa. 53 is spoken not by the sufferer (the Servant) himself but by others who, though aware in general of what had happened to the Servant, were not actual witnesses of his life in prison. It is impossible for the modern reader to know precisely why there is no reference in this poem to the Servant's prayer for help; but its absence does not constitute a reason for denying the character of individual thanksgiving to the poem.

c. The description of the act of deliverance.

This element is invariably present in the individual psalms of thanksgiving. This is so of necessity, since the divine action which it describes is that which occasions the entire act of thanksgiving of which the recital of the psalm is a constituent part. It is the action which has been asked for in the preceding lamentation, and which has now been performed. It usually refers to God in the third person: the words are addressed by the speaker to those who are present with him, with the intention of bringing them into the act of thanksgiving to share it with him. Occasionally, however, it is addressed to God in the form of a prayer of thanksgiving. A further characteristic of this part of the thanksgiving psalm is that it is usually expressed in general terms, using words like "save", "deliver" etc. and avoiding details.

In Isa. 53 there is only one brief direct statement about this action. It occurs at the very beginning of the poem, in verse 1: "To whom has the arm of Yahweh been revealed?". This is also the position in which it occurs in Ps. 30; 40; 116; Jonah 2. As in the other psalms of thanksgiving it is expressed in very general terms. The interrogative form, which is unique, is to be explained partly by the fact that the speakers have not expected the Servant's deliverance and use this form to indicate their astonishment at the turn of events, and partly by the fact that it is they who speak and not the one who has experienced the deliverance: the identity of the latter is thus revealed (although in another sense concealed) in a striking way which an affirmative statement would be incapable of expressing.

The fact of Yahweh's act of deliverance of the Servant, though not again expressed directly in the form of a statement, is however also implicit in the latter part of the poem, verses 10b-12.[61] Here the fate of the Servant is expressed in two ways: 1. in statements about the Servant's future, expressed mainly in third person singular imperfects of which he is the subject: "he will see offspring living to a great age" (יראה זרע יאריך ימים); "and the will of Yahweh will prosper through his agency" (וחפץ יהוה בידו יצלח), verse 10b ; "he will see light" (יראה אור);[62] "he will be satisfied" (ישבע), verse 11a ; 2. in a divine oracle in which Yahweh speaks in the first person: "I will allot to him..., and he shall participate in sharing out, spoil" (אחלק-לו ... ו ... יחלק שלל), verse 12a).[63]

i. *Statements by the speaker in an individual thanksgiving psalm about his future life* now that God has performed the act which has delivered him from distress are — apart from the very frequent assertion that he will praise God and offer him thanksgiving — rare. However, something of the kind occurs in Ps. 92:13-15 (EVV 12-14), where immediately after the narrative describing the act of deliverance (verses 11f. [EVV 10f.]) the speaker makes a more generalized statement, not admittedly about himself alone but about the "righteous man" (צדיק , an expression which obviously includes himself). This statement begins (verse 13) in the singular with imperfect verbs (יפרח , "will flourish"; ישגה , "will grow tall"), though in later verses plural verbs are used. The happy and prosperous life of the righteous is expressed in similes and metaphors drawn from plant life, and in particular the image of trees planted in the temple courts is used. Long life and exceptional vigour in old age are promised through this imagery (verse 15), and this may be compared with the statement in Isa. 53:10b that the Servant "will see offspring living to a great age". Another example of a statement by the speaker about his future life is Ps. 116:9, where after the reference to his deliverance in verse 8 he says "I will walk before Yahweh in the lands of the living" (אתהלך לפני יהוה בארצות החיים): compare the language of Isa. 53:8b.

A further link between this section of Isa. 53 and the individual thanksgiving psalm may be the use of the expression חפץ יהוה in verse 10b: "the will of Yahweh will prosper through his agency". Although חפץ יהוה is probably to be translated by "the will of Yahweh" here,[64] the idea that Yahweh "delights" in his Servant is almost certainly also present, since the phrase occurs in a context in which the Servant is promised his reward. In some of the individual psalms of thanksgiving the idea of Yahweh's delighting in a person is similarly associated with his act of deliverance, although in these cases it is the verb חפץ rather than the noun which is used. In Ps. 18:20 (EVV 19), in the narrative describing the act of deliverance, the speaker exclaims, "he delivered me, because he delighted in me" (יחלצני כי חפץ בי). In Ps. 41:12 (EVV 11) the speaker similarly attributes his rescue to

Yahweh's favour: "By this I know that thou hast delighted in me (כי־חפצת‎ בי‎), in that my enemy has not triumphed over me". A similar connection between Yahweh's favour and his act of deliverance is made in Psalm 22 in the mocking words spoken to the speaker and quoted by him in the individual lament which precedes the thanksgiving: "He committed his cause to Yahweh; let him deliver him, for he delights in him!" (יצילהו כי חפץ בו‎ , verse 9 [EVV 8]).

ii. *The divine oracle* is not normally an element of the individual thanksgiving. Nevertheless there are in the Psalter divine oracles which correspond wholly or partly to the divine oracle in Isa. 53:11b-12.

There are at least seven examples of the divine oracle in the Psalms which are worthy of investigation in this connection. They are: 12:6 (EVV 5); 32:8f.; 46:11 (EVV 10); 60:8-10 (EVV 6-8) (= 108:8-10 [EVV 7-9]); 68:23-24 (EVV 22-23); 75:3f. (EVV 2f.); 91:14-16.[65]

The classification of some of these psalms is a matter of dispute. However, it is generally agreed that Psalm 32 is an individual thanksgiving. Verses 8f. of this psalm, in spite of their didactic tone, are to be regarded, with Kraus and Delekat,[66] as a divine speech. They are not an "oracle of salvation" of the type which Gunkel[67] presupposed as the reply to the individual lamentation, mediated by the priest, and of which Begrich[68] found traces in the Psalms and numerous actual — though isolated — examples in Deutero-Isaiah; but they promise divine guidance and so are appropriate as an answer to a confession of sin (verses 3-5). The fact that they occur in a psalm of thanksgiving, following an acknowledgement of God's act of deliverance (verse 7), suggests that they are a quotation from the oracle which God has already spoken,[69] and which the speaker now quotes as confirmation of his confidence that God will help and guide all those who put their trust in him and pray to him. This example suggests the possibility that the divine oracle in Isa. 53:11f. may also be a quotation from an earlier oracle. Another example of such a quotation occurs in Ps. 75, in a corporate thanksgiving: the oracle in verses 3f. (EVV 2f.) serves to confirm the confidence with which the speakers praise God in the previous verse. Ps. 12:6 (EVV 5), on the other hand, is probably not a quotation of such an oracle but the oracle itself in its proper place, where it answers the complaint made in what is probably a corporate lamentation.[70]

Psalm 60 is a corporate lamentation.[71] The divine oracle (verses 8-10 [EVV 6-8]) is embedded in the lamentation itself. Various explanations have been given of this; Kraus may be right in his suggestion that this is a quotation of a much earlier oracle pronounced on a previous occasion when God had come to the help of his people, and now quoted as a reminder to God of what he had done for them in the past, in order to strengthen the present appeal.

Two other psalms which contain oracles of this kind are more difficult to classify. It may however be agreed that in Psalm 68, verses 20f. (EVV 19f.), which follow a reference to a theophany (verses 18f. [EVV 17f.]), have the form of a corporate thanksgiving. This is followed by an expression of confidence (verse 22 [EVV 21]). The divine oracle which then follows (verses 23f. [EVV 22f.]) may then be understood as a quotation of an oracle of salvation whose purpose is, like that of the oracle in Ps. 75:3f., to confirm or justify the confidence which has just been expressed.[72]

Psalm 46, which Gunkel classified as a Hymn and also as a "Song of Zion" containing prophetic elements,[73] is seen by Kraus as basically a "collective song of confidence". The precise cultic occasion for which it was composed remains a matter of dispute;[74] but the divine oracle of salvation (verse 11 [EVV 10]) follows an assertion of confidence in God's protection of his people (verse 10 [EVV 9]) which is then repeated in the following verse (12 [EVV 11]). It is not possible to say whether the oracle is a quotation or whether it is in its original place in the liturgical sequence.

The oracle in Ps. 91:14-16 comes at the end of the psalm. Once again the character of the psalm is disputed;[75] but it seems to be a liturgical composition in which in the first section (verses 1-13) a worshipper is addressed by a priest or by another layman or perhaps by both[76] and assured that if he trusts in God he will be protected by him from all kinds of misfortune and attack. The final oracle then follows in the liturgical sequence: the assurances made in the earlier address are now confirmed by a priestly oracle of assurance in which God himself speaks.[77] It is of particular interest to note that in verse 16 there are striking verbal similarities to Isa. 53: not, it is true, to the oracle itself, which begins in verse 11b, but to the promises made by the human speakers in verses 10, 11a. In the psalm, God makes the promise concerning the worshipper, "With long life I will satisfy him, and show him my salvation" (ארך ימים אשביעהו ואראהו בישועתי). These words are strongly reminiscent of Isa. 53:10f., which speaks of length of life (יאריך ימים) and "satisfaction" (ישבע) as the reward of the Servant (or his descendants).[78] It is also possible that "show him my salvation" (ואראהו בישועתי) in the psalm oracle also finds an echo in "he shall see (light)" (יראה אור) in Isa. 53:11.[79]

A further comment is relevant on the significance of the verb שבע, "to be sated, satisfied". This verb has a special place in the vocabulary of the thanksgiving psalms. In addition to Ps. 91:16 it is also found in the following psalms: in the thanksgiving section of Ps. 22 the worshipper, after thanking God for what he has done (verse 26 [EVV 25]) makes the more general confident assertion that "the afflicted shall eat and be satisfied" (יאכלו ענוים וישבעו , verse 27 [EVV 26]) when they seek Yahweh; in Ps. 63 in a

similar context the worshipper proclaims, "I am satisfied (תשבע נפשי)
as with rich food" (verse 6 [EVV 5]); in Ps. 107:9 the chorus in a thanksgiving ceremony praise God "because he satisfies the one who is thirsty
(השביע נפש שקקה) and fills the hungry with good things". Correspondingly in Ps. 90:14, in a communal lamentation, the worshippers call on God
to take pity on them and cry, "Satisfy us in the morning with thy faithful
love" (שבענו בבקר חסדך).

In the psalms considered above, most of which are either individual lamentations or thanksgivings or related in some way to these classes of psalm,
the divine oracles thus serve a variety of purposes. Four of them, however
(46:11; 68:23f.; 75:3f.; 91:14-16) are used like the oracle in Isa. 53 to confirm with divine authority the confidence which has been previously expressed by the human speaker(s) in God's readiness to help. In four cases at
least (32:8f.; 60:8-10; 68:23f.; 75:3f.; possibly 46:11) the oracle does not
stand in its original place as a cultic reply to a lamentation but is quoted by
the human speaker for some particular reason. Both of these appear to be
characteristics of the oracle in Isa. 53:11b-12. Ps. 91:14-16 is particularly
close to Isa. 53 not only in vocabulary but also in the fact that it speaks in
some detail of the future career of the person under God's protection: long
life and honour.

The extent to which the oracle in Isa. 53 resembles the other oracles in
other respects may be set out as follows:

1. *In every case* the prevailing form of the verb is the first person singular
imperfect with God as the subject; in every case but one (Ps. 46:11) this imperfect has a future sense indicating what God will do.[80]

2. The oracle in Isa. 53 begins without any formal introduction of Yahweh
as the speaker. This is also true of Ps. 32:8f.; 46:11; 75:3f.; 91:14-16.

3. The oracle in Isa. 53 gives a reason for God's promise of help: "Therefore I will . . . because he exposed his life to the uttermost and was counted
as one of the rebels." A reason is also given in Ps. 12:6 ("Because the poor
are despoiled, because the needy groan, I will . . .") and Ps. 91:14 ("Because
he cleaves to me in love, I will deliver him; I will protect him, because he
knows my name").

4. In Isa. 53 the Servant is referred to in the third person. This is also true
of the recipient of the promise in Ps. 12:6; 91:14-16.

5. In Isa. 53 the oracle occurs at the conclusion of the poem. This is also
the case in Ps. 91:14-16. In Ps. 46:11 it occurs just before the end, the final
verse being a comment upon it.

From the above discussion it will be seen that Isa. 53 contains the element
of the description of God's act of deliverance, partly in the brief reference in

125

verse 1 and partly in the statement about the Servant's future in verses 10-11a; and that the divine oracle with which it concludes is not a unique element but has parallels in the Psalter, having a particularly close resemblance to that in Psalm 91.

2. The Recognition of God's Gracious Action

The other element recognized by Gunkel and later interpreters as an essential element in the individual psalm of thanksgiving is the *recognition by the worshipper of God's gracious action performed on his behalf.*[81] This is expressed in various ways. Frequently there is a call by the worshipper to the assembled congregation to share with him in praise and thanksgiving to God for his gracious action.[82] In other psalms there is a reflection on the attributes of God: his reliability, grace, greatness, character as true judge or as protector, etc.[83] This is sometimes embedded in the narrative of deliverance, but in other cases forms a distinct section of the psalm. It often corresponds closely in form and contents to the promise made by the worshipper in the individual lamentation that when he has been rescued he will offer his praise to God. It is the essential act of praise (תודה). Together with the narrative section it not only constitutes the basic cultic action to perform which the worshipper has come to the temple, but also makes the whole action an action of the worshipping community: God's gracious deeds are made known to all, and all give him thanks and praise him for it.

At first sight this element appears to be lacking in Isa. 53. But this is not entirely the case. It is represented in verse 1 in the words "Who would have believed what we have just heard?" This testifies to the performance by God of an act of redemption even greater than what had previously been believed possible. It is a recognition of God's gracious action.[84] It is also represented in verses 4-6, where the speakers meditate on or confess how God has healed them all (נרפא-לנו) and restored wholeness to them (שלומנו). The use of these two words, the verb רפא , "heal" and the noun שלום , "wholeness, well-being, is significant. "Healing" is an action for which the worshipper prays to God in certain individual lamentations.[85] Correspondingly in some of the individual thanksgivings the worshipper thanks God for having granted it.[86] שלום is also something for which the petitioner asks in the individual lamentation in Ps. 38 (verse 4 [EVV 3]) or which he confidently expects that God will give him (Ps. 55:19 [EVV 18]); and Hezekiah in his thanksgiving (Isa. 38:17) speaks of it as something which God has restored to him.[87] The speakers in Isa. 53:4-6 thus acknowledge that they themselves have been restored to a full state of well-being in consequence of the experiences undergone by the Servant, and they do this in language which belongs to the vocabulary of the individual thanksgiving psalms.

3. Conclusion

It is clear from the above analysis and comparisons with similar literature that Isa. 53 contains the essential elements which qualify it for classification as an individual psalm of thanksgiving. The two essential features – the narrative of the sufferer's past experiences and the act of recognition of God's intervention to rescue him – are both present. As often in the individual thanksgivings the narrative occupies the major portion of the composition. Various other characteristic minor motifs are also present, and at many points the expressions and style employed are those of the individual thanksgiving. Even the divine oracle at the end of the chapter, though unusual, has parallels with the lamentation/thanksgiving literature.

There is however one great difference, and that a major one, between Isa. 53 and the lamentations which we have considered up to the present: whereas in the standard individual thanksgiving the speaker is the former sufferer himself, who now comes to offer his personal thanks to God, in Isa. 53 it is a group of persons who speak. The former sufferer is not one of them: they speak of him in the third person, expressing their gratitude for what has happened to him.

This unusual feature no doubt accounts for some of the distinctive features of Isa. 53 which have been noted above. It certainly accounts for the fact that whereas in the other individual thanksgivings the speaker usually protests his innocence or admits his sins, which have led to his punishment, but obviously not both, Isa. 53 contains both a protestation of innocence and a confession of sin: the speakers emphasize the innocence of the Servant but also confess their own guilt, which was at least partly the cause of his suffering. Other features of the chapter may also be attributable to the fact that the speakers are persons other than the sufferer himself. The expression of astonishment (verse 1) is not a feature of the other examples of the individual thanksgiving – or at least not to the same extent – because a person who has previously expressed his confidence that God will come to his help can hardly later say that he is astonished that God has done so. The astonishment expressed in Isa. 53 is that of the speakers, who had not possessed this confidence and so are truly astonished. Again, the facts that there is no reference to any prayer for deliverance, and that the divine act of salvation is only alluded to indirectly – features generally, though not always, present in individual thanksgivings – may be presumed to be due to the fact that the speakers are witnesses, not of the actual experiences of the Servant during the period of his suffering, nor of the act of salvation itself, but only of the fact that deliverance has taken place, proved by the presence of the Servant among them.

But in fact Isa. 53 is not entirely unique among the psalms of thanksgiving in the Old Testament, even with regard to the special features mentioned above. The psalm of thanksgiving expressed in the third person, though less common than that in the first person, is to be found in the Old Testament. This will be the subject of the next stage of our investigation.

D. Isaiah 53 and the Thanksgiving Liturgy

1. The Third Person Psalm of Thanksgiving

It is now well established in Psalm studies that when the person who believed himself to have been delivered by God from the distress from which he had been suffering came to the Temple (where he had, normally, previously made his petition, or "psalm of lamentation") in order to pay his vow and to thank God by uttering a psalm of thanksgiving (and, at any rate in some cases, offering a sacrifice of thanksgiving) he was not alone, but came accompanied by others, at least by his own friends and/or relations.[88] Indeed, an important part of his purpose was to proclaim publicly what God had done for him: this is the main function of the narrative section of the individual psalm of thanksgiving, which refers to God in the third person and is addressed not to God but to the other persons present.[89] This personal testimony was intended to inspire in these others a renewed trust and fear of Yahweh and new reflections on his goodness, but also to inspire them to join with the individual worshipper in singing songs of praise and thanksgiving.[90] On at least some of these occasions the act of thanksgiving took place in the presence not only of a small group of friends and relations but of the whole congregation of Israel,[91] presumably gathered at a major festival.

We are justified in assuming that the congregation thus assembled did in fact respond to these exhortations and burst forth into songs of praise and thanksgiving. The subject-matter of these congregational songs can be inferred in general terms from the language used in the exhortations themselves. Occasionally the words of the song to be sung are actually prescribed: in Ps. 35:27, which is an individual lamentation, the singer is so confident of his future vindication that he anticipates the singing of such a song: "Let those who desire my vindication shout joyously and rejoice; and let them continuously say, 'Great is Yahweh, who has willed the welfare of his servant!' "

In the majority of the psalms of individual thanksgiving the precise circumstances of the ceremony at which the individual paid his thanksgiving vows are not fully described: these psalms naturally presuppose a knowledge of the ceremony. Even though reference is sometimes made to various aspects of it, such as the offering of the sacrificial victim, the modern reader is forced to rely to a large extent on his imagination.[92] This vagueness of detail applies also to what we are now justified in calling the "corporate third person thanksgiving song for the deliverance of an individual": the character of this song and its role within the totality of the ceremony are not entirely clear.

Fortunately, however, there is at least one psalm which, in spite of some differences of interpretation, enables us to some extent to form a picture of the ceremony. This is Psalm 118.[93]

Modern interpreters are generally agreed about the character of Ps. 118,[94] although the allocation of its various parts to different speakers or singers is in some cases a matter of opinion. It is, in Gunkel's phrase,[95] a *Dankfestliturgie*: that is, a composition which combines different *Gattungen* into a single whole, with different sections spoken or sung by different voices, following the action of a cultic liturgy.[96] Among the points on which there is general agreement are the following:

a. It is agreed that at least verses 5-18, with the probable exception of two short passages (verses 8f., 15f.)[97] are an individual thanksgiving.

b. Verses 19f. consist of a request by the individual worshipper for the opening of the temple gates, followed by a reply made by priest(s) or door-keepers. The worshipper wishes to enter the temple in order to offer his thanksgiving sacrifice or to pay his vows, and the guardians of the gate in reply set out briefly (cf. Pss. 15; 24) the conditions of entry: those who do so must be "righteous" (צדיקים).

c. Verse 21, spoken by the worshipper to God, thanks him for answering his prayer and coming to his help. This presupposes that the worshipper has now entered the gates.

d. Verses 22-28, which combine various different styles and alternate between "I" and "we" forms, are spoken or sung by various different persons.

i. Verses 23-25 are spoken by a group of persons, and this is probably also true of verse 22.

ii. Verse 26 is a priestly blessing on the person or persons who have now entered the gates.

iii. Verse 27 is attributed by different interpreters to different speakers. It makes a reference to the ceremonies to be performed.

iv. Verse 28 is yet another expression of thanks to God by the individual worshippper.[98]

It is thus quite clear that we have here the liturgical text of a ceremony at which an individual worshipper comes to the temple accompanied by others to offer his vows of thanksgiving before a large assembly. The ceremony involves the singing of an individual psalm of thanksgiving, a procession, a ceremony for obtaining admittance to the temple, further expressions of thanksgiving, a priestly blessing and a further ceremony connected with the altar (verse 27), probably a sacrifice. The feature which is especially relevant to the present discussion, however, is the part played by the other persons present, whether they are a body of the worshipper's friends and relations, or the entire congregation, or, as is most probable, both: and in particular the words spoken by them in verses 22-24.

These verses, which are probably a single song or psalm sung by one group of people, immediately follow the ceremony of the entering of the gate by the worshipper, and his short thanksgiving in verse 21. The opening of the gates sets the seal on the worshipper's acceptance by God: it is in a real sense the climax of the ceremony. The song of verses 22-24, then, expresses the reactions of those present, who have witnessed the reality of the rescue of the worshipper from his former distress. Brief though it is, this song may rightly be described as a "third person psalm of thanksgiving" referring to an individual's rescue and restoration by God. It has, indeed, the same basic pattern as the *first person* individual thanksgiving psalm in that it contains the two basic elements: the narrative section and the act of recognition of the debt owed to Yahweh.[99]

The narrative section is contained in verse 22: "The stone which the builders rejected has become the chief corner-stone". It has been suggested[100] that this statement has the characteristics of a wisdom saying. However this may be, it corresponds to two of the three main elements of the narrative section of the individual thanksgiving: the description of former distress (the rejected stone) and the narrative of deliverance: the "chief corner-stone" (ראש פנה)[101] is clearly the most essential and important stone in the structure of the building: in plain terms, the person previously utterly despised has been raised to a position of great eminence.[102] Verse 23a, "This is Yahweh's doing", corresponds to the act of recognition of Yahweh's gracious act in the individual psalm of thanksgiving (cf. verse 14 in the earlier part of the psalm). Verse 23b, "it is marvellous in our eyes", expresses the astonishment of the witnesses, who had, it would seem, not expected such a vindication of the worshipper to occur: we may call it a feature peculiar to the third person psalm of thanksgiving not exactly paralleled in the first person psalm. Its significance will be considered later.[103] Verse 24a reinforces the thought of the remarkable nature of the divine action, and verse 24b, formally an exhortation by the speakers to themselves to rejoice, is in fact an act of joyous worship such as the individual in the first person thanksgivings so frequently urged upon his companions.[104]

The one main feature of the first person thanksgiving psalm which does not appear here is the reference to the individual's prayer for help. It has, however, already been pointed out that this is not an invariable feature of the genre;[105] and in a third person psalm of thanksgiving such as this it is perhaps hardly to be expected. The prayer for help has already been referred to in the preceding first person thanksgiving psalm (verse 5); here the emphasis is rather on the fact of God's marvellous action and on the contrast between the former and the present states of the person who has been rescued.

Another psalm which has been understood by some interpreters as having a similar character to Ps. 118 is Ps. 107. This view is not, however, a universal one.[106] Certainly the psalm differs from Ps. 118 in that it is not possible to discern clearly behind it the structure of the ceremony of which it is said to be the liturgy. It consists to a large extent of exhortations to thank God rather than of actual acts of thanksgiving. Nevertheless it has one prominent feature which is relevant to the present discussion. The central part (verses 4-32) consists of four sections (verses 4-9, 10-16, 17-22, 23-32) each of which, in spite of the jussive plural form, has the basic characteristics of an individual thanksgiving psalm. These four sections each consist of the following elements: elements:

i. *Narrative*

a. of former distress	4f.	10-12	17f.	23-27
b. of prayer to God	6a	13a	19a	28a
c. of God's act of help	6b-7	13b-14	19b-20	28b-30

ii. *Recognition of God's action* 8f.   15f.   21f.   31f.

There can be no doubt that the persons referred to in these verses are groups of individuals: that is, they are not a community as such but persons each of whom has been delivered individually from various kinds of distress (dangerous journeys through the desert, imprisonment, sickness, storms at sea) and who has come as an individual to offer his thanksgiving. They have been grouped together into four categories, possibly because they were so numerous that time was insufficient for them to offer their thanksgivings separately, or for some other reason.[107] This is the explanation of the plural reference. Although the function of these sections within the totality of Psalm 107 is not clear, their extremely close resemblance to actual thanksgiving psalms suggests that they belong to, or at least have been modelled upon, a distinct *Gattung*: the third person thanksgiving psalm for an individual.

It may well be that the elaborate ceremony reflected in these two psalms was not used on every occasion. We have no means of knowing this, since the other individual thanksgiving psalms provide few hints of the circumstances in which they were used. The theory that these acts of thanksgiving were offered only once a year or at least only on the major feast-days when the whole congregation was assembled cannot be proved or disproved. But this question is not of essential importance for the present discussion. The evidence offered above is sufficient to show that there was a *Gattung* which may be described as the third person individual thanksgiving psalm, which in its main elements followed the structure of the first person thanksgiving. It is constantly referred to and called for by the individual psalmist both in the individual lamentation and in the individual thanksgiving, and in Ps. 118:22-24 and probably in Psalm 107 we have actual examples of it in the Psalter. In addition, Psalm 118 shows us something of its function and place in the thanksgiving ceremony. It was sung by those present – whether by the friends and intimates of the individual concerned or by the whole congregation – after he had appeared in the Temple and had sung his own song of thanksgiving, and probably before the sacrificial offering was made. It is the song of the witnesses who are moved by the sight of the individual now relieved from his distress, accepted once more by God, and ready and able once more to resume his normal life as a member of the community. In their song they remember his former distress, testify to God's act of deliverance and praise and thank God for what he has done for their companion.

2. Isaiah 53 as a Third Person Psalm of Thanksgiving

It was Begrich who first recognized that this chapter has the form of a third person psalm of thanksgiving.[108] In this connection he also pointed out another fact of the first importance: that the expression of astonishment with which the chapter begins (verse 1) also has its counterpart in the third person psalm of thanksgiving in Ps. 118:23.[109]

This similarity deserves a close scrutiny. In Ps. 118:23, after the "narrative section" in verse 22, the singers exclaim:

This is Yahweh's doing (מאת יהוה היתה זאת);
it is marvellous (נפלאת) in our eyes.

In Isa. 53:1, this time immediately *before* the narrative section, the speakers make a similar exclamation in the form of a question:

Who would have believed what we have heard
(מי האמין לשמעתנו)?
and concerning/to whom (על-מי) has Yahweh's
arm revealed itself (נגלתה)?[110]

Both passages express the speakers' astonishment at the changed state and status of the individual in question. They also resemble one another rather more closely.

a. They both refer both to what the speakers have heard and to what they have seen. In Ps. 118:23 "this" (זאת) refers to the series of events – the elevation of the despised one to great eminence – which the speakers themselves have just summarized in verse 22; but that summary itself points back to the narrative section of the preceding individual psalm of thanksgiving (verses 5-18). The speakers have in fact had a double experience: they have *heard* the individual's account of what has happened to him; and they have also *seen* the individual restored to his normal state, passing through the gates of the Temple into Yahweh's full acceptance ("it is marvellous *in our eyes*").

The speakers in Isa. 53:1 similarly speak of the double witness of hearing and seeing. First, they have heard the – almost incredible – news or report (שמעתנו, literally, "the report which has been made to us"). This most naturally refers, like the זאת of Ps. 118:23, to the Servant's own individual thanksgiving, no longer preserved except in this reference. They have also *seen* the action of God, or its consequences, which he performed on behalf of the Servant: it has been revealed to them (נגלתה). This "revelation" has clearly taken the form of the actual appearance of the Servant, whom they had regarded as actually or virtually dead and forgotten, before their very eyes. That this is the meaning of נגלתה is clear from the way in which the immediately following narrative section begins (verses 2ff.): these verses heighten the wonder of the Servant's present appearance by vividly recalling his past appearance; the emphasis is placed on what they had previously *seen* in him (תאר , ונראהו , מראה , verse 2).

b. They both express the thought that what they have heard and seen is barely credible: such a thing could only have been done through Yahweh's specially exercized divine power. The speakers in Ps. 118:23 use the Niphal of the verb פלא , which denotes that which is difficult or impossible to do or to understand, or which is wonderful or marvellous,[111] and is therefore especially appropriate in speaking[112] of Yahweh's deeds, which are beyond men's powers and comprehension. In the following verse (24) the speakers reinforce this thought with the further statement that "this is the day which Yahweh has made": a special day of rejoicing, newly created as it were specially for the purpose.

Similarly the מי האמין of Isa. 53:1 suggests that the speakers would not have believed the evidence of their ears and eyes, had they not known that Yahweh had the power (זרוע , "arm") to do that which was impossible for men to do.[113]

The above comparison suggests that the motif of the expression of astonishment may have been a regular feature of the third person thanksgiving psalm, although of course this does not mean that it was a merely formal element not matched by a genuine feeling of joyful surprise. In many cases — especially, no doubt, in cases of severe sickness, one of the most frequent subjects of the individual lamentations and thanksgivings – the recovery of the supplicant was rare, and so unexpected.

Full credit must go to Begrich for his discovery that Isa. 53 has the form of a third person thanksgiving psalm for an individual. But, as has already been noted,[114] he regarded the use of the form here merely as a literary device, and put forward an explanation of its use which does not carry conviction. In the light of the conclusions reached about the character of the chapter earlier in the present study, however, there is no longer any reason why it should not be regarded as an actual cultic thanksgiving. To this question the section which follows will be devoted.

E. The Occasion

The question of the occasion for which Isa. 53 was composed can best be approached by the formulation of a hypothesis whose probability can then be tested.

1. The Hypothesis

The Servant of Yahweh in Isaiah 53 (as in the other "Servant Songs" in Isa. 40-55) is the prophet whom we know as Deutero-Isaiah. In consequence of his anti-Babylonian prophecies, especially his prophecies of the fall of the city to the Persians, he was – as was to be expected – arrested, tried, convicted and imprisoned.[115] Whatever following he may previously have had among his fellow-exiles evaporated: his misfortune was interpreted by them (or at least by many of them) either as a sign that Yahweh had withdrawn his favour from him, or – more probably – as a sign that he had been a false prophet from the first. They therefore ceased – if indeed they had ever done so – to believe his message of the imminent deliverance of the Jewish exiles from the "prison" of Babylonian exile. They washed their hands of him, and expected never to see him again: he was "as good as dead". But a miracle occurred: the prophet was released, or escaped from prison, and appeared once more amongst his fellow-exiles as a free man.

The poem which has been preserved in ch. 53 is a third person psalm of thanksgiving composed for and sung at a religious assembly of the Jewish exiles: a *Dankfestliturgie*. The prophet had already made his appearance and offered his own individual thanksgiving psalm for his release from prison. In this psalm, which followed his, the speakers not only express astonishment at his release, relate in their own words the narrative of his former distress and Yahweh's intervention to save him, and joyfully acknowledge that gracious action – features characteristic of this type of psalm; they also give their own interpretation of the events which they commemorate, both with regard to the Servant and to themselves: if they had previously seen his misfortunes as an indication that he was a false prophet and a sinner whom God had justly punished, they now acknowledge that they themselves are the sinners in that they so readily judged him. The action of God in miraculously setting him free has now shown his sufferings in their true light as the consequence of his courageous pursuance of his vocation despite the risk which he ran, and has led to recognition of him as a true prophet, and hence to the belated acceptance of the truth of his message. In his triumph the speakers see their own future foreshadowed, for the triumphantly positive note sounded in the description of his new life of prosperity, dignity and happiness now beginning (verses 10b-12a) presupposes the immediate onset of the national restoration. No doubt it was this understanding of the role of the prophet as a sign of the truth of his own message which caused this psalm — together with the other "Servant Songs" — to be preserved among the records of his prophetic activity.

2. Justification of the Hypothesis

a. *The identification of the Servant with the prophet "Deutero-Isaiah"*

This identification, which has been assumed without argument throughout this study, is by no means a new or unusual hypothesis but has been held in the past and is held at the present time by a number, perhaps a growing number, of scholars. To present a comprehensive defence of it would require a further monograph which would do little more than traverse ground already frequently covered. All that needs to be said here is that the understanding of the character of chapter 53 in this study, while it proceeds on the assumption of that identification, also serves as additional evidence in its favour in as far as it makes better sense of the chapter than before.

b. *The evidence of the poem*

i. It has already been established that the poem represents the prophet not as one who has died, but as one who has suffered greatly but has now received divine assurance of a happy, dignified and prosperous life in the future.[116]

ii. The words and phrases used in the poem to describe his sufferings make it clear that his sufferings were not, or at least not primarily, due to sickness but to physical ill treatment.[117]

iii. A number of phrases in the poem strongly suggest that he was arrested, tried, convicted and imprisoned.[118]

iv. The attitude expressed by the speakers in the poem perfectly fits the hypothesis· they attest a. that he was a member of their community; b. that they knew him, but paid no heed to him; c. that they regarded his misfortune as a deserved divine punishment for his wickedness; d. that something has happened to show that they were mistaken; e. that they now understand that it was for them that he had put himself in danger; f. that they now recognize that he is the recipient not of God's punishment but of his special favour and that he is destined by God's will to a position of pre-eminence.[119] No other interpretation of the poem does justice to all these features.

c. *The occasion of the poem's composition and recital*

The supposition that on his release or escape from prison the prophet appeared at a *Dankfestliturgie* and recited a song of thanksgiving for his release, which was followed by the singing of a third person thanksgiving song which is chapter 53 itself corresponds to what we should expect to have happened in the light of our knowledge, incomplete though it is, of the religious customs of the Babylonian exiles. On the one hand, the existence and procedures of the *Dankfestliturgie,* including both the individual (first person) and the third person thanksgiving psalms have been sufficiently well established,[120] and there is no reason to doubt that the custom goes back to the pre-exilic period in Israel. That the poem belongs to this latter *Gattung* has also been demonstrated. On the other hand, both inherent probability and a not inconsiderable body of evidence entitle us to assume that the Babylonian exiles were free to assemble for public worship and that this worship consisted of the old familiar forms as far as this was practicable, adapted to the exigencies of the circumstances in which they found themselves.[121] The view that one of these types of worship was the thanksgiving of the individual for deliverance from distress made on a public occasion (the *Dankfestliturgie*) and that Isa. 53 was composed for use as one element in a particularly notable act of worship of this kind is therefore in no way improbable.

d. *The release or escape from prison*

We have left until last what may be regarded as the most speculative feature of our reconstruction: the supposition that Deutero-Isaiah was liberated from a Babylonian prison, either with the acquiescence of the authorities or by escaping. This hypothesis, however, is an inevitable deduction from the other, well established facts: if, as has been shown above, he was imprisoned, and if the composition and singing of chapter 53 were occasioned by his reappearance among his fellows as a free man, no other hypothesis fits the facts.

It is more probable that he was for some undisclosed reason released from prison by the competent authorities than that he escaped, since he evidently did not find it necessary afterwards to go into hiding, but appeared publicly at a Jewish religious ceremony. Such unexpected releases of prisoners from prison were by no means unusual in the ancient Near East: there are a number of references to such occurrences in the Old Testament alone.

In some cases the reason for a prisoner's release seems to have been nothing more than the whim of the ruler who had equally capriciously put him in prison. So in the Joseph Story (Gen. 37-50) the author appears to find it unremarkable that the Pharaoh who had cast into prison his butler and his baker who had in some unspecified way "offended" him (חטא), should subsequently, without giving a reason, release the butler and restore him to his office (Gen. 40:1-3, 21), while at the same time executing the baker (verse 22). In the same story another possible reason for clemency is presupposed: Joseph requests the butler, when he is restored to favour, to "make mention of him" (הזכיר) to the king, soliciting his release as a personal favour (verse 14); though Joseph's words suggest yet another possible reason for release: Joseph has been unjustly condemned (39:6-20; 40:15) and seeks, not pardon for his fault, but the recognition of his innocence. In the event, when he is released (41:1-14) it is not for any of these reasons, but because the king has been persuaded that he can be of use to him.[122] Whatever the reason, it is probable that such released prisoners, whatever their religion, attributed their change of fortune to their god(s), and duly expressed their thanks, as – on our hypothesis – did Deutero-Isaiah.

The case of the prophet Jeremiah provides a rather closer parallel with that of Deutero-Isaiah: both are historical personages, and of the same general period; both were prophets. Jeremiah, like Joseph, was useful to the king (Zedekiah), though also feared by him (Jer. 37:16f.; 38:14-28). Because of this he was enabled to obtain some relaxation of the conditions of his imprisonment, and also an assurance that he would not be executed (37:16-21; 38:16). But his release came only when the fall of Jerusalem to the Babylonians, which he had predicted, occurred, and he became, not unnaturally, *persona grata* to the Babylonians when they took the city (38:28; 39:12-14; 40:1-6).

In one respect at least the case of Jehoiachin (2 Kings 25:27-30), an even nearer contemporary of Deutero-Isaiah, is closer to that of Deutero-Isaiah than is that of Jeremiah: it was in Babylonian prisons that both Jehoiachin and Deutero-Isaiah were confined. As in the case of Pharaoh's butler in the Joseph story, no reason is given why Jehoiachin should have been released and given favourable treatment, nor are we told when or why he had been imprisoned.

The contemporaneity of Jehoiachin with Deutero-Isaiah and the fact that both presumably lived in Babylon at the same time for part of their lives so forcibly struck a number of scholars at the beginning of this century that they went so far as to identify the Servant of the "Servant Songs", or at least of

Isa. 53, with Jehoiachin.[123] Sellin – who later abandoned the theory – had concluded from a study of all four "Servant Songs" that the Servant must be a king, and consequently, in a Jewish context, a descendant of David. The figure of Jehoiachin, a contemporary king of Judah, still referred to by that title in 2 Kings 25:27 in spite of his supplanting by Zedekiah, his long exile, and the abolition of his kingdom, seemed to fit that of the Servant too well for coincidence. It is interesting to observe that although most of the scholars who at one time entertained this theory later abandoned it, and its difficulties were seen to be too great for it to become generally accepted, those who did support it saw no difficulty in a figurative interpretation of the Servant's "death" in chapter 53: Sellin saw the relevant references as figures of exile and imprisonment,[124] and Staerk[125] was an early supporter of the view, later to be widely accepted though in the context of other hypotheses about the Servant, that they have the same character as similar expressions in some of the Psalms.

It may be admitted that none of the cases reviewed above is exactly parallel to that which has been argued here about the release from prison of the prophet-Servant, Deutero-Isaiah. The latter was not a king, nor was he, as far as is known, a person of whom the king of Babylon might be expected to have had any cognizance. Taken together, however, these narratives show that the release of a prisoner in the ancient Near East, including the Babylon of the Neo-Babylonian empire, was not an entirely unusual event.

But the partial parallel with Jeremiah may also suggest a possible reason for Deutero-Isaiah's release from prison. Jeremiah, like Deutero-Isaiah, was imprisoned as a person dangerous to the state: he had announced publicly, and in the name of Yahweh, that Jerusalem would shortly fall to the Babylonians (Jer. 32:1- 6). When Jerusalem did in fact fall, he was released from prison (Jer. 39:11-14): not by the Jewish authorities, but by the victorious Babylonians, when they gained control of the city. It is at least a possibility that the reason for Deutero-Isaiah's release was a similar one. He too had prophesied the fall of a capital city of which he was an inhabitant: the fall of Babylon to the Persians. It is consequently possible that his release from prison took place at the time when Babylon fell or just before, and was the act, not of the Babylonian authorities, but of the Persian conquerors, or, perhaps more probably, of the party within Babylon, probably not confined to the priests of Marduk, who themselves also desired the fall of the city to the Persians and, as is known, co-operated with them to that end. As the Babylonian power collapsed, Deutero-Isaiah may well have been seen by this party as an ally and as a person possessing a potentially useful influence with his own community.[126] It was appropriate that he who had predicted the opening of the eyes of the blind and the bringing of the prisoners out of the dungeon (Isa. 42:7) should have been one of the first to experience the fulfilment of that prophecy.

POSTSCRIPT

The above interpretation of Isaiah 53, if accepted, has some important consequences: its status as a passage of outstanding religious and theological importance which it has enjoyed for many centuries is thereby considerably
diminished; but something is also gained. The chapter ceases to be what
modern scholars have increasingly found an embarrassment: a *corpus alienum*
within the theological world of the Old Testament. It may now find a more
modest role, together with the other three "Servant Songs", as a testimony
to certain aspects of the prophetic vocation. The Ebed Yahweh can now take
his proper place among the many "servants of Yahweh" of whom the Old
Testament speaks. Orlinsky is right when he writes: "Were it not for the
theological needs of early Christianity that brought emphasis for the first
time to the concept 'servant' in Isaiah 52-53, it is altogether doubtful that
scholars would subsequently have paid special attention and granted special
status to Second Isaiah's servant passages."[1]

Notes

Notes to the Introduction

1　It is assumed in this study that 53:1-12 constitute a distinct literary unit and that 52:13-15 (apart from אדם ... - כ in 52:14b, which has been displaced from its original position after 53:2, as many scholars agree – see *BHS*) have a separate origin. The correctness of this view, which has the support of a number of recent scholars, will become apparent as a result of the form-critical study of the chapter in Part III below. See also Part III, n.1.

2　So Orlinsky, G.R. Driver, Soggin.

3　So Orlinsky, who also maintains that the concept of vicarious suffering on the part of one man for another (or others) is not to be found in the Old Testament at all.

4　See North, *Suffering Servant, passim.* Among recent scholars, Orlinsky holds that the Servant was the prophet "Deutero-Isaiah" himself, while Driver believed that he was "some unknown Jew" (p. 105). (See notes 2 and 3 above.) Both, however, agree that this person suffered persecution at the hands of either the Babylonians or his fellow-Jews but was later triumphantly vindicated and ended his life in honour and happiness.

5　E.g. von Waldow (pp. 160-169), Fohrer, Scharbert (pp. 178-212), Kutsch, Orlinsky, Dion, Miller, Schoors.

6　Reference will be made from time to time in the pages which follow to ch. 53 as the "Fourth Servant Song". While the term "song" is not necessarily appropriate, the common view that ch. 53 belongs to a group of passages distinct from the remainder of chs. 40-55 in which the same "Servant"-figure speaks or is referred to is here accepted. Of these passages, 42:1-4; 49:1-6 and 50:4-9 are thus commonly referred to as the "First", "Second" and "Third Servant Songs". However, it is probable that some other passages in these chapters should also be included in this group, especially 50:10-11.

Notes to Part I

1 See pp. 31-57 below.

2 RSV "and he shall bear their iniquities".

3 Reading Qere.

4 Koch, "Sein Blut bleibe auf seinem Haupt".

5 Cf. Westermann, *Genesis* on Gen. 4:13.

6 Kraus, *Klagelieder*; Rudolph, *Klagelieder*; Weiser, *Klagelieder*; Plöger, *Klagelieder*; Hillers, *ad loc.*

7 This view is of course not tenable on the "corporate" view of the identity of the Servant, which sees him as a symbol or personification of the community; but it is the most natural meaning if he is an individual who is a member of that community.

8 In view of the nature of the confession and the intensity of the feelings of the speakers it is not necessary to suppose that he was absolutely sinless.

9 For a discussion of the words יצדיק צדיק עבדי לרבים , which stand in · parallelism with ועונחם הוא יסבל in verse 11 and are also generally interpreted in a vicarious sense, see pp. 66-71 below.

10 RSV "yet he bore the sin of many".

11 See the discussion in Snaith, *ad loc.*, where it is argued that עררים refers not to childlessness but to a lack of legitimate offspring qualified to perpetuate the name of the father.

12 Pp. 71-74 below.

13 See pp. 44f. below.

14 Zimmerli, "Die Eigenart . . .", pp. 9-12. See also Zimmerli, "Vorgeschichte".

15 Although the text is uncertain the phrase is clearly present here.

16 Isa. 64:5 (EVV 6), where נשא and עון are grammatically related, is not relevant here: the text is uncertain, but the exegetes are agreed that עון is the subject of the verb: "our iniquities carry us away".

17 Possibly eight, according to Zimmerli ("Die Eigenart . . .", p. 9, n. 2), who notes that there is an ambiguity in Gen. 4:13: Cain's words may be translated either by "my sin is too great to be forgiven" or (as by most translations and commentaries) by "my punishment is too great for me to bear". See the commentaries, especially Westermann, *Genesis, ad loc.*

18 *Art. cit.*; cf. also Zimmerli, *Ezechiel I*, pp. 114-117, 306f.

19 The order in which the three categories are presented here, which corresponds neither to that in Zimmerli's article nor to that in his commentary, has been adopted for the sake of clarity.

20 Pp. 30f.

21 Some commentators (e.g. Cooke on Ezek. 4:4) include ונשא את-עונה in Num. 30:16 (EVV 15) among the cases where one person bears the punishment of others; but this is not correct. Num. 30 deals with the making of vows to Yahweh and the obligation to keep them (verse 3 [EVV 2]); but most of the chapter is concerned with the specific case of vows made by a married woman and the right of her husband to declare them null and void. He has the right to do this if he does it at the time they are made (verse 13[EVV 12]), and Yahweh will then forgive the wife (יסלח-לה) for her subsequent failure to keep them. But if the husband, having first consented – by silence – to the vows later prohibits them (verse 15 [EVV 14]), *she* remains free from sin, but *he* is held guilty. The phrase used is

ונשא את-עונה (verse 16 [EVV 15]), which is often translated by "he shall bear her sin (guilt, punishment)". But this cannot be the meaning. Her guilt cannot be transferred to him since she has no guilt to bear. He bears his own guilt, that of interfering arbitrarily with her vows. ונשא את-עונה must therefore mean "he bears guilt which he has incurred with regard to her", i.e. through his attitude towards her. This is the genitive of nearer definition (G - K 128f), found also in the phrases עון הקדשים (Exod. 28:38), עון המקדש and עון כהנתכם (Num. 18:1). See pp. 33-45 below.

22 "In Szenen der Stellvertretung kann er das 'Schuld tragen' des Stellvertreters aussagen" (Ezechiel, p. 117). Cf. Zimmerli, "Vorgeschichte", pp. 239-242.

23 With regard to some items in this category Zimmerli expresses himself, both in his article and in his commentary, with various degrees of hesitation.

24 *Art. cit.*, p. 9.

25 As Reventlow argues in "Sein Blut komme ... ".

26 RSV "And Aaron shall take upon himself any guilt incurred in the holy offering".

27 Note, for example, the alternation of 3rd and 2nd persons and of singular and plural in the forms of address.

28 The only variation in this pattern is the last case, where the reference to the "flower" to be placed on the turban is not preceded by a command to make the turban: this command follows in a later verse (verse 39) without elaboration. There is no reason to suppose that this variation has any especial significance.

29 "when he goes into the holy place", verses 29, 35; "when he goes in before Yahweh", verse 30. It should be noted that as far as can be seen the references to different parts of the body ("on his shoulders", "on his heart", "on his forehead") have no other significance than that of physical location.

30 Elsewhere it means "elucidation, clarification" (Num. 6:15, 18); "record" (Esth. 6:1; Mal. 3:16 and possibly also Neh. 2:20); "memorable saying" (?) (Job 13:12); "memory" (Eccles. 1:11; 2:16). Its meaning in Isa. 57:8 is uncertain.

31 On זכרון see Childs, pp. 66-70.

32 Urim occurs alone in Num. 27:21; 1 Sam. 28:6, apparently as an abbreviation.

33 The relevant passages are: Num. 27:21; Deut. 33:8; 1 Sam. 28:6; Ezra 2:63; Neh. 7:65.

34 So for example S.R. Driver, *Exodus, ad loc.*; Hyatt, *ad loc.*; De Vaux, *Institutions II*, pp. 204f. (ET p. 352).

35 Clements, *ad loc.*

36 E.g. S.R. Driver and Hyatt.

37 Exod. 28:43; 30:20,21; Lev. 8:35; 10:6, 7, 9; 16:2, 13; Num. 4:15, 19; 18:3, 32.

38 In Exod. 28:43 the phrase ולא ישאו עון ומתו is used: if Aaron and his sons do not wear the breeches prescribed for them when they minister in the holy place, they will incur the divine punishment and so die.

39 It is interesting to observe that the Hebrew text of Ecclesiasticus referring to this passage (45:9) has the phrase לזכרון לבני עמו , which appears to be a reminiscence of זכרן לבני (אבני) ישראל in Exod. 28:12 (see above). Since the preceding words state that the bells would be heard *in* and not *coming from* the Holy of Holies (להשמיע בדביר קולו), into which Aaron alone penetrated and where he was alone with God, it seems that for the author of Ecclesiasticus it was God rather than the people who were intended to hear them. Modern translations (e.g. NEB "ringing aloud through the temple as a reminder to his people") here follow LXX: *akouston poiēsai en naō eis mnēmosunon huiois laou autou.* It should be noted that LXX has *naos*, which is LXX's normal translation of היכל , whereas the Hebrew text has דביר , "Holy of Holies".

40 See especially de Buck.

41 Noth, "Office and Vocation", p. 236 and n. 18; *Exodus*, pp. 184f. On ץ י ץ as equivalent in meaning to נ ז ר , "crown", see also Hogg.

42 See section iv below.

43 Pp. 42f.

44 Lev. 1:3; 19:5; 22:19, 29. Cf. also Isa. 56:7; 60:7; Jer. 6:20; Mal. 2:13.

45 *K - B, ad loc.*; Elliger, *Jesaja II* on Isa. 40:2.

46 RSV "You and your sons . . . shall bear iniquity in connection with the sanctuary; and you and your sons with you shall bear iniquity in connection with your priesthood ".

47 See Eissfeldt, pp. 31, 157; Noth, *Numbers, ad loc.*

48 On the secondary connection of the story of Dathan and Abiram with the rebellion of Korah see the commentaries.

49 In 16:32 the reference to Korah is generally believed to be an interpolation into the story of Dathan and Abiram.

50 17:5 (EVV 16:40); 17:27f. (EVV 12f.).

51 Zimmerli, "Die Eigenart".

52 See also pp. 45f. below on Lev. 10:16-20, where the question of a similar involuntary fault in connection with the performance of sacrificial rites is raised in narrative form.

53 RSV "and they shall bear their iniquity".

54 E.g. Holzinger, *ad loc.*

55 Wellhausen, pp. 182, 340f.

56 RSV "and has been given to you that you may bear the iniquity of the congregation, to make atonement for them before the LORD ".

57 "Allem nach handelt es sich in 16—20 um einem typischen Midrasch" (Elliger, *Leviticus, ad loc.*).

58 Elliger, *Leviticus, ad loc.*

59 The ritual of the Day of Atonement is not an exception to this statement. See pp. 48f. below.

60 De Vaux, *Sacrifices*, pp. 84f.

61 This is also the interpretation of LXX: *hina apheilēte tēn hamartian tēs sunagōgēs.* It is accepted by most modern translations and commentaries.

62 RSV "you shall bear your iniquity".

63 Zimmerli, "Die Eigenart", p. 10, n. 1.

64 E.g., verse 32 repeats what has been said in verses 29f., and there is further repetition in verse 34. The "little ones" (ף ט) of verse 31 are presumably to be identified with "your children" (ב נ י כ ם) in verse 33, a confusing variation suggesting duality of authorship. ף ט, which denotes very small children, is also inconsistent with the reference to the age of twenty as the decisive criterion of the two age-groups in verse 29.

65 ז נ ו ת , literally "fornication", is always in the Old Testament used metaphorically or symbolically of Israel's faithlessness towards Yahweh (Jer. 3:2, 9; 13:27; Ezek. 23:27; 43:7, 9; Hos. 4:11 [EVV 10] ; 6:10). Since it is never used elsewhere in the Pentateuch, and even the corresponding verb ז נ ה occurs there only rarely and always in a fixed phrase (ז נ ה אחרי , literally "fornicate after", followed by a reference to another god or gods: Lev. 17: 7; 20:5, 6; Num. 15:39; Deut. 31:16); and since it is inappropriate as a description of the kind of rebellion with which this chapter is concerned, it has been suggested (see *BHS, ad loc.*) that it should be emended to תלנותיכם , "your murmurings", a word which occurs earlier in this section (verse 27). If ז נ ו ת י כ ם is correct it must refer to quite different incidents not recorded here, a fact which would support the view that this verse is a later addition to the chapter.

66 Gray, *ad loc.*

67 *Op. cit., ad loc.*

68 It may have been the desire to make the distinction between the fate of parents and children quite clear which prompted the addition of verse 33.

69 RSV "The goat shall bear all their iniquities upon him to a solitary land".

70 P. 46 above.

71 Following Noth, *Leviticus, ad loc.*

72 It is probable that the word לחטאת here is an addition made to balance the phrase לעלה , used of the bull in the latter part of the verse. In any case the subsequent instructions make it clear that only one of the goats was a חטאת .

73 At this point there occur the words לכפר עליו , "to make atonement for it", which make no sense and are generally regarded as a mistaken intrusion into the text.

74 Whatever may be the origin of the tradition in the Mishnah (Yoma 6:2-8) that the scapegoat was killed by being pushed over a cliff, it still remains a fact that this tradition was unknown to the author(s) of Lev. 16, and it is therefore illegitimate to interpret נשא עון in 16:22 with reference to it.

75 RSV "you shall bear their punishment".

76 RSV "you (shall) bear the punishment of the house of Israel".

77 RSV "you shall . . . bear the punishment of the house of Judah".

78 Zimmerli, *Ezechiel*; Wevers, *Ezekiel, ad loc.*

79 Some commentators, e.g. Zimmerli, following Cornill and Toy, believe that the text originally contained yet another occurrence of נשא עון : they emend ושמת את-עון ונשאת את-עון בית-ישראל בית-ישראל עליו to בית-ישראל עליו in verse 4 on the grounds that since the prophet is the one who bears the עון , he can hardly also be the one who imposes it.

80 It is immaterial to the discussion whether 4:4-8 refer to a symbolic action which was actually performed or are purely literary in character.

81 See especially Fohrer, "Symbolische Handlungen" and "Prophetie und Magie".

82 This is one of the reasons why it is widely believed that it is not an original part of this section of the book. It should also be noted that the double reference to Israel and Judah in verses 5f. is almost certainly due to a later reworking of the text, and that the original reference was to Judah alone (regularly referred to by Ezekiel as "the house of Israel"). On this see the commentaries.

83 E.g. by Brunner, *ad loc.*

84 See n. 79 above.

85 It should be noted that this view would not in any case support the argument that נשא עון can be used to refer to vicarious suffering in the usual sense in which one human being suffers in the place of another.

86 On the reference to northern Israel in the present text see n. 82 above.

87 "the years of their punishment" (שני עונם , verse 5). The complex problems of the interpretation of the numbers 390 and 40 (LXX 190 and 40, with an additional 150 in verse 4), which are intended to indicate the number of years of exile for Israel and Judah respectively, do not concern us here.

88 See pp. 29f. above.

89 This is admitted by Zimmerli, ("Vorgeschichte", p. 243), who nevertheless regards Ezekiel as an "Urbild" of the Servant in Isa. 53, whose suffering he regards as atoning.

90 RSV "Why should not the son suffer for the iniquity of the father?"

91 RSV "The son shall not suffer for the iniquity of the father, nor the father suffer for the iniquity of the son".

92 For a detailed discussion of the form, structure, *Sitz im Leben* and meaning of this

chapter see especially Eichrodt, *Hesekiel*; Zimmerli, *Ezechiel*; and Reventlow, *Wächter über Israel*, pp. 108-123.

93 The question whether this was a novel teaching does not concern us here.

94 See especially Reventlow, *Wächter über Israel* and also Zimmerli, *Ezechiel* and Eichrodt, *Hesekiel*, *ad loc.*

95 Its other occurrence in Jer. 31:29 provides no clue to its meaning.

96 So Stalker, *ad loc.*

97 It is uncertain whether the proverb originated in Palestine or among the Babylonian exiles of 597 B.C. "Concerning the land of Israel" might seem to point to a Palestinian origin; but against this are firstly the fact that LXX has a different reading ("among the sons of Israel"), and secondly the fact that "concerning the land of Israel" only fits the context of the proverb's use here if it means "concerning the loss of the land of Israel". This expresses the point of view of the exiles. The fact that the proverb also occurs in Jer. 31:29 is no proof of Palestinian origin, since there it is probably a rather late addition to the book of Jeremiah.

98 The rather surprising מרע , "Why?", with which the question begins, which may express a fundamental objection by the opponent to the new teaching which seems to reject the principle of solidarity, or possibly a demand for a fuller explanation, is not relevant to the present discussion.

99 See *K–B*, p. 104, section 17.

100 In Job 7:13 Job, speaking of his attempts to achieve some degree of comfort, says, "When I say, 'My bed will comfort me, my couch will ease my complaint . . .' ". The Hebrew is ישא בשיחי משכבי , which is usually taken to mean "my couch will share" (i.e. "take some of the burden of") "my complaint . . .". If this is correct this is a third example in the Old Testament of the use of נשא ב in the sense of "share (a burden)", which thus begins to assume the status of an established idiom. But the metaphor in Job is very bold, and its poetical character perhaps gives it less force as an example.

101 Note the corresponding phrase "I will take some of the spirit" (ואצלתי מן-הרוח) in the same verse.

102 See pp. 31-33 above.

103 See pp. 42-45 above.

104 See pp. 46-48 above.

105 See pp. 50-52 above.

106 See pp. 45f. above.

107 See p. 32 above.

108 See pp. 48f. above.

109 See pp. 52-56 above.

110 See pp. 33-42 above.

111 P. 31 above.

112 See pp. 29f. above.

113 On the parallel clause ולפשעים יפגיע see pp. 71-74 below.

114 RSV "He has borne our griefs and carried our sorrows".

115 Or, "brought low by"; see Thomas, pp. 82f.

116 Neither מכאב ,"pain", nor חלי necessarily refers to organic or other naturally caused diseases. The latter is used in 2 Kings 1:2 of injuries caused by a fall. Both words are entirely suitable to describe injuries due to ill treatment. But see p. 93 below.

117 See n. 115 above.

118 P. 30.

119 See pp. 29-31 above.

120 RSV "And the LORD has laid on him the iniquity of us all ".
121 E.g. RSV (see n. 120 above); JB "and Yahweh burdened him with the sins of all of us"; NEB "but the LORD laid on him the guilt of us all".
122 See p. 63 below.
123 So many of the older commentaries and, more recently, Driver and Gray; Hölscher; Fohrer, *Hiob*; Rowley, *Job*; also NEB. Those who retain the traditional text (e.g. Dhorme; Weiser, *Hiob*; Pope) are by no means in agreement about its meaning.
124 See further pp. 71-74 below on Isa. 53:12.
125 See pp. 29ff. above.
126 RSV "But he was wounded for our transgressions".
127 RSV "he was bruised for our iniquities".
128 RSV "stricken for the transgression of my people".
129 The last of these phrases is universally regarded as corrupt. Perhaps the best solution is to emend it to נֶגַע לָמֶוֶת , transferring the final *yodh* of the preceding word עַמִי to become the verbal prefix of ינגע and following LXX in emending למו to לָמֶוֶת . This solution has the added advantage of solving the problem of the difficult "*my* people", which would then become עַם , "the people" — "as a consequence of the people's sin he was smitten to death". But whatever emendation is adopted there can be no doubt that the phrase speaks of the Servant's fate. However, it should be noted in view of the thesis of the second part of this study — that the Servant is not here regarded as having died — that למות does not necessarily have this connotation but may be a way of expressing the superlative (Thomas, "Some Further Remarks", p. 123, followed by G.R. Driver, p. 93).
130 Orlinsky, pp. 57f. In this section of his book Orlinsky gives a number of examples of the way in which these phrases are usually interpreted.
131 Von Rad, " כפלים ".
132 A further possible example of the use of the *beth pretii* in this sense is 1 Sam. 3:13, where Yahweh utters a threat that he will punish Eli and his family in the words שפט אני את-ביתו עד-עולם בעון אשר ידע : "I am about to judge his house for ever for the sin which he knew". In view of the difficulty of the phrase "which he knew" and the anomalous construct state of עון , some commentators have proposed the emendation of בעון to יען ; but there is no support for this in the MSS or Versions. The text may be correct as it stands, or it should perhaps be corrected to בעון בניו , "for the sin of his sons", following LXX. See Stoebe, *ad loc.*
133 On the question whether the *beth* of בחברתו in verse 5b is *beth pretii* see n. 138 below.
134 RSV "upon him was the chastisement that made us whole".
135 RSV "and with his stripes we are healed".
136 Isa. 6:10; 30:26; Jer. 3:22; 30:17; 33:6.
137 See Orlinsky, pp. 56f., 63.
138 Zimmerli, "Vorgeschichte", pp. 238f., regards this ב as *beth pretii*, and seems to imply that this confers a similar meaning on the three occurrences of מן- in verses 5 and 8 (see pp. 61f. above). But ובחברתו נרפא-לנו is a quite different kind of statement from the latter. If ב here means "in exchange for", the whole phrase must be translated by "we were healed in exchange for his wounding", not "he was wounded in exchange for our healing", which would be the form analogous to that of the other phrases. There is no reason to suppose that this is *beth pretii*, which used in a metaphorical sense (which would be the case here) is much less frequent than *beth instrumenti.*
139 RSV "when he makes himself an offering for sin".
140 E.g. love, hate, disgust, joy, delight, satisfaction, desire, longing, hope, indignation,

bitterness, dejection, revenge, boasting, weeping, death, exhaustion. See Westermann, נפש in *THAT II*, cols. 71-96.

141 E.g. in Jer. 3:11 the verb is צדק , "be (show oneself to be) righteous".

142 In Gen. 49:6, an unusual case because נפשי is paralleled by כברי , which is used in a similar way, and because it is vocative and not the subject of the verb, it expresses abhorrence of being associated with wicked men, and is followed by a curse. In Ps. 119:129, 167 the keeping of God's "testimonies" is associated with the feeling of wonder and love. נפשם in Isa. 46:2 is used for a different purpose, to emphasize the identity of the subject: "and they *themselves* go into captivity" (ונפשם בשבי הלכה). In 1 Sam. 20:4 the verb is אמר ; but the meaning – whether emendation to תאוה is accepted or not – seems to be "desire". Jer. 4:19 is probably corrupt.

143 בעבור תברכני נפשי , verses 19, 31. בעבור (למען) תברכך , verses 4, 25; נפשך

144 The emendation of תשים to ישים , following Vulg.'s *Si posuerit pro peccato animam suam*, would make relatively good sense. But the evidence of Vulg. is hardly sufficient to justify an emendation which would all too simply lend itself to a christological interpretation of the whole chapter. Moreover the introduction of an emendation only serves to emphasize the fact that the passage as a whole presents massive textual problems, and thus weakens the value of the phrase as evidence for the role of the Servant.

145 See van Leeuwen, especially pp. 47f.

146 So G.R. Driver, p. 96: "more or less nonsense" (referring to the translation of RSV).

147 As Kaiser appears to do (p. 118).

148 The distinction made by Kutsch (pp. 32f.) between אשם as an atonement sacrifice and as a non-sacrificial action which removes sin (*Sühneleistung*), as in 1 Sam. 6:4, 8, 17, hardly affects the point. As Kutsch recognizes, it still remains, on his interpretation, the giving of the life of the Servant which effects atonement.

149 E.g. those of Duhm, *Jesaia*; Marti; and more recently Sonne, p. 337; Müller.

150 Without word-division the traditional text has החליאמתשיםאשםנפשו .

151 Cf. Orlinsky, p. 61, n. 1: "None of these translations may be used for any theory".

152 RSV "the righteous one, my servant, (shall) make many to be accounted righteous".

153 See note 176 below.

154 For recent views on the root צדק see *inter alia* Eichrodt, *Theology* I, pp. 239-249; von Rad, *Theology* I, pp. 370-418; Fahlgren; Koch, *ṢDQ*; Schmid.

155 "cause to be acquitted (though guilty)" (Muilenburg); "make righteous, bring to righteousness" (Torrey; North, *Second Isaiah*; Thomas); "bring about a state of salvation (for)" (Fohrer, *ad loc.*).

156 See pp. 29f. above.

157 Bonnard.

158 Mowinckel, *He That Cometh*, pp. 198f.; Westermann, *ad loc.*

159 If with some commentators we follow LXX and read "*Thou* shalt not acquit the guilty", Exod. 23:7 falls into the same category as Isa. 5:23; Prov. 17:15.

160 Whether these are to be identified with the Hasidim is not relevant to the present enquiry.

161 So, e.g., Bentzen, *Daniel, ad loc.*; Ginsberg; Porteous; Plöger, *Daniel, ad loc.*; Delcor, *ad loc.*

162 Delcor, Ginsberg.

163 Hence the title of Ginsberg's article: "The Oldest Interpretation of the Suffering Servant".

164 Even if he had done so, this is no proof that his interpretation was correct.

165   Kraus, *Psalmen* on Ps. 112:3, where also צדקה probably has this meaning, and the literature there cited. In Deutero-Isaiah also צדקה/צדק has the meaning of "salvation" in a number of passages, but there it is a gift of God to those who are *un*worthy of it.

166   So Fohrer, *ad loc.*, and Kaiser, p. 124.

167   Kutsch (pp. 36f.) accepts this explanation, but goes further and maintains that the Servant showed this "knowledge" not merely by his teaching but also by his suffering. This is an unwarrantable importation into the text of ideas which are not present there but have been pressed into service in the interests of christological exegesis.

168   See the commentaries. Many interpreters take בדעתו with the preceding ישבע ; others emend to ברעתו , "through his misfortune"; and yet others, following Thomas (pp. 82f.) translate it by "humiliation" or the like. It is evident that בדעתו cannot safely be used in any argument about the meaning of יצדיק .

169   Mowinckel, *He That Cometh*, pp. 198f.

170   Described in *G–K* 53d as "inwardly transitive" or "intensive".

171   See *G–K* 53d-f.

172   E.g. Gen. 4:7; Ps. 36:4 (EVV 3); Isa. 1:17; Jer. 4:22; 13:23. If this kind of meaning may legitimately be given to יצדיק here, it is probably best to translate the phrase by "My Servant acted righteously" rather than by "My Servant showed himself to be righteous", though this distinction is not clear in biblical Hebrew, as may be seen from the passages quoted above. The imperfect is, however, probably to be taken as referring to the past rather than to the future.

173   See *G–K* 117q.

174   In both function and form it therefore resembles the infinitive absolute.

175   צָנֵפָה יצנפך צָנוֹף , Isa. 22:18; אֲסֹפָה וְאַספו , Isa. 24:22. In Isa. 22:18, where the infinitive absolute is used in addition, the word צנפה is *hapax legomenon*, but in view of the context must mean either something wound together like a ball of wool, or the state of being so wound together: "He will surely wind you tightly together as a ball" (or, "in a winding together"), "and throw you . . .". The function of צנפה is to emphasize the completeness of the action or of the state achieved by the action. Similarly in Isa. 24:22 אספה is *hapax legomenon*, and the tendency of the older commentators was to emend the text. But once again the noun emphasizes the completeness of the action or state: "And you shall be gathered together (in) a gathering", that is, "herded together, close packed" (so NEB).

176   A note on the function of ל in לרבים is perhaps necessary here. If יצדיק means "acted righteously", ל indicates the indirect object and לרבים means "for the many" or "in relation to the many", which makes adequate sense. If יצדיק means "brought to a state of salvation", ל here indicates the direct object. This usage in biblical Hebrew is almost entirely post-exilic, though its occurrence in the sixth century B.C. cannot be ruled out as impossible. לרבים therefore perhaps makes the former interpretation of יצדיק slightly more probable than the latter, but cannot be said to be decisive.

177   RSV "and made intercession for the transgressors".

178   Westermann, *ad loc.* So also North, *Second Isaiah* and Bonnard, *ad loc.* Other commentaries imply a similar view without stating it specifically.

179   See p. 60 and note 123 above.

180   On Jer. 15:11 see below, n. 184.

181   See especially de Vaux, "Les combats singuliers" on such combats and on 1 Sam. 17 in particular.

182   The meaning of הַבֵּנַיִם אִישׁ in 1 Sam. 17:4, 23 is uncertain. In view of its use in the *War Scroll* from Qumran (1QM) thirteen times it is now generally believed that the passage is

not corrupt but that this is a genuine military term. De Vaux (*art. cit.*) suggests that it may mean "champion d'un combat singulier". The word גבור is also used of Goliath in the sense of "champion" in verse 51.

183 Note also the similarities in the description of armour in 1 Sam. 17:5-7 and Isa. 59:16. The latter seems to be following an established tradition of the narration of such combats.

184 If הפגעתי בך in Jer. 15:11 is correct, and if these words are spoken by Jeremiah to Yahweh (this would involve the emendation of אמר at the beginning of this verse to אמן , following LXX and Vulg.), this would be an example of such use, but unfortunately the whole passage is corrupt, and no agreed solution of its problems has been found.

185 Job 21:15; Jer. 7:16; 27:18. In Gen. 23:8; Ruth 1:16 the Qal is used of entreaty by one human being to another. In all these cases the person to whom the entreaty is made is indicated by the preposition ב . In Gen. 23:8 the person on whose behalf the entreaty is made is indicated by ל , as in Isa. 53:12.

186 Especially Reventlow, "Prophetamt und Mittleramt"; *Liturgie und prophetisches Ich bei Jeremia.* For a contrary view see Hertzberg.

187 E.g. Amos 7:2, 5; Jer. 18:20; Ezek. 9:8; 11:13. Jeremiah was however expressly forbidden by God to intercede for Israel: Jer. 7:16; 14:11.

188 Von Waldow, *Anlass und Hintergrund.* Von Waldow's work owed much to the earlier work of Begrich ("Das priesterliche Heilsorakel" and *Studien zu Deuterojesaja,* pp. 6-18). See also Westermann, "Sprache und Struktur", pp. 117-124. The most recent study of this subject, Schoors, *I am God Your Saviour,* does not add much to the discussion of this aspect of the role of the prophet.

189 The tense sequence (perf. נשא followed by imperf. יפגיע) may be significant here, since if יפגיע is a past frequentative the intercession is separated in time from the bearing of the punishment. Unfortunately the significance of tense sequences in Hebrew poetry is still not fully understood. On the question in general see, *inter alia*, G.R. Driver, *Verbal System.* For a survey of recent work on this subject see Mettinger. On the problems of Deutero-Isaiah in particular see Saydon. Saydon discusses ולפשעים יפגיע (p. 293) and sees here a change of temporal reference from the preceding verb נשא , although he regards יפגיע as indicating a "present-future" time. On p. 296 he discusses ולא יפתח פיו in verse 7a, regarding the imperf. יפתח , which follows the perf. נגש , as "a vivid representation of a past action". But the time-sequence in both cases may be the same: ולא יפתח-פיו , "at no time (during his interrogation) did he open his mouth"; ולפשעים יפגיע , "he had always interceded for the sinners".

190 Exod. 32:11-14, 31-32; Num. 14:13-19; 21:7; Ps. 99:6; 106:23; Jer. 15:1.

191 1 Sam. 7:8f.; Ps. 99:6; Jer. 15:1.

192 This is not to deny that Moses endured suffering as a result of his role as intercessor; but no vicarious quality is attached to this suffering. It is perhaps significant that when Moses offered his own life to God (though not vicariously, but in solidarity with the people) the offer was rejected (Exod. 32:32f.). God, on the other hand, was disposed on one occasion to kill the people and make a new start with him (Exod. 32:10; Num. 14:12). There is no suggestion of vicarious suffering in the Moses narratives.

193 For a fuller discussion of the structure of the poem see Part III below.

194 For this interpretation see Parts II and III below.

195 Verse 10ab must be left out of the discussion in view of its great textual uncertainty: see pp. 63-66 above.

196 See Part III below.

197 Hooker, *Jesus and the Servant.* It should be noted that the author herself is one of the few scholars who hold, on grounds similar to those advanced in the present study, that

vicarious suffering must be excluded from the interpretation of Isa. 53, although she does not accept the view that the Servant was the prophet Deutero-Isaiah. This opinion, however, is only peripheral to her main theme, which is that the chapter was not so interpreted in the New Testament. Her views on the lateness of the appearance of a vicarious interpretation of the role of the Servant are endorsed by the Jewish scholar, H.M. Orlinsky (*op. cit.*).

198   As evidence on this point she cites Büchler, *Studies in Sin and Atonement.*

199   *Op. cit.*, p. 158.

200   *Op. cit.*, p. 154.

201   *Op. cit.*, p. 155.

202   For a survey of recent work by New Testament scholars on this subject see Hooker, pp. 1-20 and also the comments of Orlinsky, pp. 51-63. The remarks of R.J. Loewe on both Christian and Jewish interpretation in the Prolegomena to the second edition of Driver and Neubauer, vol. 2, pp. 1-38 are also relevant.

Notes to Part II

1 This is true even of those interpretations which regard the Servant as a wholly future figure: the events described in these verses are in the past when seen from the point of view which has been adopted by the author, in comparison with the events referred to in verses 10b - 12a.

2 The traditional text of verse 10a(וַיהוה ... נפשׁו) appears to speak of the Servant's sufferings and to affirm that it was Yahweh's will that he should undergo them (e.g. RSV, "Yet it was the will of the LORD to bruise him; he has put him to grief"); but some scholars have emended, repointed or re-interpreted the text in such a way as to give it a quite different sense. Thus Elliger, *Deuterojesaja in seinem Verhältnis zu Tritojesaja*, p. 7, suggested that דַּכְּאוֹ , "to crush him", should be repointed דַּכָּאוֹ , "his crushed one", so altering the meaning of וַיהוה חפץ דכאו to "But Yahweh was pleased with his crushed one". Elliger later ("Jes 53₁₀") withdrew this suggestion; but it was accepted by Begrich (*Studien*, p. 58), who also proposed the emendation of החלי to הֶחֱלִים , "he healed (him)". (In view of the discussion below on the question whether these verses refer to a resurrection of the Servant from the dead it may be noted here that the only other occurrence of חלם in the Hiphil (Isa. 38:16, Hezekiah's prayer for recovery from sickness) does not suggest that it could be used to denote resurrection from death.) G.R. Driver (p. 96) took the verb דכא here as an Aramaizing form equivalent to זכה , "was pure, justified", rendering the phrase by "But the Lord was pleased to give him the victory" (p. 104). He also accepted Begrich's proposal with regard to החלי . There is still no agreement among scholars about the rendering of this line.

3 Although the problem of the meaning of tenses in Hebrew poetry is a difficult one (see Part I, n. 189 above) the complete consistency of the use of the imperfect in verses 10b-12a makes it certain that these should be interpreted as referring to the present or future.

4 RSV "he shall see his offspring, he shall prolong his days".

5 It occurs frequently in Deuteronomy (Deut. 4:26, 40; 5:33 [30] ; 6:2; 11:9; 17:20; 22:7; 30:18; 32:47), but also elsewhere: Prov. 28:16; Eccles. 8:13. In Deut. 25:15 ימים is the subject: למען יאריכו ימיך , "that your days may be long". In 1 Kings 3:14 Yahweh is the subject: והארכתי את-ימיך , "and I will lengthen your life". In Jos. 24: 31; Judg. 2:7 אשר האריכו ימים אחרי means "who survived", i.e. "lived longer than . . .".

6 "Job . . . saw his sons, and his sons' sons, four generations". The apparent discrepancy is explained by the commentators in various ways: it is supposed that the four generations include Job's earlier family which had died early (so Fohrer, *Hiob, ad loc.*), or that a reference to Job's sons' sons' sons has been accidentally omitted from the text (so Duhm, *Hiob, ad loc.*), or that "four generations" is itself the completion of the list: "up to the fourth generation" (so Terrien, *ad loc.*).

7 See also Ps. 128:6; Prov. 13:22; 17:6.

8 E.g. Fohrer and Schoors, and, less definitely, North and G.R. Driver.

9 The reasons offered against it by Kutsch (p. 34) are not convincing.

10 E.g. Skinner, *ad loc.*; Lindblom, p. 45, Fohrer, *ad loc.*

11 This view can be held even by Fohrer, for whom the Servant is a historical person, the prophet Deutero-Isaiah himself, as well as by Lindblom, for whom he is "a fictitious person,

who . . . is conjured up in the prophet's imagination" (p. 46). Both of these writers proceed from a conviction that the idea of the resurrection of individuals from the dead could not have been present in the mind of an author living as early as the sixth century B.C. See also Fohrer, *History*, pp. 387-389 on this question.

12 So North, and also G.R. Driver, p. 105. Lindblom (p. 45, n. 66) makes a comparison with the figure of Rachel weeping over her children (Jer. 31:15); but, however Rachel is to be interpreted in that passage (as a spirit or as a vivid personification), she was the *physical* ancestress of her "children".

13 Similarly in Ps. 91:16 a divine oracle promises long life (ארך ימים) to the man who puts his trust in God. It may be significant that the verbs שבע and ראה , which occur in Isa. 53:11a, are also used in this verse: "With long life will I satisfy him (ארך ימים אשביעהו), and I will show him my salvation (ואראהו בישועתי)". See pp. 123-126 below.

14 RSV "the will of the LORD shall prosper in his hand".

15 E.g. of prophets, 2 Kings 9:36; 10:10; 14:25; 17:13, 23; 21:10; 24:2; of Moses, Lev. 10:11; Num. 4:37, 45; 9:23; 10:13; Jos. 14:2; 20:2; 21:2, 8; of Samuel, 1 Sam. 28:17.

16 RSV "he shall see the fruit of the travail of his soul".

17 Not by Thomas: see n. 23 below.

18 It is not difficult to see how אור , immediately following יראה , could have been accidentally omitted by haplography.

19 Again Thomas does not agree. See n. 23 below.

20 Pp. 97f.

21 Thomas, pp. 85f. The views of Driver and Thomas are reflected in NEB and *BHS* respectively.

22 The view that the latter verb is intended here was first put forward by C.-F. Houbigant, *Biblia Hebraica cum Notis Criticis et Versione Latina*, 1753, p. 150; but whereas he – and subsequent interpreters – proposed emendation of יראה to ירוה , Driver's and Thomas' theory of a by-form ראה would make emendation unnecessary.

23 For the arguments in favour of this view see the article cited. Thomas' translation of the whole phrase נפשו יראה מעמל is "(When) he shall have drunk deep of his anguish". Thomas might have cited in defence of his rejection of the addition of אור the incongruity of the combination of the metaphors "drink deep" and "light", a point which Driver (p. 97) brushes aside.

24 Job 3:16, 20; 33:28; Ps. 49:20 (EVV 19); 56:14 (EVV 13).

25 So in Job 22:28; 30:26; Ps. 27:1; 97:11; 112:4; Isa. 9:1 (EVV 2); 60:1; Lam. 3:2; Amos 5:18; Mic. 7:8. A similar meaning can be seen in the phrase אור פנים , meaning "favour": Job 29:24; Ps. 4:7 (EVV 6); 44:4 (EVV 3); 89:16 (EVV 15); Prov. 16:15. In some passages the meaning of אור is uncertain or controversial: אור גוים in Isa. 42:6; 49:6; אור עמים in Isa. 51:4; Isa. 2:5 (perhaps "law"); Ps. 36:10 (EVV 9), where "in thy light" perhaps means "in thy revelation".

26 Or, in Job 33:28, ראה באור .

27 In Gen. 1:4 God "saw" or inspected the light which he had created. In Job 31:26; 37:21 "see (the) light" means literally to look at the light of the sun.

28 The textual problem, on which see the commentaries, does not affect the question of the meaning of ראה באור here.

29 RSV ". . . and be satisfied; by his knowledge . . .".

30 E.g. Fohrer, Westermann, *ad loc.*

31 E.g. RSV, JB, Kutsch, Schoors, *ad loc.*

32 See pp. 66-71 above.

33 Some liberties have been taken with the wording of these translations to make comparison easier.

34 See Thomas, pp. 82f.

35 RSV "Therefore I will divide him a portion with the great, and he shall divide the spoil with the strong".

36 The normal meaning of שלל is "booty, plunder" in the literal sense. Although it is occasionally used in a derived or figurative sense (in Prov. 1:13 of stolen goods; in Isa. 10:2 of the weaker members of society as the "prey" of their rapacious oppressors; in Jer. 21:9; 38:2; 39:18; 45:5 of a person's life as his own "prey" or "booty" in the sense that he escapes with it), there is only one passage (Prov. 31:11) where the sense of something snatched away by force is wholly absent, and its use there appears so incongruous that some scholars have suggested that it cannot be the same word at all: see the survey of the discussion in McKane, *ad loc.* In Prov. 16:19 the meaning of שלל חֲלֹק is not certain, but violence is probably implied.

37 So, e.g., in the Piel, Jos. 13:7; 18:10; 19:51; 2 Sam. 6:19; 1 Kings 18:6; Isa. 34:17; Mic. 2:4; Ps. 22:19 (EVV 18); in the Qal, Deut. 4:19; 29:25 (EVV 26); Jos. 18:2; Job 39:17.

38 Piel, Gen. 49:27; Exod. 15:9; Judg. 5:30; Ps. 68:13 (EVV 12); Prov. 16:19 (all with שלל as object); Qal, Jos. 22:8 (with שלל as object); Prov. 17:2 (with נחלה as object).

39 G.R. Driver (p. 102) affirmed that the Qal and Piel of חלק are properly quite distinct in meaning, the Qal having only the sense of "receive a share" and the Piel only that of "allot as a share". This distinction, he maintained, has been obscured by the Massoretic pointing; consequently all the occurrences in MT of the Piel in the sense of "receive a share", including יְחַלֵק in Isa. 53:12, should be repointed as Qal. The point will not be discussed here; but the acceptance of Driver's theory would not remove the ambiguity inherent in יחלק in Isa. 53:12. The ambiguity of the meaning of the Piel which constituted a problem for earlier commentators would only have been turned by Driver into a different but comparable ambiguity: that of a choice between two ways of pointing an originally unpointed text.

40 Compare also the use of עם in Jos. 22:8: חִלְקוּ שְלַל-אֹיְבֵיכֶם עִם-אֲחֵיכֶם.

41 On the general question of death and resurrection in the Old Testament see, among modern works, Eichrodt, *Theology II*, pp. 495-529; Fohrer, *History*, pp. 214-222, 387-390; van Imschoot, vol. II, pp. 42-82; Martin-Achard; von Rad, *Theology I*, pp. 405-418; Ringgren, *Israelite Religion*, pp. 239-247, 322f.; Rowley, *The Faith of Israel*, pp. 150-176; Vriezen, pp. 204, 230. While it is generally recognised that an explicit doctrine of the resurrection of individuals to eternal life is found only in the very latest of the Old Testament books – in Dan. 12:2 and possibly in Isa. 26:19 – there is considerable divergence of opinion concerning the extent to which earlier texts reflect a growing movement towards such a belief. It should be noted that the relevance of the question whether a belief in the resurrection of the individual is conceivable in the sixth century B.C. is not confined to the view, which is adopted in the present study, that the Servant was an historical person contemporary with the author of Isa. 53. Even if the Servant is a past or future figure, and even if he is a personification of a community, or a purely poetical figure, the question still remains whether the concept of individual resurrection was present in the author's mind.

42 Pp. 79-85 above.

43 On the meaning of לָמַת in verse 8 see pp. 99f. below.

44 The view of Dahood (*Psalms III*, pp. XLI-LII) that the Psalms contain numerous hitherto unnoticed or ignored references to immortality and resurrection has still to be fully assessed, but has so far met with little acceptance. For a critique of his view see Vawter.

45 E.g. 2 Kings 6:1-7, in which Elisha makes an axe head to float in water.

46   Zimmerli, *Ezechiel, ad loc.* So also Fohrer, *Ezechiel, ad loc.*

47   So, e.g. – though with caution – Martin-Achard, p. 83. This work should be consulted for a survey of the history of the interpretation of the passage.

48   It was suggested by Riesenfeld that the passage was influenced by the supposed death and resurrection ritual of the Babylonian New Year Festival.

49   E.g. Weiser, *Hosea, ad loc.*; Martin-Achard, pp. 64-73. For Martin-Achard it is a belief adopted by some Israelites from Canaanite agricultural cults, which Hosea repudiates.

50   See the surveys of these views in Wolff, *Hosea, ad loc.* and in Martin-Achard.

51   See von Soden; Lambert, "Myth and Ritual".

52   Wolff, *Hosea*; Rudolph, *Hosea, ad loc.*

53   See Stamm, and also Wolff, *Hosea* and Rudolph, *Hosea, ad loc.*, where detailed evidence on the above linguistic points is given, and where the similarity of the passage to a number of psalms of lamentation is pointed out.

54   Hosea 13:14 also has been interpreted by some commentators (e.g. Weiser, *Hosea, ad loc.*; Martin-Achard, pp. 73-78) as to some degree foreshadowing a doctrine of individual resurrection, even though the theme of Yahweh's power over Sheol and death is applied here not to individuals but, metaphorically, to the nation as a whole. The uncertainty whether the first half of the verse is to be taken as a statement in the affirmative or as a question (implying a negative) does not affect this question. The verse undoubtedly affirms the power of Yahweh over death, but there is no reason to suppose that this affirmation was derived from a belief in individual resurrection, however embryonic.

55   E.g. Ps. 6:6 (EVV 5); 88:5f. (EVV 4f.); 115:17; Isa. 38:18.

56   Especially Ps. 9:14f. (EVV 13f.); 18:5-7, 17 (EVV 4-6, 16); 30:4 (EVV 3); 49:16 (EVV 15); 56:14 (EVV 13); 71:20; 86:13; 103:4; Jonah 2:3, 7 (EVV 2, 6).

57   Especially Barth, *Errettung*.

58   Dhorme, *ad loc.*; Martin-Achard, pp. 133-144; Fohrer, *Hiob, ad loc.*

59   Driver and Gray; Rowley, *Job, ad loc.*

60   Hölscher, *ad loc.*

61   Hölscher; Weiser, *Hiob, ad loc.*

62   7:9f.; 10:21f.; 14:10; 16:22.

63   Dahood, "Lexicography IX", p. 346, sees here an assertion of Yahweh's victory over Sheol.

64   Weiser, *Psalmen, ad loc.*; Martin-Achard, pp. 119-123.

65   Barth, *Errettung*, p. 154.

66   Kraus, *Psalmen, ad loc.*

67   *Op. cit.*, pp. 158ff.

68   Stamm, *Erlösen*, p. 16; von Rad, *Theology I*, p. 406; Kraus, *Psalmen, ad loc.*

69   See below on its occurrence in Ps. 73:24.

70   See Kraus, *Psalmen, ad loc.*; Barth, *Errettung*, pp. 163f.

71   E.g. Kraus, *Psalmen, ad loc.*; Martin-Achard, p. 132.

72   It should also be noted that the text of Ps. 73:24b is uncertain. The above translation "to glory" can only be obtained with difficulty without emendation. A number of emendations have been proposed which fundamentally alter the sense of the line. The translation of LXX, "thou hast taken me to thyself with glory", seems to exclude an interpretation in terms of a life after death.

73   Especially verse 2 and its possible dependence on fertility concepts expressed in such texts as the Tammuz liturgies.

74   But see the reference to Duhm's theory about these verses on p. 94 below.

75   This was pointed out by Begrich, pp. 63ff. and by more recent writers, especially

Kaiser, pp. 89ff. and Kutsch, pp. 21ff. On the form and content of the individual psalms of lamentation and thanksgiving see Gunkel, *Einleitung*, pp. 172-292 and the discussion in Part III below.

76   RSV "For he grew up before him like a young plant, and like a root out of dry ground".

77   RSV "he had no form or comeliness".

78   RSV "and his form (was marred) beyond that of the sons of men". See also p. 94 below.

79   RSV "he was despised".

80   Compare also בזה-נפש in Isa. 49:7.

81   RSV "rejected by men".

82   RSV "a man of sorrows, and acquainted with grief".

83   RSV "and as one from whom men hide their faces".

84   By Heller.

85   RSV "his appearance was so marred, beyond human semblance, and his form beyond that of the sons of men".

86   See *inter alia* Mowinckel, *The Psalms in Israel's Worship*, vol. 2, pp. 15-25.

87   Pss. 18; 30; 116; 118. Cf. also Ps. 22.

88   Duhm, *ad loc.*

89   Pp. 29-31, 58ff. above.

90   It should be noted that even if the idea of vicarious suffering were present here, this would not necessarily imply that this suffering had fatal consequences.

91   See pp. 61-74 above.

92   החלי in verse 10a is here left out of consideration because of the great uncertainty of the text and the opinion of a large number of commentators that to translate it by "he made him ill/injured him" would be unjustified. It may be remarked that if such a translation were correct it would greatly strengthen the argument that the Servant in this chapter is regarded as being still alive, since חלה always denotes a state of affairs which stops short of death, and to speak merely of impaired health at this climactic point in the poem would make the thought of the Servant's having surrendered his life as a sin-offering quite impossible.

93   On נגע למו in verse 8b see Part I, n. 129.

94   Deut. 25:2, 3; Jer. 20:2; 37:15.

95   Though not necessarily so, in view of the frequent attribution in the Old Testament of human actions to Yahweh himself: e.g. in 2 Kings 10:32 Hazael's aggression against Israel is referred to in the words "In those days *Yahweh* began to cut off (parts of) Israel".

96   Thomas, "Some Unusual Ways of Expressing the Superlative". Clines, p. 17, argues that this idiom cannot be present here, "since it would be pointless for the 'we' to say that they 'considered' the servant to be 'terribly smitten' when there was no question but that he was". But this is to misunderstand the point of the verse. The error which the speakers here confess is not one of fact — whether the Servant was beaten or not — but one of judgement: they had previously categorized him (חשבנהו) merely as a man who had undergone terrible sufferings (normally regarded as a divine punishment for sin). Now they recognize that he was not merely a notable sufferer: there were reasons for his sufferings which were quite different from those which they had imagined. A further argument in favour of Thomas' theory is the fact that אלהים is attached to only one of the three passive participles applied here to the Servant. If אלהים means "God" here the reader is required to suppose that the author intended the reference to God as the author of the Servant's sufferings to apply also to the participles which precede and follow מכה אלהים . But if

if this is the case it is difficult to understand why אלהים should have been attached to the second item in the series. It would have been more logical to attach it to the first.

97 Qal, Ps. 77:11 (EVV 10); 109:22; Piel, Ezek. 28:9; Pual, Ezek. 32:26; Poel, Isa. 51:9; Job 26:13; Poal, Isa. 53:5. But in both Ps. 77:11 and Ps. 109:22 the text is uncertain, and these two occurrences should probably be discounted. See Kraus, *Psalmen, ad loc.*

98 Ps. 77:11; 109:22. But see n. 97 above.

99 See the end of this section.

100 Driver (pp. 93f.) rightly dismisses the suggestion of Skinner that מחלל and מדכא here refer to "the fatal ravages of leprosy".

101 On the text see n.2 above.

102 On the phrase מוסר שלומנו עליו see pp. 62f. above.

103 E.g. Kaiser.

104 It is interesting to observe that these verses are quite different in this respect from the so-called "third Servant Song" (50:4-9), where in verse 6 there seems at first sight to be a circumstantial account by the Servant himself of his ill treatment by his captors. But of the four words in this verse which describe his treatment (מכים , "smiters", מרטים , "those who plucked out [hair or beard]" [1Q Is[a] has מטלים , "those who beat with rods"] , כלמות , "humiliations", רק , "spitting"), two occur relatively frequently – bearing in mind the total number of their occurrences in the Old Testament – in lamentations: כלמה (Ps. 44:16 [EVV 15]; 69:8, 20 [EVV 7, 19]) and רק (Job 30:10: this word occurs in only one other passage, Job 7:19). Moreover the phrase יתן למכהו לחי (Lam. 3:30), used of the humiliated person who is faithful to Yahweh, so closely resembles the first half of this verse (גוי נתחי למכים ולחיי למרטים) that its value as a precise account of actual events becomes doubtful, and the character of the poem as a "song of confidence" using traditional "lamentation" language clearer. This is not to say, of course, that an actual experience does not lie behind 50:4-9. But the language of 50:6 is clearly of a different order from that of 53:4-7.

105 On נגע למו see Part I, n. 129 above.

106 In almost all these cases there are textual difficulties, but there can be little doubt that the original text in each case contained either the verb חלל or the adjective חָלָל , "pierced", usually "killed".

107 G.R. Driver, pp. 93f.

108 LXX and Vulg. have "wounded"; Aq. and Targ. "profaned" (from a different root חלל); Saadia "sickened".

109 Kaiser (p. 104) also takes the view that מדכא does not refer to the actual physical death of the Servant, but his view that the word belongs to the "bildliche Gebrauch" of the lamentations cannot be accepted.

110 Cf. חלה , a cake (with a central hole); חלון , a pierced window; חליל , a flute; מחלה , hole, cave.

111 This appears also to be the view of Thomas, p. 80, who translates מחלל by "grievously injured".

112 RSV "like a lamb that is led to the slaughter, and like a sheep that before its shearers is dumb".

113 See G.R. Driver, pp. 94, 104.

114 So Torrey and. among more recent commentators, Westermann and Fohrer, *ad loc.*

115 So Dahood, "Phoenician Elements", p. 68, followed by Clines, p. 17.

116 Syntactically the fact that נאלמה is followed by "and" (ולא ...) would constitute a problem, but the majority of commentators regard the three last words of the verse (ולא יפתח פיו) as a dittograph of the identical phrase earlier in the verse. If this view

is correct it also disposes of any possible metrical problem. The use of the perfect tense here (assuming that the accentuation of נאלמה is correct) is not unusual: see Saydon, p. 292, on the use of the *qatal* form in Deutero-Isaiah. The fact that one Version (Pesh.) has a masculine verb here would carry weight only if there were other reasons for mistrusting MT.

117 In traditional Christian circles, where the whole poem was interpreted christologically, the phrase was so understood, and so contributed to liturgical formulations and to sacrificial theories of the Atonement in which the phrase "the Lamb of God" was a key phrase. Modern commentators do not generally claim it as independent evidence for the death of the Servant, but it is not infrequently used – if only implicitly – as corroborative evidence. See, e.g., Kaiser, pp. 110f., where – though for him the Servant is Israel – the word "sacrifice" (*Opfer*) is used several times in the discussion of this verse, which in fact says nothing about sacrifice at all.

118 In Ps. 38:14 (EVV 13), in an individual lamentation, the sufferer claims that he behaved like a dumb or deaf man: "But I was like a deaf man who does not hear (see *BHS*, n. *ad loc.*), and like a dumb man who does not open his mouth (לא יפחח-פיו)" in the face of the plots made against him, because he was confident that God would come to his aid. Here the motif of the sufferer's silence is used in yet another way. Clearly the motif is a feature of individual lamentations; this does not mean, however, that it cannot have a specific application to the case of a particular person: it certainly does so in Jer. 11:19.

119 RSV "By oppression and judgment he was taken away".

120 See *G–K* 119w.

121 Gen. 2:23; 3:19, 23; 2 Kings 2:10; Isa. 49:24, 25; Ezek. 15:3; Job 28:2.

122 So, e.g. Duhm, *ad loc.* (" entrückt"). See also pp. 86f. above.

123 On Ps. 49:16 (EVV 15); 73:24 see pp. 90f. above.

124 By Volz, *ad loc.* and also by Kaiser, p. 112.

125 49:24 = 49:25 (spoil taken from a tyrant). This passive sense corresponds to the sense of the active Qal.

126 If עצר means "imprisonment" as suggested above, he was presumably led *back* to prison, but now as a convicted man. If, however, as some believe, עצר means "oppression", he would have been led off to prison after some earlier ill treatment.

127 RSV "that he was cut off out of the land of the living".

128 Ps. 52:7 (EVV 5); 116:9; Isa. 38:11; Jer. 11:19.

129 Ezek. 31:14, 16, 18; 32:18, 24.

130 Ps. 52:7; Jer. 11:19. The text of Ezek. 26:20 is uncertain.

131 נחנו חתיחם בארץ חיים , with slight variations.

132 The plural phrase, which occurs only here, would seem to be the *lectio difficilior*, altered by the Versions to conform with the more frequent singular phrase.

133 G.R. Driver, p. 104.

134 See Barth, *Errettung*, pp. 103f. on this point.

135 Thirteen times if, as is probable, נגזרתי is to be read in Ps. 31:23 (EVV 22).

136 1 Kings 3:25, 26; 2 Kings 6:4.

137 On this see pp. 103f. below.

138 Soggin, "Tod und Auferstehung".

139 E.g. Exod. 12:15, 19; 30:33, 38; 31:14; Lev. 7:20, 21; 17:4, 9, 14; 18:29; 19:8.

140 Soggin also remarks (p. 351) that Jewish tradition in general has not interpreted this verse as referring to the Servant's death. That this is to a large extent the case may be verified conveniently by a study of the texts collected in Driver and Neubauer.

141 G.R. Driver, p. 95. If this is correct, its meaning would then be close to that of חדל אישים in verse 3, if that verse refers to a state of isolation imposed upon the Servant by

others. See p. 93 above.

142 *Art. cit.*, p. 95.

143 *Art. cit.*, pp. 104f.

144 It may be relevant to note that the psalmist of Ps. 142 who in verse 6 (EVV 5) addresses Yahweh as his "portion in the land of the living" in the next verse (8 [EVV 7]) refers – probably metaphorically – to his present state, from which he seeks deliverance, not as death or nearness to death but as "prison" (מסגר), promising to offer praises to God if he will release him.

145 This emendation of the meaningless בְמֹחָיו , derived from the reading of 1Q Is^a, was proposed by Albright (pp. 244ff.) and has now been almost universally accepted.

146 It is now generally accepted that עשיר here does not mean "rich". Whether it means "rabble" (Guillaume, p. 10; cf. G.R. Driver, p. 95), or whether it should be emended, e.g. to עשי רע , "doers of evil" (so, e.g., Morgenstern, p. 317) or to שעירים , "demons" (see Thomas, p. 85) or in some other way is not relevant to the present discussion. The fact that the word is parallel with רשעים , probably "criminals", is sufficient to indicate the range of meaning which it is likely to have.

147 RSV "And they made his grave with the wicked and with a rich man in his death". In the final phrase RSV follows MT (see n. 145 above).

148 The identity of the onlookers is immaterial here. Torrey identified the Servant with Israel.

149 Torrey, pp. 420f.

150 Orlinsky, p. 62; G.R. Driver, p. 95; Kaiser, p. 104; Soggin, p. 353.

151 Ps. 18:5f. (EVV 4f.); 30:4 (EVV 3); 40:3 (EVV 2); 88:5 (EVV 4); Jonah 2:3 (EVV 2).

152 For a later example of this see Tobit 8:9f.

153 Unless this is the meaning of קברים לי in Job 17:1, sometimes translated by "the grave is waiting for me" (so, e.g., NEB).

154 Translation by Lambert in *Babylonian Wisdom Literature*, p. 46.

155 It should be noted, as Torrey pointed out in the passage cited above, that in Isa. 53:9 it is not stated that the grave has been dug, but only that its place has been chosen.

156 Schaeffer, p. 267, lines 9' - 10'. The translation of the first word *pak-rat* ("was assembled") is based on a suggestion by W. von Soden in a review in *Ugaritforschungen* I, 1969, pp. 189-195. I owe this information to a private communication from Professor W.G. Lambert.

157 RSV "he poured out his soul to death, and was numbered with the transgressors".

158 Part I, n. 129 above.

159 This was already suggested, and with reference to this verse, by Torrey (p. 423), followed by Thomas ("Unusual Ways of Expressing the Superlative", p. 220; "Isaiah LIII", pp. 80, 86). It was endorsed by G.R. Driver, pp. 102f.

160 See note 159 above. Thus Torrey renders it by "utterly, to the very last degree" and Thomas by "to the uttermost".

161 Judg. 16:16; 1 Sam. 4:20; 2 Kings 20:1; Ps. 18:5f. (EVV 4f.); Jonah 4:9. The fact that the idiom is found in other Semitic languages does not prove that it existed in biblical Hebrew, nor does the example (Mark 14:34 / Matt. 26:38) from New Testament Greek.

162 Judg. 16:16; Jonah 4:9.

163 So AV, RV, RSV. JB's "surrendering himself to death" is ambiguous, but probably also implies actual death (BJ has "il s'est livré lui-même à la mort"). Only NEB, "he exposed himself to death", while also perhaps somewhat ambiguous, leans rather in the other direction: one may face death and yet survive.

164 Niphal: Isa. 32:15; Piel: Gen. 24:20; 2 Chron. 24:11; Ps. 137:7; 141:8; Isa. 3:17;

22:6; Hab. 3:13; Zeph. 2:14; Hiphil: Lev. 20:18, 19; Isa. 53:12; Hithpael: Ps. 37:35; Lam. 4:21.

165 Ps. 37:35; Isa. 22:6; Hab. 3:13; Zeph. 2:14.

166 This may also be the meaning of the reference to Nineveh in the textually uncertain Zeph. 2:14.

167 RSV "leave me not defenceless!"; JB "do not leave me exposed!"; NEB "leave me not unprotected".

168 G.R. Driver, p. 102.

169 *Art. cit.*, p. 102.

170 Pp. 85-92 above.

Notes to Part III

1 The chief reason for supposing that the poem begins in 53:1 and that 52:13-15 (apart from 52:14b, on which see the Introduction, n. 1 above) are a separate composition is that, as will be demonstrated below, chapter 53 by itself has a clear structure which leaves no place for 52:13-15. The usual view that 52:13 – 53:12 form a unit consisting of a central section comprising a human utterance framed by two speeches or oracles of Yahweh or inserted into a speech by Yahweh (sometimes designated by the term "prophetic liturgy" [see notes 10 and 11 below]) involves the acceptance of the poem as having a form without parallel in the Old Testament. This is not the case if 52:13-15 are excluded from it, as will be demonstrated below.

2 See pp. 93f. above.

3 The question where in this section Yahweh begins to speak has been exhaustively discussed by the interpreters, whose views it would be tedious to repeat here. (On the difficulties of verses 10a, 11b see pp. 63-71 above.) Yahweh is referred to in the third person in verse 10a (חפץ ויהוה) and in verse 10b (יהוה חפץ). On the other hand "My Servant" (עבדי) in verse 11b and "I will distribute" (אחלק) in verse 12a must have Yahweh as their reference, indicating that he has begun to speak. It will be suggested below that the divine speech begins in verse 11b, confirming with an oracle the human speakers' confident expectations expressed in verses 10-11a – based on the knowledge which they already possess (verse 1) of Yahweh's rescue of his Servant – that his future life will be long, happy and contented.

4 Studien, pp. 56-60, 145-151.

5 See pp. 128-134 below.

6 Begrich's words are: "Wie soll er denn anders von sich reden als in dritter Person, wenn er sich mit der Wirkung seines Todes und seiner Auferstehung auf die auseinandersetzen will, die sich von seinem direkten Wort nicht erreichen lassen?"(p. 145). It is not easy to see why the use of the third person should be more effective for this purpose than a direct prophecy spoken by the Servant about himself in the first person. What seems to be faulty in Begrich's exposition is that his own understanding of the situation in which the poem was spoken is insufficiently precise.

7 Kaiser, p. 88.

8 Pp. 113-128 below.

9 Westermann (p. 257) also sees traces of the individual psalm of thanksgiving (or "declarative psalm of praise") in 53:1-9, but concludes that the unusual features present show that this "does no more than form the background" of the composition.

10 Elliger, Deuterojesaja in seinem Verhältnis zu Tritojesaja, p. 19; Bentzen, King and Messiah, pp. 54-62; von Rad, Theology II, pp. 255f.; Fohrer, p. 160; Schoors, p. 320. Engnell, followed by Ringgren (The Messiah, pp. 50-53) further regards the chapter as a prophetical remodelling of an Israelite Annual Festival Liturgy closely resembling the Mesopotamian Tammuz liturgies.

11 For a recent definition see Fohrer, Jesaja II, p. 2. The idea that some of the prophetical books contain "liturgies" seems to have been first put forward by Gunkel in Ausgewählte Psalmen, p. 223, n. 4 to Ps. 24, where he referred to Isa. 33:14-16 and Mic. 6:8ff. as having a "liturgical" character similar to that of Ps. 24 (see pp. 45f. of the same work). He later developed the idea in "Jesaia 33", where he claimed that not only in Isa. 33 and Mic. 6, but

also in Amos, Hosea and Isa. 56-66 there are passages which have the same character. He declined to commit himself on the question whether these passages are genuine cultic material incorporated into the prophetical books or are literary imitations by the prophets themselves; though he inclined to the latter view. Mowinckel, in *Psalmenstudien II*, pp. 235ff. and later in *The Psalms in Israel's Worship I*, p. 180, expressed the latter view with regard to Isa. 33 and Mic. 6:6-8. The use of the term "prophetic liturgy" has become widespread in recent years. See, e.g., Eissfeldt, pp. 323-327, 393, 411-413, 417ff.

12 See Gunkel, *Einleitung*, pp. 407-415, and pp. 128-132 below for examples.

13 Engnell (see n. 11 above) was obliged to go to Mesopotamia for his models.

14 See pp. 128-132 below.

15 See pp. 132-134 below.

16 Lindblom, pp. 37-51.

17 *Op. cit.*, p. 46.

18 *Op. cit.*, p. 47.

19 He merely says, "There are many analogies to the allegorical pictures in Deutero-Isaiah in other parts of the literature of the Old Testament" (p. 103).

20 E.g. the oracle in verses 10-12, the extremely veiled language and the failure to make clear the identity of the person portrayed.

21 Lindblom's parallels are taken from the Gospel parables. Thus: "Nobody would ask, *Who was* the prodigal son? but, What does the prodigal son *signify?* Nor should we ask, *Who* is the suffering servant in Isa. LIII? The correct question is this: What does the suffering servant *signify?*" (p. 48; italics original).

22 It is not possible here to give an exhaustive list of all the attempts which have been made to solve the problem of the *Gattung* of Isa. 53. Some older interpreters saw it as a lamentation (e.g. Gressmann, pp. 314f.) or as a funeral dirge (e.g. Jahnow, pp. 256-265, followed by Mowinckel, *He That Cometh*, p. 220, n. 2). Mention should also be made of the theory advanced by Baltzer, "Zur formgeschichtlichen Bestimmung" (see also his *Die Biographie der Propheten*, pp. 171-177), in which he suggests that all four "Servant Songs" originally formed a single unit, which had the character of an "ideal biography", a genre familiar from Egyptian grave-inscriptions. He fails to produce Old Testament parallels — except for the book of Nehemiah, which is hardly comparable — or indeed any evidence for the existence of such a custom in ancient Israel; and he also fails to explain adequately why the "biography" should have been divided into four parts and scattered through the oracles of Deutero-Isaiah. His more precise description of 52:13 — 53:12 as formally a "trial narrative" (*Prozessberichte*) (cf. also Preuss, pp. 99-106) is also unsupported by adequate evidence.

23 Gunkel, *Einleitung*. The relevant sections are: "Die Danklieder des Einzelnen" ("individual psalms of thanksgiving"), pp. 265-292; "Das Danklied Israels" ("corporate psalm of thanksgiving"), pp. 314-323; "Die Klagelieder des Einzelnen" ("individual lamentations"), pp. 172-265 (including a section on the "Vertrauenslied" ["song of confidence"], pp. 254-256); "Die Klagelieder des Volkes" ("corporate lamentations"), pp. 117-139.

24 Of these the most relevant to the present discussion are: Schmidt, *Die Psalmen*; Barth, *Errettung*; Mowinckel, *The Psalms in Israel's Worship II*, pp. 31-43; Westermann, "Struktur und Geschichte"; Birkeland, *Evildoers*; Wevers, "Individual Complaint Psalms"; Frost, "Asseveration by Thanksgiving"; Mand, "Die Eigenständlichkeit der Danklieder"; Barth, *Einführung*; Kraus, *Psalmen*, *passim*, but especially *I*, pp. XLV-LI; Westermann, *The Praise of God*; Delekat; Lipiński, "Les psaumes d'action de grâces individuelle"; "Psaumes: formes et genres littéraires", especially cols. 72-86; Crüsemann; Beyerlin. Schmidt, *Das Gebet der Angeklagten*, published before Gunkel's *Einleitung* (1928), is also relevant.

25 Gunkel recognised "about twenty" complete examples (Ps. 18; 30; 32; 34; 40:2-12 [EVV 1-11] ; 41; 66; 92; [100] ; [107] ; 116; 118; 138; Isa. 38:10-20; Job 33:26-28; Jonah 2: 3-10 [EVV 2-9] and five from the Apocrypha and pseudepigrapha), but he also took into account parts of the alphabetical psalms 9 and 119 and a large number of thanksgivings attached to or forming part of individual psalms of lamentation, the royal Psalm 144, thanksgiving motifs in Hymns, and the corporate or national psalms of thanksgiving (*Einleitung*, p. 265, notes 2, 3, 5-8). Later scholars have extended or varied his list. In the notes which follow some explanations will be offered of some of these additions.

26 This is also true of Job 33:26-28; but these verses may not be intended to be a complete example of the genre.

27 *Op. cit.*, pp. 257, 269-271.

28 E.g. by Kaiser, pp. 93-127 *passim.*

29 The term "individual lamentation" has been held by some scholars to be too vague and also inaccurate; and it has been argued that the psalms usually included within that category really belong to two or more quite different types (see Lipiński, cols. 37ff. for a summary of research on this subject since Gunkel). But the division of these psalms into distinct groups each having a distinct function and *Sitz im Leben* presents serious problems, and no agreement has been reached on this question. They all have much in common in form, content and language, and for the present purpose they may be considered as a single group (see Kraus, *Psalmen I*, pp. XLVIII-L).

30 The divine oracle in verses 11b-12 will be considered below on pp. 123-126.

31 See pp. 92ff. above.

32 In the individual thanksgivings: Ps. 32:3f.; 41:4 (EVV 3); in the lamentations: Ps. 22: 15-18 (EVV 14-17); 32:11 (EVV 10); 38:4-12, 18 (EVV 3-11, 17); 51:10 (EVV 8); 69:30 (EVV 29); 102:4-12 (EVV 3-11); 109:24; Lam. 1:12-14; Job 18:13; cf. Job 33:19-21.

33 Ps. 38:18 (EVV 17); 41:4 (EVV 3); 69:30 (EVV 29); Lam. 1:12; Job 33:19.

34 In the individual thanksgivings, Ps. 41:6-10 (EVV 5-9). In the lamentations and related literature, Ps. 22:7-9 (EVV 6-8); 31:12 (EVV 11); 38:12 (EVV 11); 44:14-17 (EVV 13-16); 55:13-15, 21f. (EVV 12-14, 20f.); 69:9-13, 20-22 (EVV 8-12, 19-21); 102:9 (EVV 8); 109:25.

35 בזה : Ps. 119:141; בוז : Ps. 31:19 (EVV 18); 119:22; 123:3, 4; Job 12:5; 31:34.

36 בזה : Ps. 22:25 (EVV 24); 51:19 (EVV 17); 69:34 (EVV 33); 102:18 (EVV 17); 119:141.

37 Ps. 10:1, 11; 22:2, 12, 20 (EVV 1, 11, 19); 31:23 (EVV 22); 38:22 (EVV 21); 42:10 (EVV 9); 43:2; 44:10 (EVV 9); 60:3 (EVV 1); 71:9, 18; 77:8-11 (EVV 7-10); 119:8.

38 See pp. 93f. above.

39 It occurs in two individual thanksgivings. In Ps. 22:25 (EVV 24) the worshipper calls upon the congregation to praise God for not having hidden his face from him; in Ps. 30:8 (EVV 7) the statement that God hid his face as a punishment is made in the narrative section. Elsewhere in lamentation psalms (Ps. 10:11; 27:9; 69:18 [EVV 17] ; 88:15 [EVV 14] ; 102: 3 [EVV 2]) the speaker asks God not do so, complains that he has done so, or asks why he has done so.

40 Confessions of sin in individual thanksgivings: Ps. 32:1f., 5; 40:13 (EVV 12); in lamentations: Ps. 38:2, 5, 6, 19 (EVV 1, 4, 5, 18); 39:12 (EVV 11); 41:5 (EVV 4); 51:3-7, 12, 19 (EVV 1-5, 10, 17); 130:3f.; Lam. 1:18; Job 33:27. Assertions of innocence in individual thanksgivings: Ps. 18:22-25 (EVV 21-24); in lamentations: Ps. 7:4-6 (EVV 3-5); 17:1-5; 26:1-6; 35:7, 11, 19; 59:4-5 (EVV 3-4); 73:13.

41 The unusual character of Isa. 53 in this respect will be considered on pp. 132-134 below.

42 See p. 116 and note 33 above.

43 It has been noted above (Part II, n. 116) that the final words ולא יפתח פיו in
Isa. 53:7 are probably a dittograph. Even so the earlier occurrence of the phrase in this verse
is still sufficiently close to נאלמה to constitute a significant combination of phrases when
compared with the phrase in Ps. 39:10.

44 Pp. 95ff. above.

45 Kraus, *Psalmen, ad loc.* Birkeland, pp. 39f., cites it as evidence in connection with the
character of the "evildoers" in the Psalms.

46 It is interesting to observe that the same expression is used in Isa. 42:7, where someone
(thought by some scholars to be the Servant of the immediately preceding "Servant Song"
[42:1-4], by others to be the Persian king Cyrus) is to release the prisoners (that is, the
Jewish exiles): להוציא ממסגר אסיר ("to release the prisoners from prison"). The
similarity is the more striking since מסגר in the sense of "prison" occurs in only one
other passage in the Old Testament (Isa. 24:22). If, as will be argued below (pp. 134-139),
Isa. 53 is a psalm of thanksgiving for the release of the prophet from a Babylonian prison,
the speakers and those whom they represented may well have seen his rescue as a portent of
their own imminent release, which he had devoted his ministry to predicting.

47 The question was already discussed before the time of Gunkel: e.g. Duhm was inclined
to give the verse a literal interpretation. This interpretation was also defended by H. Schmidt
in the context of a comprehensive theory. His view was rejected by Gunkel (*Einleitung*, p.
195) and later by Beyerlin (pp. 34f.), but accepted as probable by Barth (*Errettung*, pp. 102-
104) and by Weiser (*Psalms*, pp. 78, 813) and Kraus (*Psalmen, ad loc.*).

48 H. Schmidt, "Erklärung des 118. Psalms", pp. 9f.

49 H. Schmidt, *Das Gebet der Angeklagten.*

50 Ps. 30:2 (EVV 1); 32:10; 40:15f. (EVV 14f.); 41:6-12 (EVV 5-11); 66:12; 92:10, 12
(EVV 9, 11); 138:7.

51 נבזה (twice, verse 3); נגוע מכה, מענה (verse 4); מחלל מדכא, (verse 5);
נגש יובל, (verse 7); נגזר לקח, possibly נגע (י) (verse 8); נמנה (verse 12).

52 מכאבינו סבלם חלינו הוא נשא; (verse 4); ועונתם הוא יסבל (verse 11);
והוא חטא-רבים נשא (verse 12).

53 ויהוה הפגיע בו אה עון כלנו (verse 6).

54 ובחברתו מוסר שלומנו עליו; (verse 5).

55 There may be other passages in Deutero-Isaiah where a failure to be specific may be
due to a need for caution: e.g. those passages about Cyrus which do not name him. On the
other hand such caution is not always shown. This apparent inconsistency may be due to
varying circumstances about which we know nothing.

56 The theme occurs in the thanksgivings in Ps. 9:14 (EVV 13); 18:6f. (EVV 4f.); 107:18;
116:3; 118:17f.; Jonah 2:3, 7 (EVV 2, 6); Isa. 38:10-12; Job 33:28; and very frequently in
the lamentations.

57 On the meaning of these statements as denoting nearness to death rather than actual
death see especially Barth, *Errettung, passim.* That the experience of imprisonment, no less
than that of sickness, was such as to induce in the prisoner the feeling of being drawn into
the sphere of death is argued convincingly in the same work, pp. 103f.

58 Pp. 95-105 above.

59 Psalms 9 and 10 probably originally constituted a single psalm. Its character as a whole
is disputed; but 9:2-7 (EVV 1-6) has the character of an individual thanksgiving.

60 It is generally agreed that Psalm 92 contains elements of both the Hymn and the thanksgiving, though with some hesitation about which of these two elements is the predominating
one (Gunkel, *Einleitung,* pp. 265, 276; *Psalmen, ad loc.*; Weiser; Kraus, *ad loc.*; Crüsemann,

p. 283, n. 1). Westermann, who does not recognise a distinction between the two types, classifies it as a "declaratory psalm of praise" (*The Praise of God*, p. 105). At least verses 11f. (EVV 10f.) must in any case be described as having the form of the narrative section of an individual thanksgiving.

61 If Begrich's emendation of verse 10a to אשם שם-את החלים בָּאוֹ חפץ ויהוה נפשו ("But Yahweh took thought for his crushed one; he healed him who made his life a guilt-offering") were accepted, this would, as Begrich himself argued (pp. 58f.) be the most important statement in the poem of God's act of deliverance. But reasons have been given above (Part II, n. 2) for not accepting the emendation.

62 On this reading see pp. 81-83 above.

63 See pp. 84f. above on the meaning of this line.

64 See p. 81 above.

65 For a detailed discussion of the divine oracle in the Psalms see Delekat, pp. 67ff.

66 Kraus, *Psalmen, ad loc.*; Delekat, pp. 74f.; denied by Gunkel, *Psalmen*, Weiser, *Psalms, ad loc.*, and others. Kraus points out that both metre and phraseology tell against the view that these verses are to be attributed to a human wisdom speaker.

67 *Einleitung*, pp. 243-247.

68 Begrich, "Das priesterliche Heilsorakel".

69 So again Kraus, *Psalmen, ad loc.*, who refers to Begrich's article for other examples of this phenomenon.

70 Kraus, *Psalmen, ad loc.*; Westermann, *The Praise of God*, pp. 62, 70, 72; Delekat, p. 239, n. 1.

71 The use of the first person singular in verse 11 (EVV 9) is hardly sufficient evidence against this classification. The first person singular here is probably to be understood collectively.

72 On the various interpretations of Ps. 68 see Kraus, *Psalmen, ad loc.*

73 Gunkel, *Einleitung*, pp. 32, 345; *Psalmen, ad loc.* See also Weiser, *Psalms, ad loc.*; Crüsemann, p. 159.

74 For details see Kraus, *Psalmen, ad loc.*

75 See again Kraus, *op. cit.* for details.

76 It is possible that verses 1f. and 3-13 are spoken by different voices.

77 See Delekat, pp. 237-239.

78 On ישבע see pp. 83f. above.

79 On (אור) יראה see pp. 81-83 above. The possibility of an echo here exists whether יראה in Isa. 53:11 and אראהו in Ps. 91:16 are understood as meaning "he will see" and "I will show him" respectively, or whether they are to be rendered (with or without emendation to ירוה , ארוהו), "he will be drenched with light", "I will drench him with my salvation", as has been suggested in both cases.

80 אקום ,אשית ,אסית (Ps. 12:6); איעצה (32:8); אשכילך ואורך; אעלזה אחלקה; ;אענהו ;אשגבהו ;אפלטהו (75:3); אשפט ;אקח (68:23); (twice) אשיב (60:8); אראהו ;אחלצהו ואכבדהו אשכיעהו (91:14-16). In Isa. 53:12 the divine promise proper begins with אחלק-לו . It should be noted that the form of these oracles does not correspond to that of the "salvation-oracles" elsewhere in Deutero-Isaiah. This may be significant as suggesting that the situation presupposed by Isa. 53 is not the same as that in which the recipient of the promise is the nation.

81 Gunkel calls this "das Bekenntnis zu Jahve als dem Retter aus der Not" (*Einleitung*, p. 272). Cf. Kraus, *Psalmen I*, p. XLVII.

82 E.g. Ps. 22:23f. (EVV 22f.); 30:5 (EVV 4); 32:11; 40:10f. (EVV 9f.); Job 33:26f.

83 E.g. Ps. 9:8-11 (EVV 7-10); 18:31ff. (EVV 30ff.); 30:6 (EVV 5); 40:5 (EVV 4);

92:6-10 (EVV 5-9); 118:8f.; 138:4-6.

84 On the meaning of שמעתנו , "what we have just heard", see pp. 132-134 below.

85 Ps. 6:3 (EVV 2); 41:5 (EVV 4).

86 Ps. 30:3 (EVV 2); 107:20; also in a passage which has the characteristics of an individual thanksgiving, Ps. 103:3.

87 Both the text and the meaning of the phrase הנה לשלום מר-לי מר are uncertain but there seems no good reason, despite the fact that it is lacking in LXX, to doubt that שלום is original and that the phrase implies that Hezekiah is expressing his gratitude to God for restoring it to him. In addition to older commentators such as Delitzsch, Scott, Fohrer (*Jesaja II*) and Kaiser (*Isaiah 13-39*) hold that Hezekiah's deliverance is here stated to have been achieved by means of his suffering. If this is the correct interpretation there is something of a parallel here to the sentiments expressed by the speakers in Isa. 53:4-6.

88 So, e.g., Gunkel, *Psalmen*, on Pss. 22; 34; 40; 107; 118; *Einleitung*, pp. 184, 266f., 273f.; Schmidt, "Erklärung des 118. Psalms"; *Psalmen*, on Pss. 22; 30; 35; 40; 66; 106; 107; 116; 118; Begrich, *Studien*, p. 65; Mowinckel, *Psalmenstudien V*, pp. 34f. ; *The Psalms in Israel's Worship II*, pp. 42f.; Kraus, *Psalmen I*, p. XLVIII and on Ps. 22; *II*, on Pss. 107; 118; Lipiński, cols. 73-75.

89 See pp. 121 ff. above.

90 Ps. 22:23-27 (EVV 22-26); 30:5 (EVV 4); 32:11; 34:3-11 (EVV 2-10); 35:27f.; 40:4, 10f. (EVV 3, 9f.); 118:29; Jer. 33:11.

91 קהל , "congregation", Ps. 22:23 (EVV 22) (parallel with אחי , "my brothers"); קהל-עם , "congregation of the people", Ps. 107:32; קהל רב , "great congregation", Ps. 22:26 (EVV 25); 35:18 (parallel with עם עצום , "great crowd"); 40:10, 11 (EVV 9, 10).

92 For a detailed survey of views of this and a detailed discussion see Lipiński, cols. 72-86.

93 On Ps. 107 see below.

94 See Gunkel, *Einleitung*, p. 412; *Psalmen, ad loc.*; Schmidt, "Erklärung des 118. Psalms"; *Psalmen, ad loc.*; Kraus, *Psalmen, ad loc.*; Lipiński, cols. 73f.

95 Gunkel, *Einleitung*, p. 274.

96 Both Targ. and the Talmud (Pesachim 119a) were aware that it was to be sung by different voices.

97 These two pairs of verses appear to interrupt the thought and break up the style, which is otherwise in the first person singular. Schmidt (*art. cit.*) regarded them as words spoken by priest and congregation in the intervals between three separate short psalms of thanksgiving spoken by three separate individuals. This is a most improbable interpretation which has not been accepted by more recent interpreters. Weiser (*Psalms*) and Kraus (*Psalmen*) regard the verses as integral parts of the individual thanksgiving, borrowing from other *Gattungen*; but Lipiński's view (col. 73) – based on the Qumran Psalms Scroll (11QPs^a) (Sanders, p. 37 and Plate XI) in which verses 1, 15f., 8f., 29 appear independently of the rest of the biblical psalm – that the original psalm consisted only of verses 2-7, 10-14, 17-28 must be taken seriously.

98 It is not necessary for present purposes to discuss in detail those points on which no agreement has been reached with regard to some of the liturgical sequences and actions presupposed in the psalm.

99 See pp. 113ff. above.

100 By Kraus and others.

101 The precise structural position and function of the "chief corner-stone" (on which see Kraus, *Psalmen, ad loc.*) are not relevant to the present discussion.

102 The question whether such a position can refer only to the king (so most recently Eaton, p. 166) is not relevant here. This type of interpretation, which identifies the individual worshipper in a number of psalms with the particular person of the king, is not at variance with the classification of these psalms as individual psalms of thanksgiving.

103 Pp. 132-134 below.

104 See the beginning of this section.

105 Pp. 120f. above.

106 Psalm 107 is interpreted by Gunkel (*Einleitung*, p. 274; *Psalmen, ad loc.*); Schmidt (*Psalmen, ad loc.*); Begrich (p. 65) and Mowinckel (*The Psalms in Israel's Worship II*, p. 42) as the liturgy of a thanksgiving ceremony at which large numbers of individuals came to pay their vows on a festival day when a great congregation was assembled. But for Weiser (*Psalms, ad loc.*) it is not an individual but a communal thanksgiving ceremony, a view which had already been shown to be erroneous by Gunkel (*Einleitung*, p. 274). The view of Kraus, however, is more worthy of attention. He regards the psalm as an introductory exhortation spoken by a priest, preceding but not strictly part of a series of separate acts of individual thanksgiving.

107 The commentaries differ on this point, which is not material to the present discussion.

108 Begrich, *Studien*. Here after an analysis of verses 1-11a (pp. 63f.) he concluded (p. 65) that this passage "einem Danklied des einzelnen nach Aufbau und Stoff aufs engste verwandt ist", with the one exception "dass nicht der Gerettene selber redet, sondern dass andere von ihm erzählen". This he took to be an indication that the passage is a "Danklied der Festteilnehmer, welches sich auf das Erleben des einzelnen Geretteten bezieht", of which Psalm 107 and Ps. 118:22f. are examples in the Psalter.

109 *Op. cit.*, p. 65.

110 On the vocabulary see Kaiser, pp. 94-96.

111 Deut. 17:8; 30:11; 2 Sam. 13:2 (difficult or impossible); 2 Sam. 1:26; Prov. 30:18; Zech. 8:6 (wonderful).

112 Gen. 18:14; Jer. 32:17, 27 (nothing is too difficult for Yahweh); Ps. 139:14 (the wonder of Yahweh and his works). The verb is also frequently used in the Hiphil of Yahweh's "doing wonders".

113 On questions beginning with מי denoting impossibility or incredulity in Deutero-Isaiah and elsewhere see Whybray, *The Heavenly Counsellor*, pp. 21-26. For an example of a refusal to believe (האמין) a report or account which had been heard (שמע) compare the words of the Queen of Sheba to Solomon in 1 Kings 10:6f., where she speaks of the reports which had been brought to her of Solomon's wisdom: "The report which I heard in my land ... was true (אמת היה הדבר אשר שמעתי בארצי) ... but I did not believe the report (ולא-האמנתי לדברים) until I came, and my eyes saw it". Later in the same verse she refers to the report as השמועה אשר שמעתי, "the report which I heard".

114 Pp. 110f. above.

115 Compare the identical treatment of Jeremiah when he prophesied the fall of Jerusalem to the Babylonians.

116 See Part II, *passim*.

117 See pp. 92ff. above.

118 See pp. 95ff. above.

119 See pp. 79-85 above.

120 See pp. 128-132 above.

121 Sacrificial worship was not, as far as is known, practised by the Jews in Babylonia. The resumption of worship mainly according to the old forms after the exile, however, can

only be explained on the hypothesis that there had been no total cessation of it in Babylonia during the exile, since much if not most of the impetus for its full restoration came from the descendants of the former exiles rather than from those who had remained in Palestine. Evidence for Jewish public worship in Babylonia itself includes direct references in the exilic literature of the Old Testament such as Ezek. 8:1ff.; 14:1ff.; 20:1ff.; the picture of conditions of life during the exile found in Jer. 29; references to the practice of holding regular fast days during the exile in Palestine (Zech. 7:3-7) and actual examples of lamentations appropriate to such occasions, e.g. in the book of Lamentations; a reference to the singing of lamentations by the exiles themselves in Ps. 137; etc. But there is also an increasing tendency on the part of scholars to regard many of Deutero-Isaiah's oracles, especially the "oracle of salvation" (*Heilsorakel*) as actual cultic oracles spoken by the prophet himself at such gatherings in reply to corporate lamentations. See, *inter alia*, von Waldow, *Anlass und Hintergrund*, *passim*; " '. . . denn ich erlöse dich' "; "The Message of Deutero-Isaiah", pp. 5f. and *passim*; Whybray, *Isaiah 40-66*, pp. 29f. and *passim*.

122 Compare the story of Ahiqar (Cowley, pp. 204-226; *ANET*, pp. 427-430). Here, although imprisonment and subsequent release are not involved, the dependence of an individual's fate upon a capricious or gullible ruler is well illustrated.

123 Especially Sellin, *Studien*, pp. 230-287; *Rätsel*, pp. 131-150; Staerk. For a brief account of these theories and references to other scholars who adopted this view see North, *The Suffering Servant*, pp. 50-53.

124 Sellin, *Studien*, pp. 258-267.

125 Staerk, p. 132.

126 In the absence of very precise information about the state of the parties in Babylon at this time and of the extent to which the pro-Persian party controlled the administration of the city it is probably useless to speculate further. At all events neither the imprisonment of Deutero-Isaiah by one party nor his subsequent release by the other seems to be inherently improbable. For a recent account of some aspects of the reign of Nabonidus see Lambert, "Nabonidus in Arabia", to which the author has very kindly drawn my attention. On what is known about punishments and prisons in the ancient Near East see the *Journal of the Economic and Social History of the Orient* 20 (1977), pp. 65-113. It should be noted that none of the articles there deals with the Late Babylonian period.

Note to Postscript

1 Orlinsky, p. 75.

Indexes

Index of Authors Cited

175

176

178